The Myth of the Maiden

THE MYTH OF THE MAIDEN
ON BEING A WOMAN

Joan E. Childs

Foreword by John Bradshaw

Health Communications, Inc.
Deerfield Beach, Florida

The following publishers have generously given permission to use extended quotations form copyrighted works: Quotes from Sam Keen, *Fire in the Belly*. Copyright ©1991 by Sam Keen. Used with permission of Bantam Books, a division of Bantam Doubleday Dell Publishing Group, Inc.; Irving Berlin, "The Girl That I Marry." Copyright by Williamson Music Co. International copyright secured. Used with permission of Williamson Music, New York; Richard Rogers and Lorenz Hart, "The Lady is a Tramp." Copyright by Williamson Music Co. International copyright secured. Used by permission of Williamson Music, New York; Leonard Cohen, "Suzanne Takes You Down." Copyright ©1967 by Bad Monk Publishing. Reprinted by permission; Erikson's stages of development, from Erik H. Erikson, *Childhood and Society*. Copyright 1950, ©1963 by W.W. Norton & Company, Inc., renewed ©1978 by Erik H. Erikson. Reprinted with the permission of W.W. Norton & Company, Inc.; Kahlil Gibran, excerpt from *The Prophet*. Copyright 1923 by Kahlil Gibran and renewed 1951 by Administrators of C.T.A. of Kahlil Gibran Estate and Mary G. Gibran. Reprinted with the permission of Alfred A. Knopf, Inc. and The National Committee of Gibran.

Library of Congress Cataloging-in-Publication Data

Childs, Joan E., (date)
    The myth of the maiden : on being a woman / Joan E. Childs : foreword by John Bradshaw.
    p. cm.
    Includes bibliographical references.
    ISBN 1-55874-315-4 (trade paper) : $9.95
    1. Childs, Joan E. 2. Feminists—United States—Biography. 3. Women—United States—Biography. 4. Feminism—United States. 5. Self-esteem in women—United States. I. Title.
HQ1413.C455A3 1995
305.42'0973'092—dc20
[B]   95-15807
                                                                      CIP

©1995 Joan E. Childs
ISBN 1-55874-315-4

Publisher: Health Communications, Inc.
            3201 S.W. 15th Street
            Deerfield Beach, Florida 33442-8190
Cover design by Robert Cannata
Cover Illustration by: Todd Bush Model: Madonna Parsons

To my mother, Minnie, and Emily Brontë.
May their souls rest in peace.

Contents

Foreword

Joan E. Childs is a woman who is committed to the work of healing humanity. Through my association with her, I know that she is a therapist of immense integrity. I respect the work she does with individuals in recovery and I am proud to say that she utilizes the ideas and philosophies I have used in my work. I have watched her continued development as a therapist with joy and pride.

I met Joan E. Childs in February of 1989, soon after my success with the television show and accompanying book *Bradshaw On: The Family* and my follow-up *Healing the Shame that Binds You*. She was visiting her daughter who was working at the Life Plus Treatment Center in Hollywood—what was to become the first John Bradshaw Center—with Kip Flock. I saw in this woman many of my own traits. She was a successful therapist who still struggled with issues in her own personal life. She was driven to accomplish many great goals, yet happiness sometimes eluded her.

Below this dichotomy in her life, however, I had a sense that she was in touch with a great truth. Her ability to use stories from her own life to support points about particular individuals and about society as a whole intrigued me. She had an intimate understanding of her clients because she herself had experienced many of the same events that plagued them. She also had an innate sense of how to help them because of her ability to put her own pain and suffering in the past and forgive herself for her mistakes.

One does not often meet an individual like Joan. Her life does not necessarily correspond to the idea of "politically or socially correct" and few would call it stable. She takes chances; she risks what she has to get what she wants. Some might call this irresponsible, but I believe it is the highest form of responsibility: she is true to herself. Come hell or high water, Joan Childs does what is right and best, both for her and for those in need of healing.

In August of that same year I gave a seminar in Ft. Lauderdale and did the planning for a major workshop that would be held in Miami that December. My final step in organizing this event was finding someone in the area that was capable of providing follow-up therapy. The first person I thought of was Joan, so I asked her if she would be interested in opening the first affiliate of the John Bradshaw Center in the United States. Though she was initially hesitant, in October she accepted the responsibility and I gave her my permission and encouragement. Three short months later she had the center up and running and had me convinced it would be a success under her direction. She never looked back and never had any doubts that she was doing the right thing.

This book is another example of her ability to accomplish what she believes is important and will help others. I knew Joan was committed to many of the ideals in my own work: healing the wounds of childhood, of shame and of a dysfunctional family. She truly understands the multi-generational nature of toxic shame and the ways in which it is passed down through families. She is an eclectic therapist who has studied many different schools of thought, and she is a master of neuro-linguistic programming.

Through her professional background, her own experiences and the experiences of the many clients she treated in therapy, she realized that there is an additional force at work in our lives, particularly among women. This force is the Myth of the Maiden.

This myth is passed down from generation to generation, just like shame and dysfunctional families, but it isn't confined to the family setting. It functions on a societal level, and has the power to cross lines of age, race, class and geography.

Much has been written about the potentially negative aspects of male archetypes—Robert Bly's *Iron John*, Sam Keen's *Fire in the Belly*, Robert Moore and Douglas Gillette's *King, Warrior, Magician, Lover*—and how men can mature and avoid damaging pitfalls. Dr. Clarissa Pinkola Estes' *Women Who Run with the Wolves*, as well as other titles, describes ways in which women can reconnect with the

Wild Woman archetype, a positive model for contemporary women. Yet rarely is the potentially damning effect of the long-accepted Myth of the Maiden explored. It is vital that the restraints of this binding archetype are revealed, particularly in contemporary society where women are finally securing some measure of equality.

When women realize that it is not viable for them to rely on men for their identity, they also realize their true nature. They hear that voice that has always been inside them, though it was drowned out by the demands of others. This idea lies at the heart of Joan's book. She has accomplished what all women—and all people—must. She has thrown off the controlling reins of others, in her case fathers (both real and symbolic) and husbands. Her journey reflects the natural evolution of so many people in recovery. She has accepted who she is, and uses what she has learned along life's twisting path to help others.

The Myth of the Maiden is a book for all readers. I hope you share it with your friends and family, both male and female, because it is an important book that will help all people to accept and love themselves. It is both an example of and instructional guide to throwing off those roles that are thrust upon us, and discovering where our true paths lie.

John Bradshaw

Acknowledgments

So many people have supported me through this, my first effort; it would be impossible to name them all. But special gratitude goes to Shelly Faithe for recovering lost text in the computer; to my secretary Marlene for making sure all bases were covered at the office so I could write; to all my children for their belief in me; to my husband, Mervyn, for his encouragement, confidence and constructive criticism; to my father, for the gift of his tenacious spirit; to my friends and clients for their written contributions; and the others, for their patience and good wishes.

I want to express my sincere appreciation and gratitude to John Bradshaw for giving me the opportunity to expand my professional growth, and for writing the foreword; to Health Communications Inc., for taking a chance in publishing my very first book; and to my editor, Marcia Ledwith for any changes and suggestions she made which enhanced the book's content.

And most of all, I want to thank my special friend, Hanif Bajwa, for his divine talent, skill and wisdom in assisting throughout this mission of writing my book. His editing and thoughts reflect and expand my own ideas. His re-frames and suggestions have enriched the writing experience and will hopefully enrich the reading experience. I am truly grateful to both Bano and Hanif Bajwa for walking me through the process so many times way into the night.

Introduction

Three years ago, my daughter Linda and I were invited to conduct a seminar in New Hope, Pennsylvania, for a group of therapists. It was there I stumbled upon Sam Keen's book, *Fire In The Belly: On Being a Man*. I finished it in three nights.

It was a fascinating account of candor and self-revelation. I suddenly realized the omnipotence of that powerful verdict of genetics, that one variation in the chromosomes; that little difference that truly made a difference. My feelings were of acceptance, that sudden sense of the magnanimous power of Creation. I knew that my womanhood was not just a chance occurrence. I had a sensation of being chosen—chosen to be a woman. It was a mystical experience and suddenly my whole life flashed before me and I realized that it was a long journey, a journey of my discovery of myself, the discovery of my being in this life, my being as a woman.

I distinctly remember looking around at the walls and furnishings of the bedroom in that bed and breakfast in Lambertville, New Jersey, after I had finished reading *Fire in the Belly*. Far beyond those walls, I had a deeper sense of the world in which I had lived for more than fifty years as a woman. I had a much closer kinship with those billions of humans who have lived on this earth in the bodies of the females. It was a fleeting sensation, but a prescience. I knew that I was destined to live this awareness. I knew I had to write. I had to share with others my experience of being a woman. Ironically, the recognition of that deeper need was triggered by a man—my book is a response to *Fire in the Belly*, but in a way it is not. It is also a sharing, however, of another viewpoint in this ongoing saga of our self-discovery.

I recall a conversation I had with Lorraine, one of the counseling center directors at the therapists' training center who later became one of my closest friends.

"I'm going to write a response to Sam Keen's book," I said as if I had known it all my life.

"Why?" she asked. "What's so special about the book that you feel it requires a response?"

"I don't know. I only know that I have something to say about being a woman, and if I don't write it, someone else will. I have just as many reflections on being a woman as he has on being a man. It's almost begging for a response. Why not?" I responded.

Keen's thesis and commentaries on men, malehood and being, translated in my mind into a reflection on women, womanhood and being. It was a powerful body experience. The sensation stayed with me and grew into an impulse for expression. Now that I have tended this fire for over two years and translated it into book form, I wonder what it was about. What triggered this impulse in me? Why, out of nowhere, did my fire begin to burn? Had it always been smoldering, waiting for a spark to ignite it?

I still wonder about these questions. They have been my preoccupation for some time. I really cannot claim to have any answers. These pages at best are just ruminations on the energy of womanhood, coupled with my insights and understanding as a psychotherapist, which became increasingly tangible for me as I moved from one writing session to another. It was a rite of revisiting my life as a woman, holding hands with my womanhood—partly sad and partly joyful, some regrets and some pride. But it was a real way of looking at life. "Womanhood," I increasingly realized, was an important part of my being.

I call writing this book a journey of my life and this is something very special. The life of a woman in this world was mostly a state and did not have the movement of a journey. In this way, I am distinguished from the generations of women who preceded me in that I was afforded the opportunity to explore the needs of myself, make decisions and bear the consequences. It is my story, the story of a woman, the story of my time as I grew and changed to meet the demands of my evolving self, coping with the new uncertainties of the swiftly changing world around me. It is autobiographical as well as didactic. It is the experience of a little girl who grew up and went to school in Miami Beach; a woman who dreamed of "living happily ever after," dreams that were shattered in a world that posed more demands than I was prepared to handle.

My dream began in the fifties, which I regard as the last decade of the Age of Innocence. Like many women, I had to cope to survive. There was a part in us which fixated on the dreams that could not be fulfilled, a fantasy that could only push us into a persona or neurosis. It was a difficult process of learning, but we grew up to have new perceptions, new self-concepts, and the joy of our new found freedom of realization.

While there was a lot of pain and anger from the disillusion and oppression, I went through years of therapy, then I eventually became a therapist; perhaps as a result of my own woundedness. I realized that much of my behavior was influenced dramatically by both familial and cultural norms and mores, much of which we understand today as dysfunctional. Dysfunctionality in family systems gets passed down generation to generation, resulting in an accumulation of toxic shame with manifestations in compulsive and neurotic behaviors.

In writing this introduction, I was struck by the similarities and parallels between the sexes, particularly those shared in the rites of passage. Although their rites differ considerably, women have expectations and responsibilities placed upon them to engage both unwittingly or willfully in their own biological, sociological and psychological rituals which foster their development.

As I considered a title for my book, the feminine response to *Fire in the Belly*, the title that came to mind immediately was *Water on the Brain*. Because I wanted to reach a wide audience of women, I quickly withdrew that title. However, there was a time in looking back at my half-century on earth that *Water on the Brain* might have been a description of where I was in terms of selfhood and personal development. There might have even been a time, after my fifth pregnancy, when *Babies in the Belly* would have been most appropriate.

Not too long ago women were totally subjected to the power of others; our fathers often controlled our mothers; our mothers often manipulated our fathers; our husbands dominated our relationships; religions and cultures chose our mates; governments controlled our rights; and families, based upon generations of tradition, dictated and predetermined our actions and future. It's a wonder God even bothered to give us a brain, for until the last few decades, we certainly didn't seem to need one.

Sheltered by tradition, repressed by Victorianism and other social legacies, and carrying the feminine collective unconscious, a fire in our bellies began to burn, gathering strength, accruing fuel for the great feminine explosion (the movement), and alas for some, the "great nervous breakdowns." Like the Phoenix, we rose, giving birth to the twentieth, and now twenty-first century Joan of Arcs who helped raise our female conscious and unconscious minds, alerting our water-damaged brains that we do have choices. Oppression breeds rage; rage breeds radicalism; radicalism forces change; change is brought about by revolution. But standing alongside the revolutionaries in an uneasy alliance will be the submissive and the subservient. The truth is, we need the balance.

Now that the dust is settling and women can reflect on what has happened, we can make our own choices, recognizing the outcomes and consequences. We have all paid the price for unenlightenment, revolution and extremism. Our history will serve as a road map to the future. Women, all of us, one way or another, have empowered ourselves to become pathfinders and pioneers in a movement that will pave the way to a better future for our sons and daughters to hopefully reap the benefits of our mistakes.

Special Note to the Reader

Due to the fact that this book is somewhat autobiographical in content for the expressed purpose of illustrating information, much of the material is not in chronological order, and may leave the reader wondering about the sequence of events. Due to this fact, I have decided to include a list of characters for reference purposes.

The men in my life are as follows:

Carl . . . . . 1st husband, married 1959, divorced, 1961
Jack . . . . . 2nd husband, father of all five children; married 1962, divorced 1975
Tom . . . . . 3rd husband, married 1976, divorced, 1980
Phil . . . . . significant other, 1980-1985
Mervyn . . . fourth husband, married, 1987-

My apologies to those not mentioned. No insult intended. You all made a difference in my life, and I have not one regret for ever having known each of you.

I heard a thousand blended notes
While in a grove I sate reclined,
In that sweet mood when pleasant thoughts
Bring sad thoughts to the mind.

To her fair works did Nature link
The human soul that through me ran;
And much it grieved my heart I think
What man has made of man.

Lines Written in Early Spring
William Wordsworth (1770-1850)

Part I

Chapter 1

WELCOME TO MY WORLD: THE MYTH OF MY TIME

Ah! the true rule is—a true wife in her husband's house is his servant; it is in his heart she is queen. Whatever of the best he conceives, it is her part to be; whatever of the highest he can hope, it is hers to promise; all that is dark in him she must purge into purity; all that is failing in him she must strengthen into trust; from her, through all the world's clamor, she must win his praise; in her, through all the world's warfare, he must find his peace.

—John Ruskin (1819-1900)

Women's roles have changed so dramatically in my generation that it has been a challenge to know where and who we really are.

I grew up in South Beach. South Beach was to Miami Beach what the East Side was to Manhattan; Delancy was to Brooklyn; 4th and Snyder was to Philadelphia; Fairfax to Chicago; and 12th Street to Detroit. Most of us had immigrant grandparents with misgiven names as they came through Ellis Island at the turn of the century. Most were from Eastern Europe. Mine were from Poland and Russia. Most of us heard Yiddish spoken at home, especially when we were not supposed to understand the nature of the conversation. Yet, most of us could understand in spite of their best intentions. Most of us could rarely speak it, and most of us were the last this century to have heard it spoken.

Between the ages of 12 and 17, I lived on 1st and Jefferson, an address which shamed me. It represented the "have nots" in a society that had a majority of "haves." The metaphorical Mason/Dixon

line was at Lincoln Road and almost everyone who lived south of
Lincoln Road was poor. Everyone who lived north was rich, or at
least appeared to be to those of us who lived south. My only saving
grace was the fact that 145 Jefferson Avenue was closer to 2nd street
than to 1st Street. This somehow gave me permission to say "2nd
and Jefferson" when asked where I lived. 1st Street bordered the
projects on Biscayne Street. Strangely enough, Biscayne Street,
where the housing projects were, was the address of Joe's Stone
Crabs, still one of Florida's most expensive and popular restaurants.
This didn't make matters better for those of us who lived in the
neighborhood. It only accentuated our differences. I remember sitting on the curb as a child watching the limousines and fancy cars
pull up to the valet service. I was in awe of the glamorous people
and wondered where they all came from. I didn't have my first stone
crab until I was 26, and when I did, I realized why the crowds came.

In spite of all this, and the fact that we lived in a city which prac-
ticed de facto apartheid, Miami Beach was the best of all possible
worlds.

We grew up in a time of innocence, surrounded by glamour,
sophistication and safety. In the evenings, we walked the beaches
along Ocean Drive and skated in Flamingo Park without a thought
of rape, mugging or theft. I never knew the meaning of anti-
Semitism. Most of the people living in Miami Beach were Jewish.
The school population was primarily Jewish. Hardly anyone showed
up during the Jewish holidays. Even the Gentiles tended to stay
home during the Jewish high holy days.

The most delinquent act ever committed at my high school was
the burning of a tee shirt thrown on the tomb of the unknown sol-
dier. The boys of Miami Beach High were protesting a rule pro-
hibiting them from wearing tee shirts to school. Even in the best of
all possible worlds, however, Miami Beach was also a cauldron of
dysfunctionality and co-dependency. Cloaked in idealism, we were
constantly looking for ways to make our dreams come true.

Growing up in South Beach in the 1950s, girls dreamed of finding husbands, having babies and living happily ever after. If the first
goal was not attained by age 20 or 21, we felt either inadequate or
afraid. Perhaps both. Even if girls went to college, it was with the
expectation of either finding a husband or satisfying their parents.

Although some went in search of a career, most did not. When asked what I was taking up in college, my father would humorously reply, "space." When asked what degree I hoped to obtain, he would say an "MRS." When I was placed on academic probation as a result of substandard grades, he refused to subsidize my education any longer. He viewed my probation as a failure, advising me that if I wanted a degree, it would be my financial responsibility. Because I married Carl, my first husband, only one year after entering the University of Miami, my father foresaw two possibilities for me: The first was that I would terminate my schooling; the second, perhaps either my husband or his family would assume financial responsibility where he left off. To him, academic probation was a valid reason to cut off my funds. Neither prediction was accurate, however. I paid for my own tuition, and coincidentally, my grade point average dramatically improved.

My parents programmed me to marry a rich man—preferably a doctor, but nobody ever suggested a rich butcher. One of my father's platitudes was, "It's just as easy to marry a rich man as a poor one." My personal agenda was to get out of South Beach as fast as I could. My ticket out was to find a man who didn't live there.

Men were expected to be opportunities for advancement, security blankets and keys to personal happiness. All I needed to do was pick the right one. Ha! Even if I had picked the right one, none of those expectations were remotely realistic.

I grew up in a dysfunctional family. My father's entreaties to recruit a husband didn't pay off to either his or my satisfaction. Eventually I did marry the soon-to-become (and then to "unbecome") rich Jewish doctor, but there was one before him, two following him and a live-in love, blended gingerly with five confused children. Not exactly what the 1950s platitudes promised. Didn't all the movies of the 1940s and 1950s have happy endings? What the hell went wrong? How did this nice Jewish girl from South Beach with roots in the Bronx and the best of intentions, so exhaustively fumble her dreams, hopes and fantasies?

Joseph Campbell writes about *The Power of Myth*. Perhaps the myth of the 1950s was bolstered by the roles men were expected to play—modern-day white knights saving damsels in distress and slaying dragons, warriors going into corporate battles, doctors saving lives and stamping out disease, and masters of the universe, making millions on Wall Street. We were under a spell, mystified with a magical belief system woven together by our time, our histories and our culture. The burden was on men, the mighty hunters and warriors to actualize women's expectations to live happily ever after. By the 1970s, the myth was just that—a myth. Oh, the disappointment, the disillusionment; what bitterness. Our wounded men, now incapable of heroic deeds of valor—became insufficient little warriors unable to fulfill the hopes, dreams and fantasies of the 1950s women.

Those of us who made it and found our misguided fortunes of marriage and family were safely enshrined in one-bedroom apartments, nursing our adults of the 1990s. So safe were we, tucked away in those apartments, dazed by the shocking assassinations of John F. Kennedy, Martin Luther King and Bobby Kennedy. Awed by the astronauts landing on the moon, and oblivious to or confused by the righteous condemnation of a war that eventually drove us into a personal and social revolution, the 1960s and 1970s gave rise to an interminable drug culture and the near demise of the next two generations.

We walked carriages around the parks and raised money for cancer hospitals, Israel and banning the bomb. We played mahjongg, bowled once a week and had more babies. Each day we lost a little bit more of ourselves as we waited ever so patiently for our men to come home and make us happy.

By the very nature of gender, women were set up by society to become co-dependent. In Judaism, men who traditionally chant the morning prayers recite, "Thank you God for not making me a woman." (Some may refute this interpretation, suggesting that the prayer's intention is to "thank God for making me a man," meaning a "human being," using "man" to denote both sexes as in "mankind.") In contrast, according to the Kabbalah, the ancient Jewish mystical philosophical tradition rejected by some modern Judaic thought, God counts all the tears of women. This patriarchal philosophy, like it or not, permeates throughout the collective unconscious of my heritage. Its personification is entrenched throughout the Judeo-Christian-Islamic culture. This is not to say that honor and tribute have not been given to women. Pathfinders like Gloria Steinem, Melodie Beattie, Alice Miller, Betty Friedan, Marilyn

French and Phyllis Chessler have been able to heighten the awareness of both men and women to help promote a clearer and broad-
er understanding of how our families and society unwittingly led a
whole gender down the primrose path to co-dependency.

Men didn't escape the plague either. The myth of the maiden
was perpetuated, too, by the myth of manhood. Marriage vows
exemplify how our belief system served to disillusion and disap-
point us: "Do you promise to love, honor and obey, till death do
you part?"

Most of us didn't have a clue to what we were committing to at
the time of marriage, but we happily responded "I do" without ever
realizing the long-term implications. How can anyone ever be
expected to make such a commitment to another human being without knowing first who they are themselves?

Now, after we've finally dried our tears, grieved our lost dreams
and bore witness to our own children's pain from abandonment, we
seek enlightenment to bring about whatever change we can for our
future and the future of our children.

Chapter 2

ON BECOMING A WOMAN: RITES OF PASSAGE

One is not born a women. One becomes one.

—Simone De Beauvoir (1908-1986)

If an anthropologist from Mars were to study earth cultures, she would not only find a social obsession with manliness, but with femininity as well. She would find that womanhood is considered risky business, double-edged and nerve-racking. Society expects so much from women that most feel like failures before they reach full maturity. Unlike men, women live with the constant fear of being labeled an "old maid," "just a housewife," or "childless." Most everywhere they live, they are under pressure to prove themselves by establishing mastery over the home, the nursery and the job. Women, too, are expected to "provide, protect, procreate," as well as carry, labor and nurse while managing a career and simultaneously servicing a husband.

Act like a lady. You're too fat. You're too thin. Tuck in your tummy. Don't let him know you're interested. Be a teacher. Marry a doctor. Have lots of kids. Do it while you're young. Wait until you have a career. Wait for the right one. Don't be so picky. Have your nose done. Get a breast reduction. Get some implants. Have a tummy tuck. Go to Weight Watchers. Join a gym. Get some hair extensions. Try hair weaving. Get a job. Stay at home with your kids. Try both. See a therapist. Get a divorce. Have an affair. Have a nervous break-down. It will get you off your feet for a while. You'll be able to think.

Be sure you find a female shrink.

As with men, our Martian anthropologist would also find nearly every ancient and modern tribe and nation rife with formal rites and informal customs designed to turn females into women. She would find little girls dressed up in big-girl dresses, competing for Little Miss Something. Big girls half-clad in swimwear competing for Miss or Mrs. Something. She would find women encouraged to expose their buns, enlarge their breasts, develop their brains, lose their virginity, lose themselves, be strong (but not too strong, lest they be considered bitchy), be educated (but not too smart), helpless (but not invalid), coquettish (but calculating), bewitching (but not sleazy), seductive (but not whorish), and competitive (but not too pushy).

It wasn't until I was 27 that I felt some shame about my nose. It took less than three minutes. Until then, I had actually liked it. My second husband Jack and I were having dinner with a handsome Italian man with whom he had some business dealings. Over dinner, the man casually mentioned, after making some observations about my looks, that my nose tended to join my upper lip when I smiled. "You would look so much prettier if you had the tip of your nose shortened."

As if God himself had spoken, I didn't question his judgment or perception, but instead ran the next day to a plastic surgeon. Imagine someone suggesting that my teeth were too large, or my jaw too small. That's all I needed to propel myself into a plastic surgeon's office. Absolutely insane, I was ready to mutilate myself at a moment's notice. This is not to say that plastic surgery isn't a blessing, but to think how willing I was to rewrite nature on the advice of a man I barely knew is incomprehensible.

Unlike men, women did not have to separate from their fathers to prove their femaleness. Rather, they were encouraged to go from Daddy to husband without ever making the separation delineating the difference. (*The Doll House*, by Henrik Ibsen, exemplifies well this cultural phenomenon.) Nor were women expected to leave their mothers in order to claim their individuality. Rather, they were encouraged to emulate their mothers, and become carbon copies for future suitors and husbands. "I want a girl just like the girl that married dear old Dad"[2] is more truth than myth. It's part of our multigenerational dysfunctional pattern. Those of us that didn't want any part of Mom's persona or nature, inherited it anyway, even with a conscious effort to avoid doing so. An effort to become exactly the opposite is just the same as an effort to be alike. As John Bradshaw says, "One hundred eighty degrees from crazy is still crazy."

For whatever reason, I chose not to use my mother as a role model for femininity. She was too plain, too dowdy and too old-fashioned. Sexual repression stripped from her any glamour. Instead I chose to emulate Rita Hayworth, Yvonne DeCarlo, and Vivien Leigh. This collage included quite a mixed bag: A sex goddess, alcoholic, nymphomaniac and psychotic. Mother would have been a much better choice. I ran from my miserable existence at 42 Collins Avenue, where I lived in poverty and pestilence, straight to the Plaza Theater one block away, where I could fall into the arms of Larry Parks and Clark Gable, escaping the horrendous heat of Miami Beach and the horror of Lizzie the Landlady, who hated children. By 13, I could do the Dance of the Seven Veils from the movie, "Song of Scheherazade," fall into a dead faint just like Susan Hayward did in "I'll Cry Tomorrow," and recite everyone's lines from "Gone With The Wind." I was cast and groomed to become a love and sex addict without any clue to my destiny.

As we moved toward the present, particularly during the last three decades, society demanded more and more of women. The fantasies of the 1950s had become shallow and demeaning by the 1970s. Housewifery, Hadassah and PTA were bypassed by career, carpooling and the expectation to manage both. The "Super Mom" title was the new myth. Super Mom meant managing motherhood and career and looking like a million bucks.

Let me tell you how I did it. Never alone. There was always a man in my life. When I left Jack I already had Tom. (He would become my third husband.) When I heard a voice inside me say, "You are going to die if you stay in this marriage with Jack," I did what all healthy organisms do. I tried to find a way to survive. Nature, we know, abhors a vacuum. So when I became aware of mine, I looked for truth and passion elsewhere. Passion is my motivation for change and salvation. It's germane to my existence. If you want to change, look for truth and passion within.

My therapist, of course, labeled this need for change dependency, the therapeutic jargon preceding co-dependency, and now known as mystification. (I hope it stays put until I at least finish this book.) He likened my behavior to an addiction and convinced me that I was "acting out," a term he used often to describe my "pathology" (another favorite of his). He said "acting out" is taking a feeling and translating it into a behavior. Furthermore, he indicated in no uncertain terms that it was unhealthy. For me, "acting out" was as destructive as it might have been at one time salvation. Today, however, I can thank that "dependent" part of myself for saving my life. Sometimes our neurosis can save our life if it doesn't destroy us first.

When I divorced Jack, I had five children all under the age of 12, a six-bedroom, five-bath home awarded to me by the court, but not enough money to keep it, and no way to get my equity out because nobody wanted to buy it. I was desperate. My only out was to find someone to rescue me. Enter Tom.

Tom was miserably married for the second time to a rather controlling, castrating and emasculating (his adjectives, as I recall) woman with two children from a previous marriage and a son from their union. We met in group therapy and broke the cardinal rule of having an affair with a fellow patient. Our guilt forced us to reveal our secret to the other members. Our penance was marriage.

Tom was everything Jack wasn't. He was Episcopalian, Canadian, artistic, sensitive, polite and humble. Raised in an alcoholic family with an absent, philandering father and a sexually repressed, provincial, but seductive mother, Tom learned to withdraw from social situations. He carried this behavior into our marriage. To make matters worse, he had attended an English boarding school where he learned to be rigid, passive and repressed. He was practically an only child. (His only brother came many years later.) He had never been to a bar mitzvah, seen or read anything about the Holocaust, or ever heard of Golda Meir. This is the man I married.

In spite of our different values, traditions, customs and problems, we stayed together for five years. He needed a Jewish wife and I needed a Gentile husband. I helped him launch a career. He helped me launch mine. He started a design company with my support, and I began my master's degree program with his. Together, we kept the house, managed a family life and gave up smoking. He experienced his first bar mitzvah with all the accoutrements. He donned a yarmulke (skull cap) and talis (prayer shawl). He learned to dance the hora, read from the Haggadah and say "shalom." As he did all this in my home, my neighborhood, with my children, in my customs, he vanished from my body and my soul. His immersion in a culture so foreign to him made him withdraw emotionally, physically and spiritually as a protective mechanism. We went out in public together, but didn't communicate. We slept in the same bed, but didn't have sex. We shared a home, but not a life. It was not long before Tom vanished from his own soul. Eventually the old pathology resurfaced, both his and mine, and the marriage failed. I'd like to think it was his inability to believe the Holocaust actually occurred, but in fact, it was our unresolved toxic dysfunction from our respective histories that gave way to more unhealthy behavior. He retreated; I acted out. He withdrew and smoked pot; I found a lover.

There were clues everywhere. The big one was in Mexico. Tom had developed a business relationship with a German developer in Cancun. He was the designer for several projects. Henri, the developer, was a master scuba diver, bon vivant and alcoholic. I was dying in this marriage. Tom was having fantasies about sex with young girls. I had three daughters. Scuba diving seemed like a good idea, in spite of the fact that I was frightened to death of fish, not to mention sharks and barracuda. Henri was handsome. Tom was absent. I was empty. The die was cast. Mexico has no rules or regulations concerning diving. I had no rules for myself. Once again, I had no self.

We went into the sea. It was early afternoon. The weather was bad. Not weather for diving. I suggested we not go. I had just learned only one week earlier the prevailing conditions for not going diving. These were them. I was castigated for my suggestions. I acquiesced and abandoned my thoughts, needs, desires, self and common sense.

We dove into 150 feet of murky water. Before I could reach the bottom, Tom and Henri were gone. All I could see was Gerado, Henri's Mexican partner who, by this time, was several feet in front of me. Self-preservation led me to follow him. Half an hour later my mouth became dry. I was afraid, but I continued to follow Gerado. The ocean floor was barren. No reef in sight. My fear mounted. I continued to ignore it. My throat felt parched. I wanted to surface. I signaled to Gerado. We swam to the top and emerged into swells nearly ten feet high. There was no boat in sight. There was no sound of the boat within earshot. We had drifted for several miles toward the coast of Isla Mujeres, a small island off the coast of Cancun. Gerado quickly put his spear in my hand. "Hold on to this," he shouted in Spanish. I grabbed it tightly.

"Let's go back to the bottom," I shouted back. "There's no current on the bottom. We can crawl for awhile." I remembered our instructor told us to do this if ever we got caught in a current.

We had enough air to crawl on the bottom for at least twenty minutes. Gerado refused. He wanted me to stay afloat so the boat could find us in case they were looking. I, of course, obliged until I had no strength left to paddle and hold up my weights and tank. For at least an hour I paddled, spitting out water through my snorkel and pleading with Gerado to drop the equipment and swim toward the shore. It was useless. He was determined to float on top. I decided to swim back alone. I gave Gerado my equipment to hold. He insisted I not drop it.

My gear now consisted of a snorkel, goggles, life jacket and flippers. I was fighting for my life—a metaphor of my marriage. It was getting dark. I could see the Cancun shore. Still no boat. No motor or engine. No Henri, no Tom. I cursed myself over and over, "You asshole. How the hell did you get out here in the middle of the Gulf of Mexico? Mother of five children. Goddamn therapist. Idiot! Shit!" Periodically, I would look down at the sea floor. I saw the sharks, lemon sharks, with their bellies clinging to the ocean floor, undisturbed by my presence. There alongside me, swam a dozen barracuda, escorting me with curiosity and indifference. "Don't panic," I said to myself. "It won't help. Stay calm. Just keep swimming. This must be a fucking nightmare."

I remembered our diving instructor told us never to swim against the current, but diagonally instead. I swam hard, turning over on my back from time to time, trying to catch my breath and conserve my energy. Along with the waves, terror and anger swept over me. The sun was setting. Still so far to go. Then the sound of an engine . . .

"Are you alright?" Henri shouted in his defined German accent.

The anger tore through me like a blade. I felt my rage. I felt my power. "You goddamn Nazi! You fucking abandoned me."

Suddenly I realized I had a voice. I reclaimed my fear. I reclaimed my anger. Now I could protect myself. I had my power. What a price to pay for being a nice girl. Co-dependency can kill. Never again.

You might be wondering what happened to Gerado. Well, believe it or not, we found him. I led the boat precisely to where I thought he might be in the current I had befriended. As we rode back in silence together, at some point he asked, "Did you ever think you were going to die?"

"No. Why? Did you?"

"Yes. I even had a vision, as clear as a bell."

Rosemary, Gerado's wife, was six months pregnant. He described the scene he had visualized while lost at sea. He saw his not-yet-born son at age 20 or 21, talking to his friends. He heard his friend ask, "What was your father like?"

"I don't know," his son replied. "My father died three months before I was born."

Gerado died exactly three months after his son, Gerado, Jr. was born. He was killed in an automobile accident.

Who are society's role models of womanhood? How do we define ourselves? If a poll were taken by People magazine to determine the most ideal women of our time, who do you think would win? Madonna? Marilyn? Perhaps Hillary? Or maybe Oprah? Di? Barbara or Liz? Surely some would choose Gloria Steinem or Anita Hill. Of course Mother Theresa would get at least first runner up. One can be grateful that at least some of these women have truly changed some stereotypical views about women. The saddest perhaps, was Marilyn, who died never knowing who she was. And yet, her exquisite persona as the archetypal sex goddess lives on in the minds of both men and women.

Whereas women like Betty Friedan, Marianne Williamson, Margaret Mead, Lynne Andrews, Virginia Satir, Barbara Brennan, Jean Houston and many others who have truly affected both personal and social change would not likely even be mentioned. Most readers of *People* would probably have never even heard of them. As Keen points out, neither manhood nor womanhood is experienced in a social vacuum. We are judged, valued and experienced by our communities, which are often a reflection of our times. What may have been the ideal woman 30 years ago, is identified as co-dependent today. Norms and mores that may be cherished today may become ridiculed in 20 years. Are we then the reflections of our times? Or are the times a reflection of ourselves?

In the movie, "10," Bo Derek is cast as one man's fantasy of a "10." Perhaps if the movie had been produced in the 1960s we would have seen Sophia Loren in that role. And what if the producer had been blind? As Keats said, "Beauty is in the eyes of the beholder." Not only do we judge others as a product of our social times, but also as projections of our own models of the world.

There is a part of my personality that I will refer to as "Delores." Our personalities are made up of several parts and I've named mine to show them respect and consideration. A well-integrated personality is not only aware of its different parts, it also has access to and deep respect for them. Delores represents my shadow side or dark side: a hidden and powerful part of my personality.

Each one of us has a Delores persona, though we may not be aware of it. It's not the nicest part of our personality. It may even be that seedy part we pretend doesn't exist. It's usually the part that was unacceptable to our parents, and ultimately became unacceptable and perhaps even abhorrent to us. Because of this most people rid themselves of it, or at least think they do. You see, the shadow is an energy, and not unlike any other kind of energy, it can never disappear. It just hides behind us, growing larger as we pretend it's not really there, waiting to lunge into our lives when we least expect, in the most indecorous ways.

Much has been written about the shadow or dark side. Psychotherapists acknowledge and honor its presence, and stress the importance of owning this part of ourselves if we are to become fully integrated, whole beings. It is when we split off from this part of our personality and disown it that we lose our true selves. Sooner or later this disowned part of ourself finds its way back to infiltrate our personality, and it can become dangerous and ominous if not allowed admittance and recognition. A good example of this can be seen in Robert Louis Stevenson's famous work *Dr. Jekyll and Mr. Hyde.*

Throughout this book I will refer to Delores, as she is a very important and powerful part of me.

When Delores ruled my world, she was ruthless. Her energy caused havoc and destruction, reinforcing the alienation with my authenticity and power. She assumed I was worthless without her—an airhead, a "mental midget" as Jack called me. She believed my father's words, "You are nothing without him." Words that he used to discourage me from divorcing Jack. Delores declared war on my spirit. She became insatiable, forging her way triumphantly through male conquests. Each conquest fueled my thirsty ego, but the more it drank, the emptier my spirit became. She tricked me into thinking I was powerful, worthwhile and desirable. She possessed me, controlled my behavior, convoluted my thinking, twisted my values, distorted my judgment, interrupted my logic, manipulated my relationships and wove a blanket of denial so large that it took nearly 20 years in recovery to peel it off. And I didn't even know she was there.

Delores had a mission, only I wasn't aware of it. You see, behind her lived a maiden who grew up believing the myth that she was nothing without a man; a sort of perennial damsel in distress. This was the illusion that gave birth to Delores, that part in me John Bradshaw refers to as "the wounded child," which had to adapt in order to survive. It was perfectly natural for me to create Delores. She was every man's desire and would see to it that Joan's needs were met. I created what I thought would be a "perfect ten." What I didn't realize was that inside me there already was a "perfect ten" before she arrived.

The crazy thing was that in spite of the havoc she wrought, I had to learn to love her. I had to discover that it was her who helped me survive. She gave me strength. She was my genius, my power and my obedient friend—a sort of guardian angel who simultaneously wove a devil's web. She became my life force. I needed to contain her, acknowledge her, embrace her and let her know I loved her—children need their parents' love when they least deserve it. But how do we do it? How do we embrace our shadow? How do we love our most despicable parts? How do we honor the dark side when we're not even aware of its presence?

I recall well my first night in a therapy group. I had been reluctant to attend. My therapist made it a condition of treatment. I began attending in 1973, about one year after my fifth child, Aaron, was born. The group began promptly at 6:30 p.m. and I was advised to be on time. Wanting to make a good impression, I arrived on time, wearing my new rhinestone-studded patchwork jeans with matching halter top. The cut-away jacket, revealed ample cleavage accentuated by a large Indian squash blossom silver and turquoise necklace with, of course, matching dangling earrings. Atop my head was a wig, fashionably styled into two elongated ponytails, each held together by a three-inch bright pink leather ponytail clip, with leather strands braided into the ponytails. The ponytails fell loosely and deliberately over each breast.

Now for the shoes. Remember the four-inch platforms? Well these were denim-colored, with pink stripes to match the leather ponytail clips, not to mention my matching pink polished toenails.

My pancake makeup was two-toned. Tan #1 to achieve a soft, flawless, olive skin tone, contoured with Tan #2 to simulate Cherokee high cheek bones. The final touches were three, yes three, pairs of false eyelashes, bordered with black eyeliner to contour my perfectly round eyes to appear almond-shaped.

Enter Delores. The room went silent. No one spoke for at least three minutes. It seemed like ten. All eyes were upon me. Finally someone broke the silence. Clearing his throat, "Why do you need to draw such attention to yourself?"

"Who me?" I responded capriciously.

About five years later in a sensitivity training class in graduate school, Delores and I made our second debut, this time sporting an off-white, ankle-length, Indian gauze skirt and blouse, decorated with a brightly colored African medallion and, of course, matching dangling earrings. I had at least ten gold-filled bangles on my left wrist. The wig was now replaced by a mini-hair fall, combed discreetly into my own shoulder-length hair. The blouson bodice this time covered my cleavage. Platforms were out. Thin-strapped sandals were in.

I had just completed my fifth uninterrupted year of psychotherapy, with the exception of time off for the divorce hearing and a two-week honeymoon with Tom (which my therapist, Dr. McKinley, charged me for). By this time, I had made Delores' acquaintance. We were just becoming friends.

That familiar silence followed my entrance into class. We all sat in a circle on the floor. I could hardly believe it when a man asked, "Why do you find it necessary to draw such attention to yourself?"

"Oh my God." I thought. "Deja vu." I looked directly at my inquisitor and asked, "Why does it bother you?"

I had accepted her. Delores was OK. I even liked her. She had stick-to-itiveness, conviction, perspicuity and tenacity. I decided to keep her around and cultivate this hidden treasure. I would turn her into an Eliza Doolittle. Add a little class, education and humility. Perhaps I could tone her down a bit. Why, she'd be quite a lady by the time we were done. She might even become my teacher one day. I had finally begun a meaningful relationship with myself. But not until I understood that the myth of the maiden was just that, a myth. Without this knowledge, the rebirth of my self could not have occurred.

I would suggest that perhaps the most ideal women in the world today are the women who know who they are. Women who have developed healthy relationships with themselves. Women who experience a life force, a self.

In his book, *The Teachings of Don Juan: A Yaqui Way of Knowledge,* Carlos Castaneda speaks of all life paths being the same: they lead nowhere. But one, he explains, has a heart. It is the path containing all that we love. One makes for a joyful journey, the other does not. Women who follow the path with a heart are traveling a path of value. These are the exemplary women. Women who are knowing follow this path. Women who trust their intuitive nature follow this path. Clarissa Pinkola Estes, Jungian analyst and author of *Women Who Run With The Wolves,* espouses this path. She speaks of "the wild woman," an archetype, a natural force, biologically and inherently part of our life force, who somehow gets repressed, neglected or abandoned as a result of becoming civilized into our families and communities. Author and psychiatrist Alice Miller might say the wild woman gets destroyed by the poisonous pedagogy in multigenerational family dysfunction.

John Bradshaw speaks of the "wonder child." That part of our forgotten selves that re-emerges after the healing of the "wounded child," the part that got lost in the shuffle of growing up, and became frozen in time due to shame and abuse. Once recognized, reclaimed, healed and championed, the wonder child becomes our free spirit "to be" again, instead of "to do." It may be looked at as "a calling," whose voice cannot be silenced no matter how purposeful our attempts to squelch it. It demands acknowledgment and threatens destruction if it is ignored. It is a field of dreams, which may not be logical or rational; an energy source deep beneath the surface of our skin, waiting, burrowing, lurching and haunting, summoning us like ghosts in our souls who become increasingly less patient and tolerant of our denial and fears. Sometimes, the screams are so loud that they waken us in the night, invading our dreams, our cells, our organs, disturbing our thoughts, damaging our bodies and interfering with the quality of our lives. "Listen, pay attention!" it demands. "No longer will I let you remain apathetic to me. I will never cease to remind you of my existence. I will destroy you unless you acknowledge me!"

> And the raven, never flitting, still is sitting, still is sitting
> On the pallid bust of Pallas, just above my chamber door;
> And his eyes have all the seeming of a demon that is dreaming,
> And the lamplight o'er him streaming throws his shadow on the floor;
> And my soul from out that shadow that lies floating on the floor
> Shall be lifted—nevermore!
>
> *The Raven, Edgar Allan Poe*

The wild woman, not unlike the wonder child, is in our DNA, and needs only permission on a very deep level to emerge. The energy of the wild woman can only be released as the false self dies. Once we come in touch with this powerful part of ourselves, we are free to begin our heroine's journey.

Look into the mirror and you will see a goddess. Look deeper into the mirror and behold Cleopatra, Demeter, Aphrodite, Joan of Arc and Delilah. Look again and see Artemis, Athena and Hestia. Gaze upon yourself and meet Hera, Persephone, Carmen and Madame Bovary. Within your body and beneath the layers of your psyche lie the archetypes of all womanhood woven into your genes, chromosomes, molecular inheritance and divine images. The same molecules and atoms that occupied space in the bodies of Bathsheba, Salome, Ruth and Esther share space in you. You are the sum and substance of thousands of years of womanhood. You are the container of combined archeological legacies carrying the tears, passion and joys of the ones before you. Look back and see your sisters carrying their forgotten dreams, their sorrows and their unrequited loves. We are the inheritors of their wisdom, their triumphs and their glory. We are the heirs of the way womanhood has been defined.

My earliest idols were Yvonne DeCarlo and Rita Hayworth, Hollywood glamour queens of the 1940s who personified Aphrodite, even before I knew about goddesses. My six-year-old mortal soul responded to the images of these two women projected ten times their size on a movie screen in some forgotten theaters in South Beach. My heart sang out with their songs. My feet moved in rhythm with their dances. Places in my heart were born before I could name them.

At age six I embraced their identities. I had not one moment of doubt of who I was and wanted to become. At that time I remember saying, "I'd give anything to be able to dance like Scheherazade. I want to be just like her." It was in that moment that I unequivocally knew my identity. There seemed a visceral connection. I would be a goddess or die. Such conviction! How at six did I know more about my identity than perhaps today?

At age 12 I wanted to be Vivien Leigh. I could recite everyone's dialogue in "Gone With The Wind." Although I admired Melanie's virtuous character and kindness, there was no doubt that Scarlett was my mentor. She had the life force I would emulate. How I delighted in dressing up like Scarlett. I would place each leg into one of my mother's half slips, using rubber bands at the base of the knees and thighs to give the illusion of pantaloons. I packed my pubescent bosom into a brasselette that simulated Scarlett's corset. I covered my make-shift pantaloons with several horsehair crinolines and topped those with a lace and ruffled cotton one to match Scarlett's voluminous plantation petticoat. I'd use an umbrella as a parasol. Wearing white socks and black patent leather shoes, holding the opened "parasol," I'd saunter down my street, truly believing that I could win the heart of Rhett if only given the chance.

About a year later I discovered Jennifer Jones and jumped right into the part. Charlton Heston made my heart sing even more than

Yvonne DeCarlo and Rita Hayworth had done seven years previously, and Jennifer Jones knew how to conquer him.

How at such young ages did I have such a sense of self? Unfortunately, I had a terrible time convincing everyone else to accept my authentic self. I eventually learned to doubt my own choices, abandon my intuition, and I became civilized and wounded. I lost the connection with my true self; discovered at six and lost by the time I was eighteen. By the grace of God, I managed to secure a few fancies deep beneath my conscious awareness. Once the coast was clear, they re-emerged. There was a price to pay for the delay, however. My confidence was shattered. My self-esteem was practically nonexistent. The damage was done. I am reminded of T. S. Eliot's *Four Quartets*, ". . . and the end of all our exploring will be to arrive where we started and know the place for the first time."

On Being a Daughter

Oh, my son's my son 'till he gets him a wife,
But my daughter's my daughter all her life.

—Dinah Maria Mulock Craik (1826-1887)

My mother died on January 12, 1993. I'll never get the memory of my dying mother out of my mind. She lay helpless in a designated hospice bed, in the same room with another woman who was not so designated. She had been in a coma for six days. My oldest daughter Linda, my brother Mickey and my mother's sister Marian were gathered around her. I had finally agreed to remove all support systems. The feeding tube was the last to go.

"How can I allow her to starve to death?" I pleaded tearfully with my aunt.

"It will only prolong it," she whispered sympathetically.

I looked at my mother's frail, almost skeletal, body lying and dying in this last resting place. Her dyed brown hair was dry and brittle. The gray bled through. There was the streak of white just above her brow that she claimed gave her an identity. My second daughter Emily, a hairdresser, would lovingly brush my mother's hair everyday, and speak to her of fond memories from her childhood, recalling times my mother had shared with her—but my mother never responded.

There was perspiration beading on her brow. The acrid smell still lingers in my mind. Her mouth was slightly open. Her lips were parched and cracked from all the tubing and medication. Her eyes were half open. She stared, but could see or hear nothing. That's what the doctors who barely saw her told me. I'll never really know for sure. On this last day of her life no doctor came.

Her breathing was shallow. The only sign that she had difficulty breathing was the translucent green oxygen mask on her nose. This I couldn't allow them to take away. The nurse said it was redundant anyway. I needed to leave something attached to her to assure myself that I wasn't just letting her die. The oxygen mask was more for me than for her. This was my mother, breathing just enough to stay alive for a few more hours.

The night before, I alternated sleeping on her bed near her legs and downstairs in the ICU waiting room on the worn sectionals. It's funny how even in my state of grief and despair, I noticed how annoying it was when those sectionals kept separating when I lied down on the cracks. I still remember that.

My brother and I shared our memories and grief. Linda was my spiritual support. This was her grandmother. Her grief was as deep as mine. We took turns checking on my mother.

She looked the same. Her body trembled. Her fever was 106. How much longer? Maybe we should have kept the antibiotics going a little longer. What if we waited just a few more days to see if perhaps her strength could have returned? These questions and more haunted my thoughts hour after hour.

My mother had rheumatoid arthritis since she was 60. I always felt the disease was an expression of things she never expressed throughout her life. Her body wore her pain, her anger and her unspoken disappointments. My mother was giving up. Now she was 77. Her fight was nearly over. She caught a cold on New Year's Eve. 12 days later she would be dead from pneumonia.

Everyday we waited. I watched my father's face go pale each time he came into her room. I saw his eyes fill with tears, and I knew his heart was breaking. I never saw my father cry before. He was sobbing. His grief had no restraints. He buried his face in my brother's chest and cried. He was nearly 85. My brother wept with him. Imagine. I saw my father's wife of 56 years, my mother, his kindred spirit and best friend breaking his heart before my eyes.

"Don't leave me, Minnie. I need you. You're the best. Please don't leave me," he cried.

It's hard to watch your father's heart break.

We came in. All of us. Her six grandchildren, my father, my brother and sister-in-law, her two sisters, my husband and I. We crowded around her bed along with the machines. There were tubes resembling plastic tentacles attached to a different part of her limp body. One for breathing, one for feeding, one for draining and one for suctioning. Others just made deliberate sounds to remind us that her life was being measured minute by minute, second by second.

We took each sound so seriously, as if it gave us new data and information each time it shifted rhythm. Information we would not be able to interpret anyway. High-tech, mechanical noises, beeps and air sounds that seemed to beat to refrains of "Que Sera, Sera," her favorite song that we sang to her each day.

"Minnie," I whispered, cradling her in my arms. "Minnie me, Minnie me, a booga," my first baby gibberish words I had learned when I wanted her attention. I spoke these words again, at age 53, over and over, gently stroking her delicate, frail legs. I had hoped to hit a chord. Some small entry. Anything, just to make contact. To let her know she wasn't alone.

Only two months earlier my parents had signed their living wills. I knew my mother's wishes. I wanted to honor them. But it was so subjective. How could I determine if her illness was terminal and hopeless? At what point can we make that judgment that decides a person's life or death? They all looked to me to decide. They all gave opinions, but the final decision would be mine. I consulted with the doctors—who were as ambivalent as we were. No one wanted that responsibility. Everyone agreed, however, it was best to pull the machines and let her go. We all agreed to do it on the sixth day, Monday, January 11. The doctors and I signed the necessary papers. Even though we were all in agreement, and both my father and brother also signed the papers, I felt like the designated decision maker. I felt like her executioner—daughter and her executioner. What if I was wrong? I prayed and asked her to forgive me. My mother's vitality was gone. Her spirit had vanished. She wasn't able to breathe on her own, but there was no evidence of brain death. I prayed again. I don't remember not praying. I knew this was not the quality of life she would want.

"Your mother wouldn't want to live like this," my Aunt Marian said. "You're only prolonging this."

This was my mother, not hers. Yet, I needed and wanted the guidance and support. But how could I justify this?

I honored her living will and we waited. The waiting seemed endless. I felt guilty and confused. Had I done the right thing? I kept praying. That was my only comfort.

My mother and I had never really been close. I felt no real kindred spirit with her. I was everything she disowned and she was what I disowned. Our generation gap felt like two. The early injunctions not heard but felt were "don't feel." As a child, feelings were minimized and often ridiculed, but rarely validated.

"Sarah Heartburn. That's what I'll call you," she would often say if I showed my emotions or expressed any feeling that might have touched her own spiritual wounds. There was never any display of affection or an "I love you"—but I knew she loved me. Her love came in unseen or unspoken messages. She saved it for my children, and what she couldn't give to me, she gave to them in double doses.

It was difficult being the daughter of a mother who had never learned to express her needs or emotions. Making her happy was easy. It required little effort. Hang up the wash. Take it down. Fold it. Keep the apartment clean. Don't leave dishes in the sink. Don't be who you really are. Don't be honest with your feelings. I never experienced the bonding with my mother that I feel with my daughters. I guess the missing ingredient was truth. It was never safe to be honest with her. Sharing myself would have highlighted our differences. Differences that she feared and abhorred. Honesty elicited punishment. Punishment meant guilt or silence. Therefore, I learned to withhold or delete information. Consequently, intimacy was sacrificed.

She came to me in a dream the other night. She put her arms around me and kissed me. She told me she loved me.

"Mom!" I cried. "What are you doing? Why are you holding me now?"

"Because I never did when you needed me."

The day before she died, my two aunts and I took a drive out to Sawgrass Mills, a sprawling outlet mall in suburban Fort Lauderdale, just to get away from the morbid surroundings. We were driving in a heavy downpour, a rarity in January in South Florida. Visibility on the road was so bad that I seriously thought about turning around. I had never been to this particular shopping center before, so I was uncertain about my direction and whereabouts. It felt like a metaphor of my state of being. I anguished over my ambivalence at the hospital again and again. My aunts tried hard to reassure me.

"You're doing the right thing," they both said. "Honestly, your mother wouldn't want to live like this. There's no dignity."

Tears were streaming down my face as I pulled into the parking area. Then something very strange occurred. Suddenly, in the middle of this heavy rainstorm, out of nowhere appeared the most perfect and complete rainbow I had ever seen arching clear across the sky. I then realized my mother was gone. She had shed her light and being through the miracle of the rainbow. I interpreted it as the permission from her I so desperately needed to turn off the machines.

It took 53 years for me to realize I was a lot closer to my mother than I thought I had been. It took 53 years of my life and her death to become the daughter I was never allowed to be.

On Being a Wife

The girl that I marry will have to be as soft and pink as a nursery.
The girl that I call my own will wear satins and laces and smell of cologne.
Her nails will be polished and in her hair, she'll wear a gardenia and I'll be there. 'Stead of flittin' I'll be sittin'
Next to her and she'll purr like a kitten
—A doll I can carry the girl that I marry must be.

—Irving Berlin

I was 12 years old when my father told me the reason he married my mother was because she kept her drawers so clean and neat.

I knew I was doomed if that was the criteria men had for the woman they wanted to marry. My drawers were a perennial disaster.

My mother's hands always smelled like Clorox or Oxydol soap. She washed the floors on her hands and knees, vacuumed daily, lined the garbage cans with newspapers (after she washed them down with Pine Sol) and hung the clothes outside. She ironed everything, including my father's boxer shorts. She never bought name brands, prime cut meats, Bing cherries (too expensive), or any product that wasn't kosher. On Sundays, she would relieve my father in the hotel he had managed for 25 years, so he could have a day off (which would be hell for me because he made me practice the accordion for two hours on those days). For this effort, she earned eight dollars. She knew how to make a dollar into two, and two meals into three. She never went out to dinner or to the theater, except an occasional movie, and that wasn't until I was 12 and old enough to babysit my brother. She rarely bought herself a new dress, and if she did, it never cost more than $25, and had to be on sale from Hartley's Department Store. She stressed the importance of having one "better" dress rather than five cheap dresses.

On the day she succeeded in talking my father into buying their first piece of property, at 145 Jefferson Avenue, an eight-unit apartment house consisting of four one-bedroom apartments and four efficiencies, she promised him she would go to work to help contribute to the mortgage payments. That scared my father to death. When I was 12 she also found a job with an attorney on Lincoln Road and became his secretary—a job which lasted 37 years. She never spent a dime without asking my father's permission, continued to relieve him on Sundays at the hotel, and taught me how to line the garbage pails, hang the clothes and iron my father's boxer shorts. I never did any of it as well as she, and yet more than anything, I wanted to be a housewife and mother. Somehow I knew I would never have the chance to dance like Yvonne DeCarlo did in "Song of Scheherazade."

My role model at this time was my cousin Yvette, who was three years older than me. Whatever she did or had, I wanted. But whatever that may have been, we couldn't afford. Her father, my father's older brother, was rich and prominent in the community. They pretended we didn't exist. Of course, this only made me want what she had, and I didn't have, even more.

When she graduated high school, she attended college at the University of Alabama; and so did I when I graduated. When she was 19, she married a young man named Carl. The wedding was at the Fountainbleu Hotel. I would also marry a man named Carl at the Fountainbleu Hotel when I was 19. She had 200 people at her wedding. I had 20. This was the end of my role modeling. Her marriage lasted 35 years. Mine lasted two.

How I envied Yvette. I wanted to be her instead of me. I wanted to wear her clothes, live in her two-story house on Alton Road and switch fathers. She played the piano and I was stuck with a 120-base black accordian. Funny how things turn out. Thank God I wasn't her. Her son died at age 27. He was struck by lightning. He left a wife five months pregnant. And after 35 years of marriage her husband, Carl, left her.

When Carl and I were married, we moved in with his parents in Bay Harbor, a quantum leap from South Beach. Carl's mother, Rose, taught me about Joy dishwashing detergent, Wallace sterling, Waterford crystal and Lenox china. She taught me how to set a table, select a menu and prepare a meal that tasted like it was prepared by a gourmet chef. She loved me. Her husband, Milton, loved me. Her son, my husband Carl, unfortunately did not. He loved Mallowmars, Bob Cousy and "Gunsmoke." My culinary and domestic training I owe to Rose. I was grateful to abandon Oxydol, kosher soap and generic brands. I was 19 before I ever tasted Heinz ketchup, Bing cherries or a shrimp cocktail.

My maternal grandfather came to America from Poland in 1904. He traveled over here with his best friend, Sammy Goldfish, who did his best to convince my grandfather to follow him to California, where Sammy had heard about the nickelodeon. My grandfather, afraid that his fiancee (my grandmother), would then change her mind about following him to the United States, decided against it. Instead, he decided to stick to his original plans of settling in Gloversville, a small town in upstate New York, noted for glove manufacturing, which had been my grandfather's trade in Warsaw. It was a decision that he probably lived to regret for the rest of his life. Sammy Goldfish soon changed his name to Samuel Goldwyn. Another quirk of fate.

My grandmother, looking for ways to raise my grandfather's spirits after long, tedious hours at the factory, day after day, would surreptitiously plant a five dollar bill on the porch stairs moments before he returned home from work. Knowing his day was the same as the day before, and wanting to lift up his spirits, she would call her children to the window moments before his arrival so they could all watch the excitement on his face when he discovered the money.

"Eva," he would shout from the front porch, waving the bill frantically to the family. "Zee vus ich hub gafindt!" *Look what I found.*

"Vus hus de gafindt?" *What have you found?* she would ask, as she and the children would laugh. I often wondered if my grandfather went along with the charade to keep up my grandmother's need to be needed.

And so it went. My grandmother would find ways to make life a little bit easier for my grandfather. It was the least she could do after he brought her to America.

My mother, too, focused on being a caretaker. She supported my father's personal and professional development like a guardian angel hidden in the wings of his shadows, never too intrusive, but with just enough restraint and encouragement to make his personal achievements and successes look like his own. She took the backseat to all his efforts, which she quietly initiated each and every time.

When he took his first risk and entered the stock market in 1938, it was she who said "Yes, do it!" When he moved to Florida and worked 12 hours a day, six days a week at a hotel that he shared in a partnership with three other people, one of whom was his older brother, it was she who worked the 12 hours on the seventh day so he could rest. His rest was more important than hers. When he feared that he might lose all his savings by buying an apartment building that she wanted so they could accrue equity and live rent free, it was she who committed to working as long as need be, promising to contribute her full paycheck toward whatever he needed to overcome his fear. Her commitment lasted as long as the final mortgage payment: 37 years. And when she died, 56 years after they were married, it was she, only nights before her death, who nursed his flu, tended to his dinner and brought him tea while her flu turned into double viral pneumonia. Martyr? Co-dependent? Perhaps. Caretaker for sure.

During one of the most precarious times during my marriage to Jack, I looked to my parents in a desperate cry for help. My mental state was so compromised that getting up each day was an effort. I chewed Valium to get through the mess. This particular day I had chewed one too many. I called my parents for help. My mother asked my father to accompany her.

"Gene," she said to my father who sat practicing at his organ, "Joni is having so many problems. We need to go and help her. Please come with me."

He maintained his position, as if in a trance, his body moving steadily up and down to the euphonious sounds emanating from his new Hammond.

"You go," he replied, even after she had pleaded several times. "You'll tell me all about it when you come home."

And so she nursed me all day alone. She listened to my woes, counseled me, tended to my five children, helped with lunch and dinner, baths, bedtime stories, and then wearily drove home by herself that evening. There she found my father, still sitting and playing the organ, exactly as she had left him hours before, moving to the music.

"Oh Gene," she cried. "My God, the problems that girl has. She's depressed. The children are depressed. Jack doesn't come home at night. There's no family life. She cries all day and wants to leave him. What are we going to do?"

"That's nice," he commented from the organ stool to the refrain of "Tico Tico." "That's nice."

On Being a Mother

So this is what I will do. I will gather together my past and look. I will see a thing that has already happened. The pain that cut my spirit loose. I will hold that pain in my hand until it becomes hard and shiny, more clear. And then my fierceness can come back, to my golden side, my black side. I will use this sharp pain to penetrate my daughter's tough skin and cut her tiger spirit loose. She will fight me, because this is the nature of two tigers. But I will win and give her my spirit, because this is the way a mother loves her daughter.

—Amy Tan, The Joy Luck Club

I don't think I was a good mother. Certainly not the kind of mother I would have liked to have been. I abandoned my children. Not intentionally or even consciously, but intentions aren't relevant when you are in search for truth. I wasn't present for them. I emotionally abused them, neglected them and there were times I even hit them. I lacked the maturity to understand and be responsive to their needs. I lacked the insight to be responsive to my own. I expected too much from them. I became enraged when the house was messy. I made them responsible for my feelings. I often lost my temper. I didn't get up early enough to prepare them for school adequately, and many times arrived late or left them stranded at places that I had forgotten about.

Contrary to popular belief, motherhood doesn't come naturally to all women. And even if it did, circumstances often affect its efficacy. The myth of motherhood has promulgated guilt, anxiety and feelings of inadequacy.

I knew nothing about parenting, my most important role in life. I knew more about purchasing a car than raising children. What I knew, intrinsically, came by way of the 40,000-year-old woman who resided within my soul. She along with perhaps Demeter, the maternal goddess, Ruth, Esther, Leah, Sarah and Rebecca raised my children. They were my unconscious maternal teachers, guiding me through unfamiliar territory. They guided me through those dark and treacherous years, steering me like a ship in troubled waters to a safe harbor. I was dead inside. My marriage was dead. The only life I could produce was in my uterus. Then I felt alive, worthy and productive. Not a reason to have children. Mothers are to meet the needs of their children. A child's purpose is not to fill the empty life of its mother. Carl Jung once said that the most damaging effects on the family are the unlived lives of the parents.

So in 1973 I got a life. My best friend, Phyllis, then a social work major at Barry University, found a therapist for herself. She urged me to get some help.

"You're out of touch with your feelings," she said.

I had no idea what the hell she was talking about, but somehow, I knew she was right. So I went to see her therapist, Dr. McKinley, and wound up in therapy for eight years. Part of my recovery was self-discovery. My first job was to love myself. Once accomplished,

I could give of myself to my emotionally starved children. Motherhood is like healthy narcissism. The more you love yourself, the more you can love your child. Self-love is something we don't usually bring into motherhood. Most of us evolve into parenthood with barely a sense of self. This doesn't make for a healthy marriage, let alone healthy parenting. We look to our children to make up the deficits in ourselves and our marriages.

I wanted a baby almost as soon as I was married. Why the rush? I suspect the lonely nights, my culture and my mother were the reasons. My mother said, "Have five children. Four for you, and one for me. Your father only wanted two. Have five." So I did. Then she had the nerve to tell me that one mother can take care of five children, but five children can't take care of one mother. Looking back, not only was she wrong, but I think my five children did a much better job of taking care of me than I did of them.

Our lives are usually so contaminated with unresolved conflicts from our source relationships that unless we work out these leftovers before marriage and family, we are going to contaminate our own families with our past problems. Motherhood is fertile ground for repeating these destructive patterns. Every person contemplating having children should heed this warning: BECOME A PERSON BEFORE YOU BECOME A PARENT.

And what of this divine gift called motherhood? Are there words to describe the first time you feel life within your womb? That unexpected sudden shift of movement in your belly? Are there words to recount the first time you hear your baby's heartbeat, or see the faint fetal image projected on a monitor? Each day I was continuously amazed at the metamorphosis of my mind and body. He or she had infiltrated my territory. That innocent, unsuspecting little human being in the making had wrought more havoc on my body and mind than anything I had ever known before. I thought to myself, Will I have any peace? But then, more than precious peace arrives when you hear that first cry of life. Then you feel the vitality as you realize it was your life force that has given birth to yet another. You are the co-creator of life. Woman is divinely able to procreate the species. We are the vessels that transport new beings and souls into life, blessed with a gift no man can ever know. But then again, without their life force we carry nothing.

I didn't plan on having five children in eight and a half years. Albeit, my mother gave me the injunction, there was never a conscious effort on my part to reproduce within a specific time table. In fact, after the fourth baby, I was advised by my physician not to have anymore children because it was determined that I had a "boggy" uterus, among other unpleasant side effects of having four children so close together. Therefore, precautions were taken to avoid another pregnancy. I was fitted for an IUD, and nine months later, my son Aaron was born with it wrapped around his wrist.

The circumstances surrounding this pregnancy were quite unusual. Due to a condition I had called hyperlipidemia, I had been selected to become part of a control group at a local hospital to participate in a study to determine the effects of a new drug that was being tested for this condition. Never believing I would become pregnant, especially with the latest hardware, I agreed to become part of the study. When it was discovered that I was indeed pregnant, the doctors performing the study were anxious for me to continue; there had never been anyone pregnant in a study such as this for results to be measured and reported. My personal obstetrician and internist advised me to terminate either the study or the pregnancy, believing it would not be in my best interest to continue both. Both physicians were leaning more toward terminating the pregnancy based on my medical history and the unknown effect on pregnant women using this experimental drug. My husband, Jack, agreed with them. Florida did not permit elective abortions in 1971, so we made arrangements to have it done in New York.

As we were getting into the car to go to the airport, suddenly my inner voice shouted loud and clear, "Have this baby!"

Jack had just finished loading the car with our luggage and was opening the door for me to get in. My face must have gone white. I couldn't move.

"Get in," he said matter-of-factly. "Come on, get in. You look like you're going to faint."

"I'm not going," I said.

He looked at me as if he hadn't heard what I said.

"Get in. Let's go. We're running late. We'll miss the plane."

"No. I can't. I won't," I replied vehemently.

"Have you lost your mind? Get in the car. Let's go!"

"No. I can't. I'm not going. That's all there is to it."

"You must have gone crazy. What's gotten into you? You know the risk is too dangerous. We're batting a thousand with four beautiful healthy children. Why the hell do you want to take a chance with your health and the health of a baby? Let's go! Now!" he screamed.

I ran down the block listening to Jack as he shouted from the car. He followed me for a while, but when he realized it was hopeless, I found myself walking alone somewhere familiar in the neighborhood.

Seven months later, Aaron was born. He weighed nine pounds. His black hair stood straight up on his head, like Indian feathers, so the nurses called him Geronimo. He smiled before he ever opened his eyes. His Hebrew name was Abraham, after my Uncle Abe, who had died only six weeks before. He was my favorite uncle, and he and his wife Gertie were childless. She had died a few years before him. So I named the baby Aaron Gregory.

Five days after the delivery, and three days before Aaron's circumcision, I hemorrhaged. I called Jack at the office and he came home and rushed me to the hospital. Because I had just eaten a large meal, there was some reluctance to anesthetize me too heavily. They were going to pack my uterus, and if necessary, perform a hysterectomy.

I remember the tube going down my throat. Then, in what seemed like only seconds, I felt myself rising out of my body. I rose to the right corner of the operating room, and watched the operation. I saw my legs in stirrups, the doctors and nurses surrounding the operating table, and heard their voices and the mechanical sounds of the machines. Suddenly, I saw a golden, white light emanating from what looked like a long tunnel. I began to walk through the tunnel. It looked so long, but I could see the outlet to the other side. As I approached, I heard voices. There, in what looked like a courtroom, I saw my Uncle Abe. I saw other old men who looked like sages with white beards getting ready to hold a hearing or a meeting. As soon as he saw me he yelled to me in Yiddish, "*Gey avech.*" Go away, waving his arm with his palm stretched out. "*Gey avech. Gey tsrick. Siz nish dein czite. Gey tsrick.*" Go back. It's not your time.

"I want to go with you," I said. "Let me go with you."

"*No. Di kenst nit kimmen. Gey tsrick tzu dein meshpucha.*" You can't come. Go back to your family.

He was adamant, so I returned and re-entered my body. When I awoke in the recovery room, my mother was alongside my bed. The rails were up, and I was crying. "Mom, I saw him. I saw Uncle Abe. He argued my case before God, or someone who looked like he might be God. He told me to go back. It wasn't my time. I just had a child who needed to be born. He needed me, and I was to go back."

My mother had tears in her eyes too. She tried to console me.

I found out later that before he came to the United States, my Uncle Abe had been married in Poland and had a child. My Aunt Gertie was his second wife. His first wife died in childbirth. She hemorrhaged a few days after the delivery. The child had died too.

Could it be that women are determined to be caretakers, rescuers and relentless friends and nurturers? Is it in our genes, chromosomes and DNA to fall deeper into our feelings, our madness and passion? Could it be that in spite of women's lib, equal rights and empowerment we still run home when the house alarm goes off, call our girlfriends about our boyfriends, stay home from work if the baby is sick, make the car pool arrangements, bring the cleaning in before work and pick up dinner on the way home?

Demeter, Mary, Ruth, Sarah, Naomi, Golda Meir and Eleanor Roosevelt were women of valor, women of honor, women of power and women of change. But given a choice, I'd bet their husbands, children and family problems kept them awake nights more than any other worry.

How do we know to call home when we sense some danger? How do we know when to call the doctor before anyone needs to advise us? How do we know how to rock a child in our arms if we ourselves may never have been rocked? How do we know how to wake up seconds before we hear the baby's cry? How do we know when it's time to turn off the life support system? To wipe a brow. To hold a hand. To say "I'm sorry." To say, "I love you."

I believe women are genetically, biologically, chemically and certainly sociologically designed to be agents of nurturing. Demeter, the archetypal goddess/mother woven into the soul of most women thankfully remains constant as our eternal well of giving. And, if her expression is denied, it can have significant repercussions on our emotional well-being.

Once I felt her presence, without even knowing her name, I never seemed to be able to let her go. When I became pregnant with Aaron, I chose, in spite of my doctors' warnings, to have this child. Foolish. Perhaps. But some force within, (perhaps Demeter), caused me to ignore medical reasoning and fulfill my need to have this child. As my life changed through divorce and other circumstances, I abandoned this child I was once willing to die for. This abandonment gave rise to illness in both of us, until one day I could no longer avoid acknowledging the obvious.

Aaron was the fifth of five children. The first latchkey kid on the block. At age seven, I told him to go directly home after school and wait there until an older sibling arrived an hour later. His older brother, Tim, angry about his own abandonment issues, brought home his aggression and frustration, displacing these unconscious forces on his younger brother, using him as a scapegoat to vent his feelings. Often, Tim would bring home his friends who would collectively bully Aaron to release their frustration. Although there was usually a woman present who had worked for me as a domestic for many years, her limited authority had little impact on protecting Aaron from the mental and physical abuse he endured for so many years. He had no one there to protect him.

I was in graduate school until late in the evening. Their father, by this time, had lost his license to practice medicine in Florida. He was forced to move to Missouri, the only state that accepted his license. My inability to balance home and school life, coupled with a lack of maturity kept me from being an effective nurturer for any of my children. Aaron, being the youngest, received nothing, except whatever nurturing the other siblings could provide and an occasional visit from my mother, who in spite of her own limitations, gave whatever she could. The financial and emotional stress of these living conditions, together with my single parenthood, prompted my decision to invite my lover at the time, Tom, to move in with me and my children. Neither of us really needed this. Now I had an Episcopalian boyfriend living in a Jewish neighborhood with five Jewish kids, all of whom were attending either Sunday school or

Hebrew school. One was preparing for a bat mitzvah, another was being forced against his will to begin his studies for his bar mitzvah. Add to this, their father Jack filed for bankruptcy, which meant little or no child support. Compounded with Tom's decision to begin his own business, we did what most co-dependents would do. We got married.

In the meantime, Aaron was being more and more neglected, as were the other children. He found the refrigerator as a source of love to fill up his emptiness. By the time he was 13 and ready for his bar mitzvah, it was difficult to fit him for a suit. By this time, Tom and I were already divorced, and I was now living with an ex-seminarian, Italian food broker from South Philadelphia who was in serious trouble with the IRS. His wife and two kids lived less than a half mile away. Phil moved in two days after Tom left. This was my kid's third father figure in six years. Confused? Imagine the impact this must have had on the children.

At 16, Aaron weighed over 250 pounds. His growth, both vertically and horizontally, could no longer be supported by his skeletal system. Coming off the bus one day from school, his right leg buckled, causing a slippage of the hip into the femur. He developed pain in the knee from the misalignment caused by the accident, thus obscuring the real problem. Not giving his injury the attention it deserved, I discounted the severity of the problem and told him to stay off his feet. After a few days with no change, I suggested he see his father, who by now had returned to Florida to resume his practice after seven years in Missouri. His father, looking for the problem in the knee, missed the fracture.

Aaron was referred to a specialist, who also missed the diagnosis. His treatment consisted of lying in an adult crib, straddled to a metal traction bar with no other activity or physical therapy. He was released after a week without any improvement, but it was apparent something was terribly wrong. By this time, I had a new boyfriend, Mervyn, who would become my fourth husband. He saw the problem and advised me to consult a children's orthopedic specialist.

Aaron had a hip operation that left him with a leg one inch shorter than the other. His left foot turned out at a 45 degree angle, so he could no longer ride a bicycle. He had a noticeable limp and two metal pins in his upper leg. This abominable condition, coupled with his excessive weight, diminished his sense of self-value and resulted in chronic depression. He had not yet turned 17. This was the child I was unwilling to abort when advised to do so.

Once again Demeter had invaded my soul. Here I was nurturing the souls of others, unable to give my child the nurturing he so desperately needed. Aaron agreed to attend an eating disorder treatment program for adolescents. During Family Week, a time designated for the families of patients to interact and become educated about eating disorders, we had an opportunity to resolve some old issues. I came each day with an exuberance that I had so long been lacking. But his father never came. His excuse was that he couldn't afford the time away from his busy practice. Mervyn, Aaron's fourth father figure, accompanied me instead.

Caught in a fantasy mother/child bond, Aaron was unable to acknowledge that I had abandoned him. Children tend to deify and mythologize their parents. They see them as perfect. Therefore when children are punished or abused, they blame themselves, not their parents. This is a normal response in childhood and is best described in a book called *The Fantasy Bond*, by Robert Firestone. John Bradshaw refers to this work quite often.

Aaron was doing what all children must do: Feel that they matter and that their parents are OK. Unwilling to give up the fantasy and demythologize me, or allow himself and others to see me as less than perfect, and perhaps even neglectful, he became caught in a conflict between truth and fantasy. Each day he manipulated the arrangement of seats and timing, so that he could avoid confronting me as was expected of him and all the other adolescents on the unit.

It was now Friday, the last day of Family Week. The therapist looked at Aaron, whose discomfort was like a neon sign.

"Well, Aaron," he said. "You have managed to avoid this confrontation for five days. Now the time has run out. So, look at your mother and tell her what she did and what you needed that you didn't get."

Aaron was turning colors. He was fidgeting, twisting and turning. He grimaced and tears welled up.

"Tell your mother, Aaron. Look in her eyes and tell your mother what you needed that you didn't get. Tell your mother what she did."

Silence. No truth.

"Aaron. We're running out of time. Do you want to get well?"

"Yes."

"Then tell your mother. Now!"

"I can't," he said.

"Why not?"

"Because it hurts so much," he cried with tears streaming down his swollen face. "I love my mother. I don't want to hurt her. She did the best she could. Please, don't make me say it."

"Look at your mother, Aaron," the therapist demanded. "Speak your truth and tell her what you have never been able to tell her. Do it now."

Aaron slowly shifted his face up to meet my eyes. Tears were already in mine. I knew this was so important to his recovery. I waited with a heart full of sadness. I saw my son's pain. I leaned forward as if to give him the permission he needed. I waited.

"Mom," he said. "You, you . . . you . . . ab . . . aba . . . aban . . ."

"Aaron," Jim the therapist shouted. "Tell her. Tell your mother." Weeping, unable to contain his grief, he quietly said, "You abandoned me, Mom."

"What did you say, Aaron? I didn't hear you. Your mother didn't hear you. Say it again, louder."

There were no more words. Only the sounds of repressed anguish, loneliness, sorrow, anger and shame. His eyes were filled with tears as he held his head down into his hands.

"Don't hold your head down," said the therapist. "Look into her eyes. Hold your head up. You've done nothing wrong. Give your mother back her shame and tell her what you never had the resources to tell her. Tell her the truth."

His grief continued to eat up his words. But I heard them in spite of the sniffling, choking and gagging. I heard his truth clearly, and I was so grateful—it would become his healer.

I looked in his swollen red eyes, walked over to my son, put my arms around him and said, "You're right. Aaron. You are right. I did abandon you. I wish it could have been different. You deserved a mother and a father. You had neither. I'm so sorry I couldn't be there for you growing up, protecting you and loving you the way you needed to be loved."

And the healing began. He was validated, legitimized. His truth had been received and embraced by the person who meant the most to him. His mother, now his nurturer. Thank you Demeter. You saved my son's life.

On Being a Madonna and Whore

I can do this. This too, like all the above is in our DNA. We are socially, morally, psychologically and exquisitely schizophrenic. We have that permission. We're all Madonnas and whores. It's a delightful co-existence. Delores is my whore, and Sarah is my Madonna. They can both take you for a ride on a wave of sheer joy. They can both cause you pain and grief. They are polar opposites.

One time, during a very rough period in my marriage to Jack, I had been acting out dangerously and destructively. Delores was out of control again. She seemed to go wild when certain needs were not being met. She was on a rampage, and I nearly ran into a problem.

I had decided to meet Tom in New York after Jack had canceled plans to take me to New York. Jack thought a week in New York might give us a chance to see if there was any life left in our marriage. It was a half-hearted attempt to rekindle a long-gone flame. That Jack suddenly changed plans the day before we were to leave for "business" reasons infuriated me, so I immediately invited Tom to join me. I was "acting out" my anger by translating it into a behavior. Jack and I had reservations at the Americana Hotel on Seventh Avenue. Jack suggested I fly up, see a few shows, shop, and he would join me in four or five days. (This was Jack's modus operandi.) He would take his feelings of guilt, translate them into a behavior and give me permission to spend money to absolve his guilt. So now we have my anger and his guilt being transformed into behaviors that were counterproductive, destructive and undermining the chance for any marital reconstruction and reconciliation that might have occurred if we had both dealt with our feelings instead of acting them out. (But what did we know?)

I agreed, but added Tom to the deal. For five days and four nights, Tom and I did the Big Apple. We dined out every evening, went to the theater and danced at Dionysus, a Greek night club that Jack and I visited every trip we made to New York. We walked through the safer parts of Central Park, and shared a hansom cab ride. We visited museums and art galleries, strolled down Fifth Avenue, shopped at Barney's, Bergdoff's and Bloomies, lunched at Tavern on the Green, attended the opera, and of course, took a boat ride around Manhattan. Delores was in charge of the trip. She chose what I would wear. (And I might add, her taste was more than provocative—it was whorish.) She planned the nature of each evening, filling the night with a sensuality that bordered on madness. Tom's Episcopalian ethics and sense of decency were compromised, and soon completely vanished.

For five days and four nights we behaved like two lascivious rascals. On the fifth day, Tom left and Jack arrived. Both from the same airport at approximately the same time. The two men crossed paths at LaGuardia, neither seeing the other.

The first evening Jack arrived, we went out on the town again. My dress again was revealing and flashy. The only change from the night before was the man on my arm. Hotel security had been paying close attention. It was hard to miss me. That evening upon returning from Dionysus, the same Greek supper club Tom and I had been to the night before, two plainclothes policemen greeted me in the elevator. Holding the elevator doors open, one spoke with an air of authority and arrogance, while the other just smiled.

"Miss, are you a guest in this hotel?"

I stared at them with a quizzical and confused look and said nothing.

"This is my wife and of course she's a guest in this hotel," Jack sternly replied.

"Forgive the intrusion. We just needed to check." The elevator doors closed.

"What do you think that was about?" I asked innocently.

"They thought you were a hooker and were going to arrest you if I hadn't just saved your ass."

"Why would they think that?" I said naively. And then it hit me like a bolt of lightning. I put my head in my hand, and heard myself say in silence, "That was very stupid!"

Jack loved the whorish look. He was sort of a Damon Runyon character himself, a Nathan Detroit, and my look complemented his flashy style. It was sometimes difficult to tell him apart from the pit bosses or me from a call girl. He loved Delores' style, but I'm not sure he appreciated her behavior.

Phil, who called himself "the Italian Stallion," a la Sylvester Stallone, preferred the madonna in me. It offended him if I dared to even exhibit one glimpse of Delores. This was hard for me to understand because it was Delores who conquered him in the first place. As soon as the conquest was made, he only allowed her in the bedroom. He assumed ownership of me, and I gave him permission as one would a master. He requested Delores on demand, when it suited him. Otherwise she was banished. This Roman Catholic, recovering seminarian from South Philly, who gave up the priesthood because God made a few too many demands on him, projected the unacceptable parts of his personality (even Jesus would have been more tolerant) onto me. Then under the guise of "class," he declared a personal war on Delores in an effort to avoid dealing with his own disowned parts. I was his shadow and he nearly destroyed me. After he put a gun to my head one very disturbing evening, I ended the relationship. When Delores and Sarah got together and integrated our forces, we threw him out. We've been a team together ever since, committing never to repress either part. I needed them both. Together, we stood a chance. Like Jesus taught when the inside is like the outside, and the outside is like the inside, then you're in heaven.

On Being a Goddess

There are goddesses in every woman. Look within, and you may see Artemis, the goddess of the hunt and the moon. She is your independent nature. She drives you to success. She is what D. H. Lawrence described as the "bitch goddess." He actually used this term to describe the male appetite for success, as if it were inherently male-oriented, but driven by some feminine force. Artemis is her own person, belonging to no one. She can be found in the lives of Gloria Steinem, Barbra Streisand, Simone de Beauvoir, Golda Meir, Margaret Mead and Virginia Satir. She is the lioness, the explorer, unafraid to be who she is. She doesn't need a man's approval to feel like a woman. She can feel whole without a man. She needs no approval from others. She feels strongly about principles and causes. She radiates autonomy.

You may be influenced by Athena, goddess of wisdom and craft, indulging your left brain, ruling your head rather than your heart. There seems to be a shortage of Athenas in many of us. These archetypes are practical, level-headed and confident. They exercise good judgment and discipline. They do not represent our male or "animus." They are simply a natural part of our femininity that demonstrates clear thinking, initiative and follow-through. They tend to select successful men as partners. In her book, *Goddesses in Everywoman,* Dr. Jean Shindoda Bolen writes that these women look upon men who are poets, dreamers, sensitive, tender-hearted, or neurotic as "losers". She identifies Jackie Kennedy as an Athenian woman.

Perhaps you are dominated by Aphrodite, the goddess of love and beauty, and the most beautiful of all. She is the archetypal lover, falling in love quite easily, frequently and deeply. She too often abandons herself to a man, not feeling fulfilled as a woman without a man in her life. She gives herself permission to love, to be beautiful, sexy and creative. The Romans called her "Venus." Woman as "sex symbol" is her archetype. She embodied Jean Harlow, Marilyn Monroe, Brigitte Bardot and Elizabeth Taylor. Aphrodite implores you to create and procreate. Aphrodite inhabits both glamorous and plain-looking women. Her magnetism and charismatic charm make her irresistible to men. She is disarming, engaging and sensual. She usually attracts the wrong men. Don't despair however. You can always call upon other goddesses to help make the right choice. It was my misfortune to always give her the final say. I had to learn how to cultivate Athena and Artemis to lend balance in my love life. Aphrodite was a menace to me. It was difficult to contain her. She is strong-willed and tends to follow her heart, rather than her head.

Perhaps you are driven by Hera, the goddess of marriage. Idealized by culture and tradition until the women's movement, she perhaps is one of the dominant archetypes for Jewish, Christian and certainly Moslem women. "Whither thou goest, I goest" and "Hell hath no fury like a woman scorned" are expressions of Hera. Ruth, Medea, Nancy Reagan and Donna Reed all reflect Hera. This goddess seems to have lost her popularity since the women's movement.

Hestia, goddess of the hearth, is best exemplified by a good old-fashioned girl. Usually introverted, content with day-to-day living, taking pleasure in traditional roles, enjoying cooking, cleaning and making a comfortable homelife. These are truly enjoyable experiences for these women. They need little stimulation outside of their personal lives. They make wonderful wives, but can be neglected in their efforts to please. In today's terminology, we would say they are candidates for co-dependency, only they don't seem to mind. They seem to maintain an inner peace and tranquility. Hestia's strengths are patience and inner-centeredness. She enjoys time alone, and offers you the gift of introvertedness and splendid solitude. Unfortunately, most of us too often disown this treasure of solitude within, and won't stop moving long enough to allow her entry.

Dr. Bolen defines Persephone as the maiden and queen of the underworld. She describes her as "compliant in action and passive in attitude." She is malleable and has an extraordinary need to please others. She is adaptable, conforming, demure and ever-changing, depending on the expectations of others, especially men. She seems to lack a sense of who she really is, which makes her somewhat unpredictable. She does not see herself, therefore, does not reflect. She is harmonious, avoiding conflict at any cost, saying no when she means yes, and yes when she means no, so as not to "rock the boat." She is the perennial "damsel in distress," wearing a neon sign that says, "Take care of me." Eternally youthful, playful, coquettish and narcissistic, she can be seductive and engaging. According to Melodie Beattie, author of *Co-dependent No More*, Persephone is a prime characteristic of co-dependency. She is easily recognizable. Most of us have or have had mothers or mothers-in-law like her.

Demeter, the goddess of grain and the maternal archetype has been my most important goddess. She has given me the greatest gift of life: My children. Her force dominated my existence and if I could, I would still keep her in the forefront. Time being inexorable, she has lost some of her energy. I miss her, and will forever be grateful to her. She has led me to the computer and along with Sam Keen, placed a fire in my belly, this time to write. My fingers dance to the beat of a new drummer, but I recognize that familiar energy. It is still her, challenging me to new beginnings with new hopes and revelations.

On Being a Teacher and Healer

I never really wanted to be a teacher, but it was one of my two options. "Be a doctor or a teacher," my father ordered me. "Or be a teacher and marry a doctor."

"OK. I'll be a teacher."

I entered the work force as an elementary school teacher in 1961. I was already married two years to my first husband, Carl. Things were not going well.

My first teaching job was at Biscayne Elementary School. I was given a third grade class of refugee children from Cuba. They also threw a few other foreign kids in with them. None of them spoke English. And I didn't speak Spanish, let alone Hungarian, French and Hebrew. There they were all staring me in the face, 38 Cuban, Hungarian, Belgian and Israeli noisy and confused eight-year-olds. There I was, 21 years old, two weeks out of college and scared to death. Most of the children's families had just fled Cuba. They were barely settled and my job was to teach them reading, writing and arithmetic.

When I divorced Carl, the Mallomar Kid, I found a job teaching the first grade.

"Miss Gilbert," I said as I wrote it on the board to children who had not yet learned to read. "Miss Gilbert. That's my name."

There they were. 36 little six-year-olds posing as first graders. Only two knew how to hold a pencil. Not one knew how to write his or her name. Half couldn't tie their shoe laces. A motley crew.

There I was. 22 years old. Just divorced, and just six months experience teaching school. What a challenge! I realized that I was responsible for 36 children learning how to read and write. I would be the one to introduce them to the ABCs, teach them their numbers and how to write from 1 to 100. I would show them how plants grow, how kittens are born, how one plus one equals two, how to spell *dog* and *cat*, how to tie their shoelaces and blow their noses. I would even buy their lunches when they forgot their lunch money. They would grow up and always remember their first grade teacher because I gave them something no one would ever take away from them.

Then I married Jack and had my own children. The subjects changed, but the teaching continued. "Hold it this way. Not that way. And move it this way, up and down . . . You'll love the water. Just blow bubbles. I won't let you go . . . Wipe it this way. Not that way. Bend over as far as you can and open up that tushie. Do it three times and then check. If there's any brown spots, do it again. And, don't forget to flush." How'd you like to have five little behinds to teach how to clean?

How many "Let me kiss the boo boos" were there? How many fairy tales did I tell? How many recitals did I attend? How many lectures did I deliver on chewing with your mouth closed, turning the lights off, taking out the garbage, feeding the dog and taking him for a walk? How many fights over what belongs to who, taking things that don't belong to you, and not telling the truth? I was Mommy and somehow we managed. Jack and I divorced, and I married Tom.

"Girls develop faster than boys, honey. But don't worry. They catch up soon enough."

"The difference between alcohol and pot is that what I'm doing is legal, and what you want to do is not!"

"You have to push it all the way inside, and make sure the string is hanging."

"Let me teach you how to wash your undies . . . Let me teach you how to hang up the blouse you borrowed from me, without asking permission . . . Let me show you how to separate the colors from the white, so they won't bleed all over the new bras and panties I just bought you . . . I know he takes your things without asking, but he's only here with us every other weekend . . . You can put up with it for Tom's sake, can't you? His daddy lives with us, so think how it feels to him. Put yourself in his place . . ." Time passed . . .

The first call I received was from her girlfriends; three of them on one line.

"There's something wrong with Linda. We think it's pretty serious. I think she's freaked out," one said nervously. She was their spokesperson. Then one at a time, and sometimes in unison they said, "Something's really wrong."

They told me that they had just brought her back from the emergency room of a local hospital in Los Angeles. They called an ambulance when they realized she was hysterical and out of control.

"Just go with the paramedics," they urged. "It'll be alright. Don't make a scene for God's sake. Just go."

She made a scene. An awful scene. And the one that forced her friends to call 911.

Of course the first thing they checked for were drugs. The tests were negative. However, she did admit to smoking pot—something she rarely did. The doctor said her behavior was drug-induced, concluding from her history and physical that she was under a great deal of stress. He released her.

Something had occurred that evening with a man, someone she hardly knew. It might have been the marijuana which acted as the catalyst for this episode. I was to learn about it later.

The second phone call came just two days later from another girlfriend. "I'm really worried about Linda," Ellen said cautiously. "Maybe she should go home."

"What's going on?" I asked, afraid of a response I was not ready to hear.

"She hasn't bathed or washed her hair for several days. She appears disoriented. She can hardly complete sentences, as if she were in a trance or altered state," Ellen said with constraint. I suppose she was trying hard not to alarm me. It didn't work.

"Do you think she's capable of getting on a plane?" I asked, hoping for an affirmative answer. It was the same week John Bradshaw was to appear at the Miami Beach Convention Center. I was sponsoring the event. We expected between three to four thousand people during the four-day convention. My role as sponsor was that of a producer. Without my presence, the event would be compromised. I had been preparing for this week for one year and had invested nearly eighty thousand dollars of my husband's money. My career and counseling center were being launched and promoted and all our efforts were coming to fruition in two days.

"I think she'll be able to do it. I'll make all the arrangements. I'll take her to the airport, and see that she gets on the plane," Ellen said.

"Let me talk to her," I said. " Linda, how are you feeling, honey? Do you think you can fly home alone, or would you prefer I come out to get you?"

Her responses were disjointed, inaudible and incoherent. She was still having difficulty completing sentences. I called her supervisor at the John Bradshaw Center in Los Angeles, where she worked, to have someone check on her and assess if she was capable of flying alone. They told me she had not been to work that day and would send someone right over. A few hours later they called to tell me she was quite disoriented. They believed that the best treatment would be for her to come home.

Her father and I met her at the airport in Miami. She was rigid, frightened and mistrustful when we approached her.

"The people on the plane were moving around in slow motion," she said. "I'm so scared, Mom."

She told me she was the fallen angel. I was horrified. Her father nearly collapsed when he saw the condition she was in. I took her home with me that evening, but realized almost immediately that she needed to be hospitalized. She was in a state of terror. She had been working full-time as a therapist at the treatment center, an inpatient facility for co-dependency, doing highly intensive "original pain" work with patients who had been severely abused during their lives. Many had been sexually abused, and some had ritual and cult histories. She was studying for her Ph.D., going to school at night, and had just broken up with her fiance after all the wedding plans had been finalized. Just 26 years old, and she'd had a complete breakdown.

How to heal my child?

Almost immediately after hospitalization and medication, she began to respond. She related the story of how she landed in the emergency room in Los Angeles. She called it a "Kundalini" experience, a metaphysical change in the body and mind that occurs when a surge of energy rushes up the spine. I knew very little about the subject, only what I had read in some of Joseph Campbell's literature. She felt that she had broken through a barrier of this life and had fallen into another dimension. That other dimension she referred to as the dark side.

She said that she felt she had a spiritual death, and she was afraid she would not return. By all standards of modern psychiatry, this would have been diagnosed as a psychosis. However, by yogis, shamans, Eastern and even Native American practices, this is hardly considered psychotic. It is the expansion of mind, body and spirit, where all the chakras, the body's energy centers, are jolted with a force so great that a dimension of higher consciousness is created in the individual. Nicola Kester, a writer for *Common Boundary*, a New Age magazine, writes, "The raising to Kundalini, the famed 'serpent power' of the yogis, is one of the most spectacular and powerful occurrences in spiritual practice. It has been thought to be the result of Eastern practices which were often arduous, prolonged and limited to the most serious seekers."

That doesn't seem to be the case anymore. It seems to happen to many people who least expect it. Gopi Krishna, whose own life was changed dramatically by Kundalini, believes its purpose is the transformation of the person whom it awakens. It is said to break through blocks in a spontaneous, sudden fashion, causing the person to become traumatized. Kester writes, "Classic Hindu tests describe Kundalini as the cosmic energy that sleeps in each individual but awakens in only few. Some Hindu texts use the metaphor of a coiled serpent sleeping at the base of the spine. When this energy awakens, they say, it rises up the spine, surges through the chakras, and bursts in the head in an illumination of light that brings, 'enlightenment.' Thus transformed, the individual becomes deeply attuned to the spiritual truths of the universe and may be capable of many intellectual, physical and psychic wonders for which some yogis are famous." This is what my daughter said had happened to her the night she was taken to the emergency room.

Linda had invited an acquaintance named Simon to her apartment. They had known each other casually for some time, having met at a place called "Dance Home," an expressive dance hall. She had taken me there once, and I remember noticing how many weirdos attended. Not only did they dance expressively, but they dressed expressively. Anything went. Having just broken her engagement, feeling vulnerable, lonely and needy, she asked Simon over. He played the guitar, sang folk songs to her and they smoked marijuana. What might have been an hallucination (an interpretation made by the physician on call at the hospital), appeared to her as a terrifyingly real nightmare.

She told me she was looking into Simon's face as he began chanting the same melody over and over again. His face began to divide into lightness and darkness, as if split down the middle. She interpreted it as the yin and yang. The light side she thought, reflected his inner child, and the dark appeared like a skeleton. He began talking about suicide, as if he had been contemplating the idea. This frightened her and she suspected he might have been using her to help work through this issue. He began to sing to her and tell her that his wounded child needed healing. Knowing she was a therapist experienced in inner child work, he pleaded with her for healing. She thought he may be using her as a channel to pull her life force into him, to save his soul. She thought her soul would leave her. She imagined there were two bodies, but only one soul. That's when she felt most vulnerable.

"Don't die, Simon. Don't die. God will save you," she remembers saying to him.

"You mean I won't go to jail?" he asked.

This statement terrified her. She told me they both got down on their hands and knees and prayed. Then she told me that he took her hand and placed it over his heart. At that moment she felt the energy surge up through her spine. She felt as if an electrical current ran up her back and through the center of her right palm. All the light disappeared from his face and she could see only the darkness. She thought she was looking into the dungeon of his soul. There were no boundaries between them. She felt as if her soul was being raped.

Her fear mounted and she thought that the world was coming to an end. She ran out of her apartment, into the courtyard through the complex screaming at the top of her lungs. "Help, help!" she cried. "Somebody. Please help me!"

Nobody came. She felt she was in a ghost town or the twilight zone. It was late, nearly midnight. Surely, someone should be able to hear her she thought, but no one came. Suddenly, she saw what she described as seven spirits who appeared to be almost floating. They were both men and women. All were wearing black.

"Come with us, Linda," they whispered in unison. "Come with us."

"Go away! Go away!" she screamed. "God will save you. God will save you."

"We're you're friends. Come with us. We'll protect you. Don't be afraid."

She recounted all this to me, and I didn't know how to respond. I just listened. That was all I could do. I felt any judgment or challenge would alienate her, and I needed to keep her close to me. I was the only grounding she had—me, her family and the trilifon (anti-psychotic medication). What was real for her, became real to me. I never let her think she was crazy.

"Mom," she would cry. "The bed is moving. Can you feel how it shakes? My arms can feel the blood running through my veins."

I remembered "The Exorcist" and feared the worst. I began to question my own mental state. I rented "Altered States" with William Hurt, and "2001, A Space Odyssey" so she would know that I understood her experience. She thanked me. We began a new bond. She could share her experience, her interpretations and her beliefs without judgment, criticism or shame. What if her perceptions were accurate? I thought. What if she did have a metaphysical experience? Who could really say? And most of all, how much did it really matter? Her mental health was all I cared about.

She still had a hard time trusting, and was still somewhat paranoid, but now had the strength to observe and challenge her reality. I noticed slight changes in her every day. She was able to define her paranoia and recognize it when it happened. She then felt safer with it and began to embrace it as she worked through the integration process. Indeed it was part of her; a part she needed to explore and understand.

She wanted to see Brian Weiss, the psychiatrist who wrote the book *Many Lives, Many Masters*. I knew getting an appointment would be next to impossible, but I called and, to my surprise, the secretary told me to bring her in the following day. Weiss, who spent nearly two hours with us, was nurturing, reassuring and supportive. He told her it was most important to stay grounded. Yes, she had an extraordinary experience, but how she would use it would be the most meaningful.

Linda and I both knew her life would never be the same again. She needed to take a close look as to why this happened. This was a calling and a lesson to be learned.

That spring, I took her to our cabin in North Carolina in the Blue Ridge Mountains. We went to the pond where I often meditate. There wasn't a ripple. I directed her to a spot on the ground so she could look through the tall twin birch trees into the sun. There was the white light.

"Look into the light, Linda," I said softly. "Look into the light and ask God to heal you."

She began to cry, her body trembling. "Mom," she said. "I can feel the light. It feels good."

"Shhh," I whispered. "Just go into the light and ask for healing."

We both were motionless. I stood above her holding my head into the light too. I prayed, "Please, dear God, give me the wisdom and the power to help heal my daughter. Show me the way, and teach me how. She is my child and yours too. Help me."

I took her to the mountain where I had once felt God's presence. We walked together for a long time. When we headed back to the cabin she laid down next to the rhododendron bushes. They were budding with lilac and crimson flowers waiting to burst open. She rolled in the grass trying to connect to the earth for her own grounding and support. I noticed a crown of dried grass and leaves just beside her. It had probably gathered around the wheel of the lawnmower at the last cutting and had fallen off, drying into a perfect circle. I picked it up and placed the crown on her head.

"This is God's way of letting you know everything is okay. He left a perfect crown for you to find," I said gently. She still has the crown.

On Being a Working Woman

Because of their age-long training in human relations—for that is what feminine intuition really is—women have a special contribution to make to any group enterprise.

— Margaret Mead

I was 13 years old when I lied about my age in order to apply for working papers. 14 was the legal working age. I knew early on that my parents would never be able to keep me in the style I had chosen to live in. My options were few. I needed to work. It was now evident that I was indeed poor, and by comparison to the rest of the beach kids, very poor. My likes and dislikes were already established by the movie stars I admired. My dream was to look like a movie star too. This took money—money my parents did not have.

I took a job as a roll girl, serving sweet rolls and bread at Curry's Restaurant on 74th Street and Collins Avenue; which is still in business today. All I needed was a white blouse, black skirt and bus fare. On weekends I would play the accordion at different hotels and occasionally land a club date on one of the cruise ships sailing to Nassau. My pay depended on my ability to perform. My ability to perform depended on the weather conditions. If the seas were smooth, I'd be okay. If the seas were rough, I was out of the money.

I was never without work throughout my teen years. When I knew I was going away to college and needed a competitive wardrobe, I went to work the summer I graduated from high school for Bell Telephone as a long distance operator. As soon as I received my paycheck, I'd run to Hartley's Department Store, three blocks away, where I had six Haymaker skirts and blouses on layaway. I would deposit my entire paycheck with them until the items were paid for. By the end of the summer, I had purchased six dresses, seven pairs of shoes and enough underwear to last a full year at school. When the train pulled out from the Miami station headed for Tuscaloosa, Alabama, none of the passengers could tell I came from South Beach. I made sure of that.

All the women in my family worked in addition to raising families and being homemakers—my grandmothers, my mother and all my aunts. My maternal grandmother had been trained in Poland by the Organization for Rehabilitation and Training (ORT), a Jewish-American women's organization that helped develop working skills for Jewish Europeans who intended to immigrate to the United States. Jews were not permitted to own land or property in Poland, so many had been trained as tradesmen or craftsmen, skills handed down from one generation to the next. Women usually maintained the home and looked after the children. Most were unprepared to enter the workforce after arriving in America.

ORT trained my grandmother to sew leather gloves. She worked in the glove factory with my grandfather in Gloversville, New York. He cut. She sewed. Several years later, they moved to Coney Island and opened a delicatessen. She worked alongside my grandfather until they moved to St. Louis, where she ran the family candy store. In the meantime, she had a son and three daughters. When they moved back to Gloversville, she volunteered her services as a Chevra

Kadisha, a person who prepares Jews for ritual burial by bathing them and sewing their traditional shrouds.

My paternal grandmother came to this country from Russia as a seamstress. My paternal grandfather, from the Russian aristocracy, never learned a trade. Boys from aristocracy were destined to study the Torah. Consequently, he went to synagogue everyday to study the Holy Book. My grandmother earned a living sewing American flags in her two-room railroad flat on New York's East Side.

It was dark each morning when my grandmother walked to the subway to go to the factory. She was a dress finisher, and after that she sewed draperies. It was dark when she returned at night. To augment her income, she leased out rooms to borders. Every penny counted. There was never enough money, food, clothing or room for the children. My father told me he would face two chairs together to use as his bed. He was born blind and suffered every childhood disease imaginable—all because of malnutrition. His eyesight was restored only because a neighbor lady took care of him and nursed him back to health. His youngest sister was put in an orphanage to help defray expenses. Things were so bad that at 14 my father lied about his age to join the navy. He never finished high school.

My mother left Gloversville before she turned 20. She somehow managed to get through a two-year course in secretarial studies. She was smart enough, I'm told, to skip a grade in high school. But poverty prevented her from going any further with her education. She worked full-time as a secretary for a large cosmetics company until she married my father in 1936.

She began working again part-time as a legal secretary about the same time I decided to lie about my age so I could start work, as well. I was 12. She was 36. She kept that same job for another 37 years on a full-time basis. Even when she was crippled with rheumatoid arthritis, she returned many times after her retirement to help out whenever her former employer summoned her.

I can still hear the clicking of her heels and see her carrying grocery bags in both arms coming home at the end of the day. She would take the bus each way so that my father could drive the car to work. She would pick up the groceries, carry them home, prepare dinner and wash the dishes. She did laundry two to three times a week, ironing in the evenings. The house always smelled clean and fresh.

We had a lady come in and clean one day every other week. Her name was Sally. None of us ever saw her. For 20 years, Sally would come religiously every other week. My mother would leave her the key under the mat and money on the kitchen table. Sally would come, clean and leave.

One day, my mother and Sally traveled on the same bus. Mom didn't recognize Sally because she had only seen her on a few occasions. Sally recognized my mother, however, because of the family portraits around the house.

"Well, hello Mizz Gilbert," she said.

"I'm so sorry," my mother replied. "Your voice sounds familiar, but I honestly don't know who you are."

"Why Mizz Gilbert!" she exclaimed. "Sho' 'nuff, I'm Sally, your housekeeper. Don't you know me?"

The rite of work came to me without any ceremony. I inherited a collective-unconscious work ethic from all the women in my family. Working was never an option. We did it because it had to be done.

On Being a Psychotherapist

My first client as a social worker was Ed Mannstein, a German-American brakeman for Florida East Coast Railroad, who drove Peterbilt trucks cross-country during time off from the railroad. He drank Beck's beer, used profanity, was a Little League coach for his son's team, played first violin in the Milwaukee orchestra and loved Mozart. He had been referred to me by a home health agency I had contracted with while I was trying to build a private practice.

Ed had just been discharged from the hospital after having his left leg amputated as a result of a railroad injury. The train missed his testicles by one inch. He had a stump so short that it was questionable if he was even a candidate for a prosthesis.

Ed lived in a rented home off Commercial Boulevard in Fort Lauderdale, a good 30 miles from my office. As part of his after-care, the home health agency provided a social worker along with all the other custodial services. While Ed was with his home health aide, I was driving around his neighborhood looking for his house that was hidden behind a wall of 12-foot Eureka palms. Ed had had it with his custodial care visitors, and I had had it with the search for his hidden house. We both were agitated and irritable—neither of us needed to confront the other at such a precarious moment.

I knocked at the door several times before his wife came. She spoke nervously.

"I really don't think you ought to come in now. He's not in a good mood and it might be better to come back at another time."

"Who is it, Lois? Tell 'em I don't want to see anybody. Do ya hear me?" I heard a man shout from somewhere in the back of the house.

"I have to see him now," I replied. "I just drove two hours and I can't leave without seeing him," I said in a determined voice.

"I don't think you want to do that," she said. "He's really not up to seeing anyone. He's tired from all the care he's been getting, and he just came home from the hospital today. Couldn't you come back at another time?"

I could hear his disgruntled comments mixed in with the usual four-letter words that gave me the distinct impression he didn't want to be disturbed.

The year was 1978. Delores was very much present. So when Ed's wife, Lois, saw me she might have been somewhat surprised with my appearance. There I was, dressed in gypsy clothing, high lace-up boots, wearing long colored beads, and of course, matching dangling earrings. My dark hair fell loose to the middle of my back and the make-up, coupled with the two pairs of false eyelashes, must have startled the poor woman. She didn't know what to make of me.

"Who did you say you were, again?" she asked.

"My name is Joan Childs. Home Health Service sent me to see a Mr. Ed Mannstein. Does he live here?"

"Yes, but I don't think he wants to be disturbed right now. Why are you here?"

"I'm the social worker. And I need to see him now."

She stared at me with disbelief, trying desperately to talk me out of the visit, while cacophonous sounds emanated from the back room.

Exasperated with lost patience, I pushed past her while she covered her face in her hands. I followed the sounds to the back room, which was completely dark. The drapes were drawn tight, and the patient was tucked tightly under the sheets and blanket. I switched on the light and introduced myself. "I'm Joan Childs. I was sent here by your home health service agency. I've been driving around looking for this place for nearly three hours." (It had really been two, but I tended to exaggerate.) The patient, startled, sat up and said,

"Who the hell are you?"

"I just told you. I'm Joan Childs, your social worker. Your home health service ordered me. I drove 30 miles to see you and got lost because your home was hidden behind the palm trees. Now I'm here, like it or not. You might as well reconcile that fact. I don't get paid unless I see the patient. You're the patient and I need the money."

That's how this client/therapist relationship began. I thought he was a noncompliant, resistant patient, and he thought I was a hooker. From that moment everything improved.

I saw him twice a week. Our visits were more like friendly afternoon chats than therapy. I wasn't even aware of the therapeutic value. He shared his music with me, *Deutschegrammophon* records he had collected all his life. He always had a bottle of Beck's in his hand and Mozart or Mendelssohn on the phonograph as he hobbled on his crutches towards the door to let me in. He was bitter about the loss of his left leg, and as time went on he realized more and more about the implications of this loss. No more trucking. No more coaching. No more carousing. He was beginning to feel powerless, and he became more depressed. He covered up his anger with anti-Semitic jokes, knowing I was Jewish. He took pride in his arrogance, telling me how he was bringing up his children as bigots and racists.

Despite his black humor, I grew fond of this six-foot, two-inch, half-shaven, bloodshot-eyed, foul-mouthed, intelligent, gentle human being, who, in spite of his gruffness, was a tender-hearted, fragile man with a passion for life that was slowly disappearing before my eyes. During each visit it was easier to see his loss of life force. As the passion dissipated, the depression grew, the drinking increased and the music changed to Tchaikovsky and Wagner. The signs were there, and I didn't want to see them. I visited with him twice a week without fail. The visits were supposed to be for 45 minutes. I often stayed two hours.

One day when I arrived, Ed was drunk. His eyes were bloodshot.

He hadn't shaved for perhaps three days. Slumped in a chair, he sat with a bottle of Beck's in one hand, and a .38 revolver in the other. I went into the dark room. There was no music playing and he was alone. Lois had gone to her mother's for the day with their son, Paul.

"Ed, what's wrong? Tell me, please," I begged.

"It's no use, Joni. All the days are the same now. There are no good ones left. I have no reason to live."

Stunned, not knowing what to do or what to say I burst into tears. He stood up and grabbed his crutches, hobbled over and looked at me with the same concern I had when I looked at him.

"It's OK, darlin'," he said as he took me in his arms holding my head against his chest. "It's OK . . . "

"No, no. It's not OK. You want to kill yourself, and I'm not able to help. I've failed you. I'm new at this and you needed an experienced professional, and I couldn't do it," I cried. "Oh Ed, please don't kill yourself. I'll never be able to live with myself. What am I going to do?"

So preoccupied with my reaction, he forgot about his own pain and he began to nurture me. He comforted me for what seemed to be at least a quarter of an hour, offering me tea, and doing anything he could to restore my mood.

Thank God I am a woman. I had the chemistry and the societal permission to have these authentic naked emotions. This emotional response was the therapy my soul dictated. It worked.

Several months later, after the healing process had finally begun, Ed had to consider the idea of a prosthesis. The thought of an artificial leg was abhorrent to him. He flatly refused to even consider the idea. During these months, I continued my biweekly visits to his home.

"Never. Do you hear me? Never! Not even over my dead body! You'll never see me in a fake leg!"

His physiotherapist urged me to convince him of the importance and value of a prosthesis, suggesting that Ed could resume many activities he used to enjoy. Only his pride and stubbornness kept him from returning to a productive life. I had to find a way to elicit the response I was looking for.

During the months we worked together, Ed shared so much of himself with me. I recognized early on how important his German heritage was to him. He would tease me about being Jewish and having to put up with an arrogant "kraut."

"What's a nice Jewish girl like you spending all this time with an anti-Semite? Didn't your mother ever teach you about us Nazis?" he would say in jest. "Why don't you come to the German-American Club and learn how to polka the way it was meant to be danced?"

I would usually smile and avoid answering. He asked me to come to the German Club nearly every time we were together, always including my husband Tom in the invitation. When he became impatient with my refusals, I had to explain in my best social work "practices and procedures" language, that it was unprofessional for a therapist to attend social functions with clients.

"Screw that," he retorted. "Nobody's gonna find out, and I can show off my Jewish social worker to all my buddies. Come on, Childs, give a guy a break."

I had an opening. And I seized it.

"OK, hotshot. You want this Jewish social worker to come to your German Octoberfest? I'll make a deal with you. You put on that prosthesis, and not only will I come, I'll even dance with you. Screw policy, practice and procedures. Screw ethics. Make me a deal you pigheaded, goddamn Nazi. Put your money where your mouth is!"

Two months later in mid-October, all dressed up in masquerade, wearing my maternal grandmother's Victorian lace wedding dress with my hair coiffed high in a Gibson style, framed with a wide brim white lace bonnet, escorted by my husband Tom and my parents, I gracefully walked into the German Club. There he was, halfway across the room, seated with Lois at a table. He struggled to his feet and stood unsteadily, wearing the new prosthesis. I walked over slowly and deliberately, raised the right side of my evening gown, curtseyed and said,

"Mr. Mannstein, sir. May I have this dance?"

"With pleasure, my dear Mrs. Childs."

He bowed politely, placed his arm around my waist and we danced our first polka together. The man with the wooden leg and his Jewish social worker. The crowd gathered around us on the dance floor. Cheers, tears and applause accompanied the oom-pah-pah band as it played the "Beer Barrel Polka." The man with the wooden leg and the Jewish social worker became a legend at the German-American Club.

I am a psychotherapist. It is my life's work. I can change the colors of people's minds. My work is an extension of me. It is the voice of my soul. I give birth each time I see a client. I am a co-creator. I am doing God's work and I make a difference.

On Being a Friend

Each friend represents a world in us, a world possibly not born until they arrive, and it is only by this meeting that a new world is born.

— Anaïs Nin (1903-1977)

We meet people and we like some of them, love some of them, dislike some of them and hate some of them. Many of us have very rational ways of explaining this process. With me, it is a wavelength, an intuition, a voice or feeling that resonates within me. Many times I don't have any conscious control over these feelings. Though I might try to reason, in the end, my intuition prevails. I enjoy this act of submission. That is the story of my life and of relations of friendship, love and regard. My friends are a mystery for me and with the passage of time, they become more mysterious. My closeness grows, and with that, so does my sense of wonder. It seems that sometimes I start looking at my friends through the eyes of a dazed visitor to a mysterious land. Their voices tickle me. Their presence enthralls me. Their observations enrich and extend my consciousness, transporting me into a different and splendid new world. The greatest blessing for me is to be with my friends.

I met Lorraine. She looks like a woman who has come down from the mountain. I call her the wise one. She is a wizard, not just in appearance, but in the feeling you get when you meet her. From deep within, she exudes a divinely guided wisdom. It is a collective wisdom that seems to encompass all of time and humanity. Although she has a classic Irish woman's face, she represents all of us. Both women and men.

She speaks in soft, low tones, with purpose and strength. Even when she speaks, she appears to be listening to you. It is like a suggestive whisper, a hypnotic trance, the deeper truth that gets conveyed through the intonation and modulation of her voice. She says a lot, but it seems that she is telling you what is already in your heart. She speaks the truth, with the slow movements of her hands and with the smile in her eyes. One only needs to watch her to understand her. Sometimes she frowns, deepening the wrinkles on her brow and beneath her smiling, soft brown eyes. She is real. She is truthful. She has conviction. She has her sense of right and wrong. Though conveyed in low whispers, her convictions are written in steel. And this is how she lives her life. There's never any second guessing. She's on the path. The path with the heart. Yes. She is a magic mystery.

I met Gretchen. Her powerful brown eyes stare with certainty, defying any other presence or viewpoint. Her expression and confidence reflect the deeper arrogance born of affluence and tradition. She is the kind that men try to "catch" when they are young. But her vulnerability is deceptive. Her strength commands all to meet her on her terms. There is the confidence of generations of royalty, self-possession and one who has fought many battles. She knows it all. She can advise you on any subject. Sometimes I wonder if even Socrates felt as omniscient as my friend. But this omniscience is not challenging or threatening. It is revealed in a slow, soft, sonorous voice of a Southern belle. Sometimes she reminds you of those jet-setting women who talk of their visit to the Uffizi and the Louvre as though it were a trip to the grocery store. She speaks of old times with reverence to her parents, heritage and traditions. But with her there is no name dropping. There is depth. There is an experience. There is a deep feeling. It is a personal lingo. It is a personal accent and insights that make one breathe deep and swallow when she talks. She really lives in the world of Keats and gilded tapestry, Victorian baths and linen, embroidered robes, antiques and original works of art. She loves beautiful things and has a way of conveying that beauty to the deepest recesses of your soul and mind. She is fun to be with; a flowing brook brimming with new observations with calm and measured reflection. Often her sentences end as if she were asking a question. She has an acerbic wit softened by a touch of ever-present humor.

One knows when a thought is final. She has this little habit of pursing her lips together, and speaking in a deeper, more defined tone that finalizes her statements.

Although born in Ohio, by her own definition she is a Southern lady. She was groomed to be a woman and she has groomed her-self to a perfection in the "Art of Womanhood." Proud of her her-itage and of her personal gifts—the latest one, acting—she knows how to love and indulge herself, and does the same for others. We never part without a kiss on the lips.

She enjoys the experience of living and sharing with friends. Her joy is infectious. Her zest is seductive. And being with her is like being in an aura of magic or on a visit to infinitely expanding unknown realms.

I met Phyllis. The first time I saw her she was with Max: an addict, a hustler and a fugitive. Something was wrong with the pic-ture, I thought to myself. She was 17. He was 29. I was 25 and six months pregnant with Emily. She was wearing tight black leather pants and a sheer zebra print shirt tied at the waist. Her straight, light red hair fell loosely to her shoulders. Phyllis and Max had stopped by my home to see Jack, who they both apparently knew. Max's right leg shook nervously up and down the entire time they waited for Jack.

I don't know why, but I had this urge to rescue her. She just did-n't fit in with Jack's usual collection of seedy looking weirdos. I wondered if her parents knew about Max. What if Linda fell prey to someone like that when she became 17? I shuddered.

Kindred spirits find each other. We soon became friends. I assumed I would become her guiding light, her mentor and teacher. But instead she became mine. She drove me to the hospital the night Emily was born while Jack maintained his position at a crap table at someone's stag party. She, not Jack, welcomed Emily to the world. She led me to Dr. McKinley, my therapist, Barry College to pursue my chosen profession, and most of all, my true self.

She was a true 1960s flower child. She loved pot, Leonard Cohen, The Beatles, The Rolling Stones, headbands and beads, nature, children, academia, Tom Wolfe and Hershey's chocolate. But most of all, she loved Bob, who became her husband. They would become the new establishment of a better tomorrow. She left Max to become one of nature's most splendid human beings. Although the years have separated us across the continent, I carry her in my heart everyday. Her spirit has kept me centered. There's always that introject, that pleasant reminder that gives me permission to trust my feelings, honor my soul and be true to myself.

Her hair is still red.

The first thing you notice about him are his eyes. They're deep, dark and penetrating. They speak to you, but only if you understand the language of the eyes can you really know him. There, from deep within, comes the soul of my kindred spirit.

Then comes his voice. It reeks of mystical magic, a power so great that if you give in as I did, you fall instantly under a spell. I haven't awakened yet. Nor do I want to.

I remember the first time I saw him, sometime in February 1992. There was no special feeling. Just that pleasant curiosity. I had been invited to join a master's training program for neurolinguistic programming, a psychotherapeutic technology using triggers to manifest certain behavior, and the invitation said the meetings would be held at the residence of someone named Meehar. My reason for attending the first meeting was simple. I wanted to meet the man who had that name.

My fantasies ran the gamut of some Middle Eastern oil tycoon, entrepreneur, or Arab sheik, to perhaps a wealthy Iranian businessman who had nothing to do with his money and time except pursue intellectual follies. I was fascinated by exotic names. Especially Islamic or Hindu names. Perhaps it was because they sounded so forbidden.

Reality proved quite different, however. Meehar was an American citizen who 16 years previously had left his native country, Pakistan, due to the persecution of his religious sect. A Moslem by birth, once he immigrated to the United States, he could no longer return and be considered a Moslem in his native country. He came to America to begin a new life. He left behind his family, friends, a feudal system and a culture thousands of years old. Once a nationally acclaimed debate champion and full professor of English literature at age 21, he had a promising career in the civil service of his native government. When he moved to New Jersey, he became a bricklayer and chimney sweeper, then dishwasher service supervisor, to real estate manager, and chief financial officer of a major corporation. He is presently executive vice president of one of the largest corporations in the world.

Of course, I knew none of this until much later in our relationship. Neurolinguistic programming training was just one of his many interests. He was a master trainer at this workshop when our paths first crossed. His interest and passion seemed to be in the field of psychology, particularly human behavior. He, along with other trainers, worked with the group teaching new techniques that we could integrate into our respective practices. As I developed a friendship with him over the months that followed, I learned that he had an impressive collection of master degrees, including English literature, economics, psychology and business administration. He also acquired a CPA, after he arrived in the United States while working 50 hours a week managing property.

So often people cross your path with intentions that seem to flourish into other outcomes. We became wonderful friends. But this was a friendship that had an altogether different definition. I was to discover, perhaps, for the first time, a new paradigm for friendship.

He spoke to me of Keats, Byron and Shelley. He recited poetry from T. S. Eliot, prose from Brontë, Shakespeare, D. H. Lawrence and Hemingway. He enjoyed sharing his knowledge with me, and I was eager to learn as much as I could. His pace was always faster than mine. But he slowed down so I could absorb the richness of these gifts. I hadn't read a tenth of what he could recite off the top of his head, yet he cherished what I gave to him. I spoke to him of Mozart, Beethoven, Mahler and Tchaikovsky. He gave me Kris Kristofferson, the Gita and the Koran. I gave him Pat Conroy and the *Prince of Tides*. Yes, he was married and so was I. But our friendship transcended any constraints.

He shared his philosophy and compared his reflections and thoughts to Jean-Paul Sartre, Gregory Bateson, Lao Tzu, Kierkegaard, Joseph Campbell and a zillion others.

Meehar's presence in the groups we co-facilitated was quiet, yet engaging. The participants revered him. He exemplified a harmonious balance of yin and yang, and his Middle Eastern looks and demeanor captivated both the men and women. He merely had to show up to affect change.

He had studied and read all that Freud had written. He read Jung, Adler, Carl Rogers, Alice Miller and so many other contributors to the field of psychology. In an instant, he could relate the comparative difference of each. All this was before he ever received his Master's Degree in psychology, which he acquired after getting his CPA while managing a real estate office. He reflected and compared the ideas and philosophies of Nietzsche, Schopenhauer, Heidegger, Plato, Socrates, Aristotle and more. His fascination with knowledge was endless. What he already knew by age 50 would take several lifetimes for most to learn.

He admired John F. Kennedy, Gandhi, Winston Churchill and Milton Erickson. He likes Tony Robbins, Richard Bandler, Madonna and Woody Allen. He loves the writings of Abraham Heschel, Peter Drucker, and says that Gregory Bateson "knocks him off his feet." (I can barely understand Gregory Bateson.) His fascinations take him into the world of astrology, acupuncture, human resources, organizational development, and of course, the Tao.

He's impressed with the commitment and works of Margaret Mead, Gloria Steinem, Jean Houston and Steven Spielberg. He can recite phrases and excerpts from the classics as if they were written in the air. He is a man of his own ideas, beliefs, values and opinions that change as often as the tide, yet stay consistent enough to make him credible and perhaps not enough to take him seriously all the time.

He's "spent a long time watching from a lonely wooden tower" and is truly a "walking contradiction, partly truth, and partly fiction; taking every wrong direction on his lonely way back home." He's crazy. He's brilliant. He's pensive, insightful, fun and a wonderful listener. He's empathic, thoughtful and generous; an asshole and a bastard. He has the heart of a poet. He's a man and a little boy. He's in his truth, yet full of deception.

He is a man for all seasons and for all time. He is my friend and kindred spirit. The sharing and exchange of our ideas, thoughts, wisdom, fears, ideals, hopes and dreams has been one of the greatest enrichments of my life. I will forever honor and cherish our friendship and communion. I am so grateful he is the man with that name.

Friendship is the most important commodity in the world. We are often defined by our friendships. Women intrinsically have the capacity of giving and receiving this gift, perhaps because we have been given this permission on a very deep level throughout history.

The qualities essential in friendship are inherent in women. Like all good things, friendship requires time to cultivate. Yet time is not the essence of true friends. Friendship transcends time, but requires truth and unconditional love. These are the principle qualities of friendship.

On Being a Self-Made Woman

"The poet says, What I do is me, for that I came."

In his chapter, "The Self-Made Man," Keen describes what defined the male in terms of character before the late 1800s: "The words most used to relate to character were: citizenship, duty, democracy, work, building, golden deeds, outdoor life, conquest, honor, reputation, morals, manners, integrity. The good man of the 18th century was the one who devoted himself to the good of the community while he 'lived a life a piety' and 'mild religion.'"

With the exception of perhaps "conquest," (except in terms of a husband), these standards applied to women as well. The word "work" might be translated to housework, and "outdoor life," perhaps to raising children. But otherwise the criteria was pretty much the same for both men and women.

By the turn of the 19th century, he writes, "the ideal man had changed dramatically. The key word was now 'self.'. . . The virtues of a self-made man were a strong ego, unbending character, and a substantial social person, four-square and solid as a brick house." Still not much difference. Whereas the Boy Scouts of America instilled the virtues of being "trustworthy, loyal, helpful, friendly, courteous, kind, obedient, cheerful, thrifty, brave, clean and reverent," the Girl Scouts of America espoused to the same.

The women of the 20th century learned quickly how to shift gears and go into the factories during war years yet stay abreast of domestic concerns and child-rearing.

Women have always honored their soulful content. Perhaps it's because we had the permission granted to us at birth. The same inherent qualities squelched in men are revered in women. The women's movement took some of those qualities from our souls and gave us characteristics that men are now looking for. Women always had them in the first place.

How do we define a self-made woman today? I take a good look at myself and wonder if that's what I've become. And at what price? The women's movement for me was a double-edged sword. In leaving the hearth, I discovered myself, but I paid a big price. The vote is not in yet, but in looking back, the road was indeed a personal struggle. In the 1950s, my roles were so defined—get married, have children, join the PTA, play mahjongg or bridge, and look real pretty on Saturday nights. Jack's roles were easy too. Kill the dragons, stamp out disease, save lives and make lots of money. We both did just that. So what happened?

This is not a blame game, but in looking back I can plainly see that my needs were not being met. Not by Jack, not by the roles designated to me by society, and not by me. There was a certain level of satisfaction I had from making babies and becoming the president of the women's auxiliary, but that wasn't enough. There was a restlessness in me that wouldn't subside. It became relentless. I would have said some time ago it was because Jack was a gambler, incapable of intimacy due to his disease. But I know now that it was only part of the truth.

After we divorced I had to take a good look at what I was going to do with the rest of my life. I mean, leaving a man when I had five children all under the age of 11 was either the most courageous thing I ever did, or the dumbest. I can't answer that yet.

But here I am, 54 years old, mother of five adult children, wife of a fourth husband, director of my own counseling center, psychotherapist, lecturer, author and making a noble effort to heal the planet.

Did I do it by myself? Heavens, no! I had a lot of help along the way, most recently from my husband Mervyn, and my dear friend, Meehar. Mervyn supports my efforts and Meehar ignites more fire in my mind than a million volumes of knowledge found in any library in the world.

When I divorced Jack in 1975, the judge awarded me $18,000 in alimony to be paid at $1,000 each month. I used that money to pay for graduate school. When I received my master's degree in social work, I made a copy of the diploma and cut it into three parts. I celebrated with a graduation party, and gave the "M" to Martha, my housekeeper, for being "Mom," while mother matriculated. The "S" went to the children, for their patience and understanding during my absence those three years, and the "W" went to Tom for his emotional and financial support (he helped pay for living expenses). They each earned a third of my diploma. Without their help I know there was no way I could have succeeded.

So is there such a thing as a self-made woman? I don't think so. For every self-made woman, look around and see all the help and support she got from her family and friends.

A 21st Century Woman: Femininity and Vocation

If you bring forth what is within you, what you bring forth will save you. If you do not bring forth what is within you, what you do not bring forth will destroy you.

—The Gnostic Gospels

I came into my vocation motivated solely by my unconscious. My chosen field of psychotherapy was an outgrowth of my own woundedness. I think this is true for most therapists. After all, it is generally understood in the industry that you can only take your clients as far as you've gone yourself. I've brought four marriages, three divorces, a five-year live-in boyfriend, five children and a stepson into my chosen profession.

I recall making the choice to jump right into private practice because I wanted to be home for the children after school and available for them in case of emergencies. I thought a job at an agency would not be flexible enough. What I didn't realize was, that once I developed my private practice, the result would be the same. My commitment was to my clients. As my practice grew, my responsibilities shifted. As the responsibilities shifted, so did my attitude.

My live-in boyfriend at that time, Phil, became "Mr. Mom" and I took on the mortgage payments, utilities, household and personal expenses. This is where it became touchy. I realized for the first time how money can affect power and control. Suddenly, I began to want things my way. I had to learn to balance men and money, motherhood and career, power and femininity, and simultaneously maintain my sanity.

The deal was how to have it all without compromising my

values, family, health, and self-esteem and having everyone I love hate me. When I neglected my kids, I felt guilty. When I acted aggressively, I felt bossy and guilty. When I neglected my clients, I felt incompetent and guilty. When I neglected my boyfriend, I felt too independent and guilty. When I neglected my parents, I felt over-responsible and guilty. When I neglected my friends, I felt lonely and guilty. And when I neglected myself, I felt unworthy and guilty. I walked around feeling guilty most of the time because I was always neglecting someone. My son, Tim, would sing "Cats In the Cradle" when I came home late from work. My father's voice, "When am I going to see you? You know, too much time we don't have," I heard in my sleep. I felt like prey in the middle of the wilderness, unprotected, confused, fragmented, angry, and worst of all, I wasn't having any fun. I was grinding my teeth at night, yelling at the kids, short with my parents, and hating sex.

If this was the promised land of the women's movement, give me chauvinism anytime. I was miserable. But it was too late for that. I had to make the best of this newfound freedom and pay the price of "feminism," which I never understood that well. I knew one thing. Something had to change.

My analyst used to say, "If the brain doesn't have enough sense to tell you when to stop, your body will." Well, mine did. Sitting in my chair one day conducting a session, I went blank. Fortunately, for me, my client was someone who had been in therapy for quite some time, so we just transferred roles. She knew exactly what to do. She drove me home. I still don't remember the whole incident. I lost a day and a half. When I came back to consciousness, I realized what burnout was all about. I had it. I had finally sold my home after a seven-year effort. I took the down payment and a Caribbean cruise with my kids, my mother and Martha. When we returned, I waited another two weeks before going back to work, and found that, in spite of my fears and panic, my clients were still there, wishing me well and happy to see me.

The world went on in spite of my absence. What a marvelous revelation. So now, what had I learned? I needed balance. Time for work and time for play. Time for friends and time for me. I needed support. Support from my family and support from my friends. If I didn't make time for them, there was no way I could get my needs met. The most important lesson I learned however, was that money was not the answer. The answer was to be free. Freedom meant giving up my ego, connecting with others, expanding myself to receive as much love as I was giving, and to just have fun.

If there's one lesson for the 21st century woman to learn, it's live your life. Like Auntie Mame so exquisitely said on her winding staircase, "Live, live, live! Life is a banquet, and most poor suckers are starving to death."

On Being a Person

How are we going to live when we give up our myth and surrender to our reality? What's the new deal going to look like? Are we ready?

Will there still be happily ever after, 'til death do us part and home is where the heart is? Or did the myth of the maiden cultivate a new maiden far from the girl that married dear old dad?

And who may she be? How many veterans of the myth will be able to transform into a 21st century woman? How many diehards will be left behind to fall into the archives of the 20th century?

Kicking and screaming, putting up a solid fight, some of us will relinquish the past with great resistance. Some will simply say, "Thank God. Let's move on." And others will stand there, scratching their heads, muttering with confusion, and get pushed into their new roles without even noticing the changes. Women born today will certainly look at their futures with a different map of the world. Babies may be born with anyone imaginable in the birthing room: Roommates, girlfriends, mothers, sisters and brothers, perhaps fathers, boyfriends and sometimes husbands. Marriages may become yearly renegotiable contracts instead of lifetime commitments. Marriage may not be the only viable option for commitment. Living together and living separately may be alternative lifestyles and new paradigms that may have more foundation than contractual marriages.

Babies will be born to women in their early 40s as often as to women in their 30s and 20s. Daycare centers at the workplace will be as common as the lunchroom and work-out room.

Each of us will be ultimately responsible for our own destiny, with no one to blame or credit except ourselves. Finally, an autonomous society where women can enjoy the friendships of men, and vice versa, without the inevitable passion pretending not to interfere with the friendship. Sexual interaction may even become a choice, rather than a pressure or expectation. Women won't have to become objectified or sexualized to matter. Women's bodies may keep their exalted positions in the minds of men, but the minds of women will have their long-due respect. A woman might be considered a person with a female body. The person will matter—not just the body.

Whatever the outcome, one thing is for certain. Women must own their male energy and be willing to negotiate contracts with that part of themselves before they look for a mate. The same is true for men. Once a woman claims her maleness, she then becomes totally fulfilled as a woman, thereby choosing a mate as an enrichment, rather than a projected part of her to make her whole. Carl Jung referred to these male and female archetypes as *anima* and *animus.* "For just as the man is compensated by a feminine element, so woman is compensated by a masculine one."

When one thinks about it, men and women are separated only by a single chromosome. We are made up of 48 chromosomes, 24 from each parent. Only one out of 48 separates us into male and female. Otherwise, we are almost identical. It is true of course, that one chromosome that determines gender makes a hell of a difference, but nevertheless, each of us has the element of the opposite. Our opposite gender parts allow us to retrieve wanted and unwanted projections onto our mates, bestowing higher levels of autonomy and individuality within our relationships. These projections are the outcomes of unresolved conflicts with either parent, carrying both positive and negative leftovers into our adult relationships. Once we see these projections as our needs and wishes, and not theirs, we can look forward to healthier relationships with fewer disappointments.

Every time I chose a mate to provide me with the missing parts of either myself or deficits in the previous relationship, I left myself open for another disappointment. It took four marriages and one live-in relationship for me to get that this wasn't about them, but about me instead. I needed to retrieve those projections I placed on them due to my own sense of need, fears and feelings of inadequacy. These were my feelings of incompleteness, not theirs. The answer is so simple it almost makes you wonder what took so long to figure it out. It's not that we're stupid. It's just that we have unrealistic expectations from old tapes and scripts telling us to "just find the right guy." I think we finally understand that there ain't no such thing as the "right" guy. Wake up and smell the coffee, gals. It's time to regroup. Take off the rose-colored glasses and look the world straight in the face, dig your heels in deep and go for it. The results might just surprise you.

Chapter 3

MANAGING MOTHERHOOD AND CAREER

I have yet to hear a man ask for advice on how to combine marriage and a career.

—Gloria Steinem

I once heard Katharine Hepburn say the reason she never married and had children was because she loved her career, and she felt one could not do both well. At the time, I thought it was a poor excuse for not being able to marry Spencer Tracy. I later realized she was right. Balancing career and motherhood is risky business.

Just as little boys are asked what they want to be when they grow up, so are little girls. Except when little girls answer these days, you might hear them respond, "I want to be a mommy and a doctor." They already have a conscious mindset about becoming both.

I began my second marriage wanting a baby as quickly as possible. I was 23, and my friends were ahead of me. I was looking for a good excuse to end my career as a teacher. Motherhood would provide me with a ticket out. I had five children in eight years.

By the time my third child was two and a half, my husband Jack announced that he needed my income and requested that I go back to teaching. The thought of it upset me. I instead asked his permission to choose something that I wanted to do. Reluctantly, he agreed. It never occurred to me why he needed my income at the time. I found out later it was to help pay the bills. His income as a doctor, as large as it was, could not cover our living expenses and

73

pay his gambling debts as well. I took a job as an interior decorator—a financial disaster. I bought more furniture than I sold.

After my divorce from Jack, I was once again faced with the dilemma of what to do. Teaching was out of the question. I already had five children, and couldn't bear the idea of 36 more. I learned that with an undergraduate degree in education, I could get my master's in social work in two years. I spent the next two and a half years at Barry College, taking care of five children, remarrying, building a pool and deck, carpooling, studying and preparing for another career—which was to become my life's work.

Developing a practice took every ounce of strength I had. I offered free presentations, lectures, seminars and workshops to anyone willing to listen. I spoke at Hadassah meetings, the Rotary Club, the school board, the Jewish Community Center and senior citizen centers. I taught adult education classes at local high schools and condominiums. I went to different doctors, clergy, teachers, principals, lawyers and even astrologers. I called the local police department, fire department and court system offering free seminars on stress, marriage and family matters, assertiveness training and the psychology of everyday life. I made up titles to fit the needs of the population I would be speaking to. I once taught a class at the local Jewish Community Center on "Sex Over Sixty," and the turnout was so great we exceeded the building's occupancy limits. Building my practice took five years. But I did it—I was full and had a waiting list. My marriage was on the rocks, my children were in trouble, but I made it. What price glory!

I can really appreciate Katharine Hepburn's insightful remark now. I wholeheartedly agree. You can't do both and do them well. One will be sacrificed for the other. This is not to say that one should stay in a bad marriage for the sake of the children. Children growing up in a dysfunctional home will re-enact the dysfunction in their adult lives. Whether one is a single parent or married, the task of balancing motherhood and career is difficult at best. I don't have any answers. Just the knowledge that one's life force can be drained if there is no support system. The men in my life were my support system. So, in spite of the hardships, adversity and losses, I am still grateful for the part they played in my life.

The High Price of Both

There is a time for work. And a time for love. That leaves no other time.

—Coco Chanel

The decision to separate and divorce is painful and difficult. Hearts wrench. Pragmatic intentions collide and create anxiety and guilt. Somewhere the self decides. The decisions rarely rest on pure logic. No lesser in value, however, are the demands of innocent victims—the children. It is hard for them to understand the moving away of one of their parents and the substitution of that with another unrelated friend or new father figure. The feelings sometimes are strong. It can be anger. It can be fear. It can be a sense of intrusion. It can be jealousy, uncontrollable rage and in some cases, it can be an abuse of the child by the friend or spouse of the parent.

What starts as an emancipation of one's dying self many times results in the high price of the loss of security and the emotional effect on the children. When I look back at those years after my divorce from Jack and Tom, it was a long struggle. While I never regretted my decision, I could not escape the pain, guilt and utter sense of emotional and financial destitution that struck every now and then. With all the objective facts on one's side, still there remains a lurking doubt, a hope and a fantasy that it might have worked. As a therapist, and in my own life, even with all the hindsight, I have seen it to be a correct decision. But that does not make it the best choice. Relationships are built on trust and optimism, and when that trust for whatever reason is not realized, one suffers pangs of regret and pain by mustering strength to say, "Good-bye."

I don't know if my professional commitment was an expression of an inner need or just a part of the struggle to strive and survive. My job became my pride and a source of great joy and fulfillment. But was my devotion to work a mechanism to repress my guilt and my pain as a mother?

During my marriage to Tom, my oldest daughter, Linda, left home to join her father in Missouri. Leaving me was her way of expressing her anger towards Tom and me. Tom's presence in her home was an intrusion. She retaliated by leaving home. The decision was impulsive, abrupt and without any consideration of consequences. She was defiant and relentless, unwilling to listen to reason and common sense. It was as if a wall came between us. It was impenetrable. She was in her junior year of high school; a cheerleader, and enjoying the best years of her adolescence. Suddenly, she was gone. I lost her, and my heart broke.

There were times the longing was so great that I would comfort myself by holding a tape recorder and talking to her as I walked the three miles to my office. I would disclose my feelings, thoughts, my impressions and the previous day's or week's events. Sometimes I talked about how the sky looked, how the air felt and identifying some sights I passed along the way. "I'm passing the water tower now. You know, the one that looms over the police station. Not the colorful one on the beach."

Somehow, this dialogue helped to heal my sorrow. Still it hurt so much. I felt I was reaping what I had sown. My beautiful daughter Linda had abandoned me, just as I had her. I found it so difficult to believe. I found it impossible to accept. How could she leave me? What had I done to deserve this excruciating sentence? How could she cut me out of her life and exile me as if I had been her perpetrator?

I recalled the days and nights I prayed she would survive my tenuous, first pregnancy. I remember the fear I felt when I began staining early during my first trimester. A doctor had once told me that I couldn't have children due to my retroverted uterus; some ominous medical terminology I didn't understand, yet it brought tears to my eyes.

"I suggest you think about adoption," he said without a shred of compassion in his voice. I cried for days. Now, in spite of his prognosis, I became pregnant.

"Please Jack. There must be something you can do. Some shot or hormone you can give me," I cried on the telephone from the teacher's lounge, while my first graders were on the playground.

Jack and I drove over to Dr. Sheldon's as soon as school was over.

"Nature has a way of taking care of these things," he said in a sympathetic voice. "Trust nature to do her job," he assured me.

I couldn't accept nature's plan. I had to find my own way.

"Please Jack. Do something. There must be something you can do. Just try," I pleaded.

Jack gave me a shot of some hormone to see if he could strengthen my pregnancy, and six months later Linda was born. She was perfect.

But I had suffered before and during her birth, and both of us had nearly died. I was in labor for 32 hours. The labor pains began far apart, but they gripped me with a force I will never forget. I spent most of that day wandering around the halls of Magnolia Hospital, a hospital in Opa Locka that Jack had been working in for the first two years of our married life. The nurses catered to me with love and tenderness, all of them so willing to help me through my very first experience in becoming a mother.

Jack was busy during that day seeing patients, making his rounds and doing routine paper work. I prayed, wondered and worried. I called my mother and asked if she would come and visit with me. I told her I was hungry and had been experiencing the labor since before five that same morning. Could she bring me a cheese sandwich? She ignored my need for her support, saying that if I was feeling hungry I could not possibly be in labor. I never did get the sandwich. I was lucky to get a conversation. I wanted her with me, but she said she couldn't leave work.

I stayed at the hospital until Jack finished his work day. When the pains were about ten minutes apart, we drove over to Osteopathic Medical Hospital, where Dr. Sheldon was waiting for me, but not before Jack insisted we stop at a drug store to purchase film for the new Polaroid and get a lesson on loading the camera. I waited in the car outside in active labor.

At the last minute something must have gone wrong. After I was given my epidural, all I can remember is the doctor telling Jack that the baby had turned, and he had just a few minutes to get her out before she suffocated.

"I have to see if I can turn the baby around. It's too late to do a C-section. I need to do a cephalic version if possible."

I looked at the large white clock on the wall. It was 1:10 A.M. She was born breech.

"It's a girl!" I heard Jack shout. "And she looks just like me."

I had an allergic reaction to the epidural and went into shock. When I awoke 48 hours later, my body was wrapped in ace bandages with Jack lying by my side.

"What happened?" I asked. "How's the baby?"

"Oh my God! You're okay," he said with relief. "She's fine. She's beautiful. Thank God you're okay. I was so worried."

More memories. It had been less than two months before Linda left that I threw her a sweet sixteen party. I had invited 40 of her friends and had spent days preparing for the event. I cooked the entire dinner myself and had invited a self-proclaimed "warlock" to entertain her guests. He read their fortunes and delighted them with stories about mystics and magic. The party was a huge success and Linda and I sat on the living room floor reviewing the evening with delight and laughter.

"Thank you so much, Mother," she said with genuine gratitude and affection. "You're the best mother any girl could ever have."

25 days later was my 40th birthday. We celebrated with my family and dear friends.

"You've only just begun, Mother. The best is yet to come. I hope I can be the kind of woman and mother you have been. You are my guiding light," she said with tears in her eyes.

One month later she was gone. One month later and nothing mattered any more. My child deserted me and there was nothing, absolutely nothing I could do about it.

I asked those questions that I am sure every mother must ask herself so many times during the evolving years of motherhood. Why? Why did I make this choice? Why did I have children? Did I need this pain and sorrow as a lesson? God is good to us by not revealing the future that would surely deter us from having children.

I distinctly remember the days after my divorce from Tom. My psychotherapy practice had grown. My work hours were long and unpredictable. I was constantly on call for my clients. There were these five beautiful children; three teenagers and two pre-adolescents, who needed my time, affection and guidance. I was a therapist. I was well aware of their nurturing needs. I made my clients aware of the abandonment that they had suffered. I encouraged them to feel the sense of loss and anger at having been neglected.

Then there were my own children. I had many questions, feelings and defense mechanisms to contain my anxiety and guilt. That is when I decided to live with Phil. He had no regular job. No regular income and a lot of baggage from his previous financial and emotional dealings. Something attracted me to him. He was naturally disposed to parenting. Perhaps the wife and his own children who lived less than a mile away would not agree. Was he a pragmatic choice dictated by my need for a companion? Now it was 1980. My practice had grown and so had my family. I had five glorious teenagers. Phil was perfect—from South Philadelphia, an ex-seminarian and Italian with an innocence that at times scared the hell out of both me and my children. But I needed a father figure for my five teenagers and maybe for myself too. He came home and cooked. I came home and collapsed.

In retrospect, however, I have a lot to thank Phil for what he did for the kids. When one of my daughters was sexually abused by someone who was once a significant other, she had enough trust and confidence in Phil to share this experience with him. While part of me was jealous and angry that she did not trust me with that information before talking to Phil, I look back with gratitude for his affection, sensitivity and presence.

All too often this is the story of struggling "super moms." We are supposed to take care of financial responsibilities and simultaneously provide for the emotional needs of the children. It's really another myth of our time.

Ashamed and afraid, unable to tell me the truth, she confided in Phil, who somehow developed a trusting relationship with her. It was he who told me about this dreadful event.

The perpetrator was no stranger. He was close to me and I had trusted him even though I had feared and suspected something like this might occur.

He had lived in our home and had seen my children grow. I had heard from his former spouse that he had told of his fantasies for little girls, and had heard him share the same while living with me. I had known and ignored it because I had watched him go through many long years of therapy. I was sure that such fantasies must have been resolved. But the worst had to happen.

During the latter years of our relationship, he had been sexually withdrawn and spoke about his fantasies. Fearful that he might act out, I made an appointment with my therapist who I had not seen for a few years. When I told him about my concern for my daughter's safety, his unfathomable response placed the onus on me and implied that I was pathological, suggesting I perhaps had some unresolved sexual fantasies about children. I was so enraged after Phil had disclosed my daughter's lamentation, that I wrote my therapist this letter:

Dear Dr. McKinley:

When I told you about my partner sharing his sexual fantasies with me concerning my daughter, you suggested that perhaps I had unresolved sexual conflicts regarding younger people (children), and sexual feelings. And then you went on to say that a "fantasy is not reality, and no one is really affected," as if to say, "What am I getting so excited about. It's no big deal," intimating that I was over-reacting to his fantasies.

Well if you don't know the reality by now, allow me to impart it to you as imparted to me by my daughter, who broke down tearfully as she related the events of that evening . . .

So, my fantasy was not to be taken so lightly after all. And, if you had any insight into the depth of his pathology and its implication, you had a professional responsibility and obligation as my therapist of five years to warn me of this, and help me acknowledge and deal with my instinctive feelings. Instead, you minimized my feelings and tried to cast guilt, doubt and blame on me. You should have told me he was sick; a lot sicker than you allowed me to believe.

Now, I know I was right—after the fact. After I agreed to allow her to spend the night against my better judgement, assuming you, as a trained analyst, must know more than me.

I'll never forgive you. His ex-wife warned me. You knew about the allegations that he had molested her teenage daughter just prior to their separation. My own feelings tried to give warning, but you persuaded me to gain "insight."

"Analyze them out and test them to reality," you said so clinically, putting the responsibility on my shoulders.

I'll tell that to my daughter one day.

Joan

I am reminded of what Alice Miller wrote in her book, *The Drama of the Gifted Child*:

"Metapsychology has no model for these processes. It is concerned with cathexis, with intrapsychic dynamics, object- and self-representations, but not with the facts that at most are taken into account as the patient's fantasies. Its concern is the meaning attached to experiences and not the reality behind them."

There is no doubt that such perpetrations can be and have been committed by the real fathers. In all cases they call for a justified outrage. It is different when such perpetration is committed by someone who has been brought into the house by the mother. The conflict of the original divorce is relived. The guilt of subjecting one's child to undeserved exposure becomes agonizing and unforgivable. It is like the revisiting of the original shame, dark and overpowering; so powerful that one wonders if with all the reasoning it was justified to have separated one's child from the father. Divorce for sure is a painful decision when the children are involved, and the pain subsists for a long time; nurtured by the merciless conditioning of our upbringing, the deep entangled roots of familial guilt and the sense of responsibility for the welfare of the children. I am sure that most of my children would agree that my decision to divorce was better than staying in an unhappy marriage with their father, but it does not wipe out the sense of guilt and pain that I suffer after nearly 20 years of my divorce. There are no absolutes in human situations. We are all capable of doing our best, according to our limited understanding. Not to grow and be a victim goes against the grain of our innate human nature. I took my chances and in some ways it was a success, but some losses I am destined to bear.

During the five years I lived with Phil, my daughter Emily repeatedly ran away from home. It seemed to be standard procedure for her. She ran away five or six times. Her obsession with running away was an effort to establish her autonomy and discharge her hostility. Trying to counsel clients, manage a household and stay up nights worrying about a fifteen-year-old's whereabouts was a trying task, and one that took its toll on all of us. Something told me to let go. I had often heard it expressed in the 12-step vernacular, but had never really understood how one lets go. Especially when you don't know where your child is. So I waited, and I prayed.

Several weeks went by and still I heard nothing. Her father sent out a dragnet and discovered her whereabouts. He insisted she be sent to him. He claimed I didn't have control over her and was unfit as a mother. She refused to go.

I often doubted my mothering skills. Jack's reminders of how ineffective I was served to inflict more guilt and self-doubt. What could I do that I didn't already do? What choices did I have? So many times I hated myself for leaving Jack. Perhaps my parents had been right for admonishing my behavior and not supporting the divorce. Just by virtue of their age, they could see the larger picture. I hated myself and God so many times for bringing these problems into my life. My nights were filled with restless sleep and constant worry.

In a way, I was grateful when Jack wanted to take over, although in my heart I knew Emily was deeply troubled and control was not the answer. At least not his version of control. The adult in me knew what I was doing or not doing was not working. Perhaps sending her to her father would be more effective. At least he was not juggling a romantic relationship and four other children. His only distraction was his work. He lived in a town that had less than 200 people—and there was little social life or diversion. The time and attention he might be able to offer her seemed to make good sense. But the mother in me went crazy. How could I send her away to a place where she knew no one? How could I go through the pain of abandonment again as I had done only a few years before with Linda? I screamed inside, feeling the torture of losing another daughter. But I had already lost her I said to myself. The therapist in me won the argument, but the mother in me hated the decision.

Phil had the job of getting her on the plane. She was obstinate. She refused to dress or pack. Phil threatened to take her on the plane exactly as she was. He did. She left the house wearing a long teeshirt, no pants or shorts, thongs, and holding a hair brush in her hands. She protested vehemently the whole way to the airport, threatening to jump out of the car at every opportunity. It became a test of wills and strength, but Phil succeeded in getting her on the plane.

I chose not to go to the airport with them. I couldn't bear the pain. I prayed that I was making the right decision. I felt I had betrayed my child. I was sending her into exile. I was punishing her by turning my back on her during a time when she needed me the most. I recalled my own adolescence. It seemed so long ago and so different. Things like this didn't seem to happen in the 1950s. At least I hadn't remembered any. No one ever ran away from home. I hadn't remembered anyone even wanting to. Things were so different then. What would my mother have done under the same circumstances? I had their support, but somewhere in the background lingered the unspoken echoes of "I told you so."

My brother came to my house that day. I was terrified and distraught. "Mickey," I cried. "Help me with this. I need help. It's killing me. I don't know how to handle her. She needs supervision. But maybe she needs me. I'm so confused," I cried. I wasn't even making sense.

He felt my pain. He wanted to be there to support me and to help me think. Reaching a decision was like tackling Mt. Everest. I thought about all the mothers who had to make the same decisions. I remembered the nights I would lecture about "Tough Love," and the suggestions I made to other parents who were dealing with incorrigible teenagers. Now it was my turn.

Just as I had anticipated, Emily was back in Miami 24 hours before her father even realized she was missing. She had managed an escape plan. Her girlfriend (the one she had stayed with during those weeks away from me) had stolen money from her mother's purse to purchase a bus ticket. Soon, Emily was on a Greyhound headed back to Miami.

Once her father discovered she was gone, he ordered another rescue mission. I told him it would be useless, just like the last effort. This time he agreed. We waited. A few weeks went by, and I began to hear through the teenage underground that Emily wanted to come home but was afraid to approach me. Strategic intervention was called for.

I gathered all sorts of memorabilia from her room, including photographs of her when she was little, her animals along the way, camp photos, anything that tied the timeline of her life together. I made a scrap book and wrote the message, "If you love someone, set them free. If they are really yours, they will return."

I had discovered (also through the teenage underground) that she had been living in a one-bedroom apartment with a Puerto Rican family of seven. By now things were tougher than she thought they would ever be. I had really let go. She was ready to come home.

Her decision to return home was negotiated with a one-year commitment to live in Missouri with her father, something she greatly protested. But she acquiesced when I stood firm. I needed to be able to trust her, and this would demonstrate if that trust could be re-established. The deal was simple. One year in Missouri with her father, faithful school attendance and a demonstration that she would apply herself to her studies. I finally had the control I had lost.

One year later—a year that felt like five to me—she returned a different child. We had established boundaries and limits.

My son Tim began skipping school. In his senior year of high school he had cut class 17 times. The principal called me in to discuss the implications, the most severe being that he would not graduate. During that meeting I began to cry. I felt impotent as a parent, without the resources to help my son. Perhaps it was the tears or perhaps it was the fear the principal instilled in Tim (I'm still not sure), but somehow Tim graduated, and I relaxed.

Some years prior, Tim had been invited to join a diving trip his teacher had arranged in the Keys. He was 15 and had just been certified for diving. I agreed to let him go. That same evening, just after Phil and I retired, the phone rang. It was 1:00 a.m. Phil answered.

"I'm scared," Tim said.

"What's going on?" Phil asked.

I was unaware of the complete conversation because I could only hear Phil's portion. After a few minutes and some specific instructions, Phil jumped out of bed and began to dress.

"What are you doing?" I asked.

"Go back to sleep. I'm going to get Tim. I'll be back in the morning," he replied.

"Why? Why are you going to get him? Is he alright? Has something happened?"

Phil related the essence of Tim's phone call. He had been suspicious that his teacher, Mr. Parker, was making sexual overtures. He was afraid that he would not be able to protect himself, so he went down to the lobby in the motel where they were staying and called

Phil to come and get him.

"Now? You're going now?" I asked.

"Yes. I'm going now. I'm not going to let him suffer in fear all night. He needs me, and I'm going."

"Well I'll go with you. It's pouring out there, and you may need my help. Islamorada is a long way from here," I said.

So, we both got dressed and headed out the door. It wasn't just raining. It was pouring. An electrical storm had hit the area and the wind was howling ferociously. Lightning lit up the sky. The rain turned to hail, and by the time we reached the expressway I was near hysterical. Phil realized that I would be no help, so he turned the car around and took me home. He left alone. Seven hours later he returned with Tim.

Twenty years later and the price gets higher. Marcia Clark, prosecuting attorney in the O.J. Simpson trial, has to maintain her professional responsibilities, manage her home, care for her children and fight for custody of her two young sons. Sharon Prost, counsel to Senator Orrin Hatch of Utah had to give up custody of her children because she was accused of workaholism. Millions of moms are struggling endlessly to manage both motherhood and career; even with the threat of losing custody of their children. Consider the consequences carefully. Managing motherhood and career without a support system can be hazardous to your mental and physical health.

Part II

Chapter 4

THE SOULFUL QUEST: A JOURNEY INTO SELF AND SAYING GOODBYE TO MYTHS

To every thing there is a season, and a time to every purpose under the heaven. A time to be born, and a time to die; a time to plant, and a time to pluck up that which is planted; A time to weep, and a time to laugh; a time to mourn, and a time to dance; A time to get, and a time to lose; a time to keep, and a time to cast away; A time to rend, and a time to sew; a time to keep silence, and a time to speak; A time to love, and a time to hate; a time of war, and a time of peace.

—Eccles. 3:1-2, 4, 6-8

Each of us moves into our journey in different ways. Some hear it like a calling, that inner voice that keeps whispering our truth, no matter how we resist it. Some like myself, don't hear the calling until long after we were guided by destiny through circumstances and synchronicity. Some know their journey from the moment they develop a conscious awareness of their life force, like Liza Minnelli or Amelia Earhart. Others find their journey through trial and error, and there are those who never seem to see the light or hear the bell. They stay loyal to the scripts and traditions assigned by their family, or they just keep trying to figure it out. They are the unlucky ones; the ones who go to their graves never knowing who they are—the Willie Lomans, who never complete their journey in this lifetime.

Each of us has a quest. Some of us know it early, others later. To be self-actualized is to follow your quest. Some of us need a map to get where we're going. Others know the way as if they carved it themselves from other lifetimes. For those of us who need help along the way, here's a map that may be helpful.

Trust your feelings. I know there are times when you can't discern which ones are the crazy ones and which are healthy. Which come from your heart, and which come from your head. When you learn to listen to your inner voice, you will never go wrong. Your inner voice presents itself in many different ways. Some of us can hear the dialogue in our head. Some can feel it in their pulse. Some see it in their dreams. Some are obsessed in their thoughts. Others need to do chair work with a Gestalt therapist. Some just get a strong feeling that won't go away no matter how much they try to avoid it. Some are born with it, or learn it so early that they never have to question their choice.

Nancy Kerrigan began skating at age six. From the moment she touched the ice, she knew she was a skater. She never second-guessed herself. 18 years later she brought home the silver medal from the Olympics.

My son, Tim, and his father before him, heard their inner voice at age three. There was never any other choice—only medicine. No matter how difficult the struggle for both, they were relentless in their quest, and as I sit here writing, my son is in his third year of medical school, after failing the MCATs three times before he was accepted. His strengths in academia were history and English.

"Be a lawyer or a political scientist," I would say. "Why must you pursue a career in medicine when every sign indicates it's not for you?"

His weakest subjects were biology and chemistry. Getting into and through medical school was like pushing Jello up hill. He came so close to losing his quest.

I remember the night he, his father and I sat on the terrace of a waterside restaurant in North Miami Beach. He had just learned that his third set of scores didn't cut it and that Jane, the love of his life, chose not to come to Miami to live with him.

"There are only two things I want most in this world," he said with a face so sorrowful I could barely keep from crying. "Jane and becoming a doctor. And I guess I can't have either."

His guardian angel must have heard him. He passed the MCATs

and was accepted into a five-year program. Jane came to live with him when he least expected it. Medical school outlasted their romance, but not their friendship. When she left him, I feared the worst.

Tim was heartsick. He found it difficult to concentrate. He stayed focused on his grief and loss of this five-year relationship. We met for lunch one afternoon during his lunch hour. I picked him up from school and we drove down 19th Avenue toward the neighborhood we had lived in from the time he was born until he was five years old. As we approached, I told him the story of his birth and the conditions surrounding my pregnancy.

I had given birth just seven months earlier, and here I was, pregnant again. It was January 1966. Emily, my second child, had been born in June 1965.

My doctor reassured me whenever I complained that I didn't feel pregnant. After all, I had two other pregnancies to compare, and this didn't feel like those.

"Stop worrying. Each pregnancy feels different. I assure you that everything's fine. Just relax," Dr. Sheldon said. But somewhere inside, I didn't trust him.

Dr. Sheldon was 39 years old and overweight. He had a white patch of hair on the top of his head, close to the frontal lobe. He said it was a birth mark. He was married with three children and was a part owner in the hospital where my husband worked during the first two years of his practice. We knew Al Sheldon for nearly four years and he was well liked by everyone that knew him.

As the months progressed, I kept complaining every third week on my appointment. In June, when I should have been feeling life and felt nothing, he finally agreed to do an internal exam, something usually not done so late in pregnancy.

"You're right. You are right," he said while feeling the size of my uterus. "This fetus hasn't grown beyond six weeks."

"Six weeks." I exclaimed. "I told you something wasn't right. I knew it. What am I going to do? Why haven't I aborted?"

"You may not. Sometimes women go to full term."

"There must be something you can do. I can't walk around four more months knowing I'm carrying a dead fetus."

He told me I could have a therapeutic abortion if three doctors agreed that the fetus had not developed.

"Then let's do it." I pleaded. "Let's do it."

It was a Friday afternoon. He arranged for the doctor's appointments with the two other physicians the same afternoon. As soon as they all agreed with his diagnosis, a therapeutic abortion was scheduled for the following Tuesday morning. Just four days away.

On Sunday morning, Dr. Sheldon had a massive heart attack and died. The community was in shock. I was too. Instead of my abortion, I attended the funeral. There I was, in maternity clothes, carrying a dead fetus and grieving for my doctor and friend. By Wednesday, I decided to call the obstetrician who had delivered Emily, my second child. I told him as much as I could, but he refused to perform an abortion without waiting a reasonable amount of time, which he determined to be three more weeks. He said he had no frame of reference to evaluate if the fetus was in fact dead. Perhaps Dr. Sheldon had made a misdiagnosis. I had no choice but to wait the three weeks. They were the longest three weeks of my life.

"Well, my dear lady. You are now nine weeks pregnant," he announced with a cigarette dangling from his lips.

"Nine weeks!" I shouted. "How is that possible?"

"Easy," he said with a smile so big that he could no longer hold the cigarette in his mouth. "We make mistakes. You simply were not pregnant when Dr. Sheldon said you were. He probably mistook your enlarged uterus for another pregnancy, when in fact, it was still coming down in size from the last baby. It's not uncommon. Doctors do make mistakes, you know."

Tim was born December 28, 1966, nearly one year after my misdiagnosed pregnancy. When he was born, he had the same birthmark on his head as Dr. Sheldon. There on the top in the exact same spot was the white patch of hair. Three weeks later it was gone. Dr. Sheldon had to die so Tim could be born. I named him, Tim Daniel, after the doctor who delivered him, Danny Stone. I don't know what kind of a doctor Tim will become, but I know one thing for sure. He will be a doctor. And he knew it all his life.

As we drove past the house that had once belonged to Dr. Sheldon, I told my son, "So much of what happens is already destined. Just accept what comes down and above all, trust your feelings."

In his book, *The Celestine Prophecy,* James Redfield suggests the first of nine insights into true spiritual awareness is becoming conscious of the coincidences in our lives. Scott Peck writes that all of us experience these coincidences, but not all are aware they are happening. Carl Jung wrote about synchronicity as patterns of the timely interfacing of events, giving larger meaning or purpose to these events. I don't think anyone really knows why these things happen, only that they do.

Those of us who are open to these happenings develop a clearer understanding of our purpose and where we are in life. I still ask myself why I didn't choose to go back to either of the other two doctors who agreed with Dr. Sheldon. I am convinced that the story above was no simple coincidence, but rather a psychic phenomenon which I am not about to question, only accept. With my acceptance comes grace and gratitude. After all, Tim was my first son. This event along with many others has taught me to let go and allow destiny to take me where I need to go. Control only interrupts the process and gets in the way. This is not about abandoning responsibility. It is only to give permission to nature to let it do its work. The ego must relinquish itself to the universe. The universe is connected to each of us, and we are one with the universe. In finding your true self, you will feel secure to dismiss your ego and become part of the whole.

From Miss America to Marilyn Van Derbur Atler

There she is, Miss America.
There she is, your ideal.

Somehow I knew I didn't have the right stuff to make the Miss America contest. I knew at a young age what constituted a winner—long legs, blonde hair, blue eyes, all American looks and talent. I knew a short, dark-haired, Semitic, brown-eyed, olive-skinned, full-breasted accordion player from Miami Beach wouldn't cut it.

America never expected their crowning choice, that lovely, tall, elegant, blond, blue-eyed beauty to have two personalities—a "day child" and a "night child." As she regally strolled down the runway in her full-length white evening gown, her full bouquet of long-stemmed red roses, wearing her jeweled crown, smiling at the audience with tears rolling down her cheeks, no one knew there lived inside this objectification of ideal womanhood a tortured little girl. Nearly every night, from her fifth to her 18th year, she had been molested by her father, a seemingly upstanding community leader and philanthropist.

The only way our beauty queen managed to survive was to split herself in half, becoming daddy's little girl by day and daddy's sexual partner by night. Never the two shall meet—until one day when the split became so great that it could no longer stay contained, it erupted into a clinical depression interfering with every aspect of her life. Her mind and body finally screamed her truth. And when it did, the world heard. Her truth could save countless others. If it could happen to Miss America, Marilyn Van Derbur, then it could happen to anyone. So Miss America 1957 became Miss America of today and gave to the world the truth that was denied so many years ago. Her truth, and that of so many others, continues to bring healing to both men and women who have been keeping the same secret she had.

From Answering Questions to Asking a Few

He's a walking contradiction, partly truth and partly fiction, taking every wrong direction on his lonely way back home.

—Kris Kristofferson

When I was growing up all the questions had easy answers:
What college will I go to? One my parents could afford.
Who will be my husband? Hopefully, a Jewish doctor.
How many children should we have? Have five, Mom says. Four for us and one for her. She always wanted four, but Dad wouldn't let her. So, I'll be a good daughter and have five.
What temple should we join? The one everyone else joins: Beth Torah.
What should I wear to the party? Something very sexy that causes great attention.

It is not that these same questions aren't being asked now, it's that so many others are included in the dialogue and the answers are not so simple. My daughters ask questions that don't even resemble the ones I asked. Their choice of college was determined on not only what was affordable, but which could provide the best education for their chosen careers, even when they weren't sure about what they wanted to do.

My second daughter, Emily, chose to quit school at age 16. The only one out of the five children who decided academia wasn't for her. This would not have been an option for me at 16. But after she ran away from home several times, failed two or three subjects and developed mononucleosis, which prevented her from attending classes for six weeks, I trusted her belief that she was not a candidate for college. I agreed to let her quit, but with the condition that she attend trade school and obtain a GED. With my encouragement, she enrolled in beauty school and became a hairdresser—although not without constant reminders from me to make sure she attended class. I knew her attendance track record was poor and that she was a risk for any kind of school. But she was destined to be a hairdresser, perhaps because it came so easy. I still had some control over her actions and she managed to complete the course in 13 months. In spite of her apathy and poor attendance, she managed to score a high grade on her exam. Today, she is a successful hair designer, happy with her career, but most of all herself.

Emily never liked to get up before noon. Today, she has a lifestyle that allows her to sleep late, work four days a week and earn a great living. And she loves what she does! I, on the other hand, lived out every assignment delegated to me by authority figures, which really meant I was living out their dreams and desires. At the age of 35 I was divorced, working in a profession I disliked, with five children and a house with no money to keep it up. Tell me, whose choice made more sense?

At this writing, my daughters are 30, 28 and 25. The questions they ask are: How can I help change the world? Am I ever going to get married? What is my role in society? Can I stand alone without a man? Must I be a mother to be accepted by society? How will I know if I made the right choices with my life's work? Can I be a single parent? Do I want to bring a child into this world without a father figure? Do I want to bring a child into this world, period? What are the things I need to think about before I make a commitment to marriage and family? Am I going to fulfill my own expectations or those of my parents? (At least they make the distinction!) Who am I and what is my purpose in this lifetime? What part of God do I manifest? What is the difference about me that makes a difference?

One daughter asks, Was I molested? Why do I lose my mind when I talk to a man? Why am I the "messy" one in the family? Why do I hurt? What is my depression about? Why couldn't I feel my own feelings and where was my anger? How did I lose my convictions and how can I get them back? Why do I have a problem focusing, concentrating and thinking if I'm supposed to be "so smart"?

By being willing to ask the questions her truth was revealed. Through her commitment to 12-step programs, years of personal work in psychotherapy, the support of family, friends, and most importantly her belief in God, the answers came and set her free.

Sam Keen writes, "To be on a quest is nothing more or less than to become an asker of questions." He subscribes to living the questions. Joseph Campbell said, "Follow your bliss." I wholeheartedly agree!

From Co-dependency to Gaining a Self

I agree with Keen that self-doubt is part of a healthy personality, and furthermore, to know one's limits and finiteness is the source of all spirituality.

One of the greatest men of our times was racked with self-doubt. His love and devotion to this country was paramount, and yet he risked dividing this nation in half. Abraham Lincoln thought of himself as a failure.

When one holds on to rigid beliefs and presuppositions, then growth is stifled. We need to examine our beliefs and values and re-evaluate their logic and applicability for where we are in our own journey. Norms and values that were proper when I was in my 20s and 30s are outdated and absurd today. If countries that were once so stubborn in their beliefs and customs can alter their paradigms, so can individuals. What was once held sacred and unrefutable, can be obsolete and meaningless in less than an average lifetime.

Did you ever believe that someday you might think that men who burned their draft cards were right when you once were convinced they were wrong? Did you ever think you would see the demise of the Soviet Union? Do you remember the fear you felt when missiles in Cuba were pointed at the United States? Did you ever believe that the Berlin Wall would come crumbling down? That apartheid in South Africa would end? That Israel would sign a peace agreement with Arafat? That a president could be Catholic? That a woman could attend the Citadel? Did you ever think that babies could come from test tubes? That free love could cause death? And that a black man would be considered for the presidency when less than 40 years ago they had to ride on the back of the bus, drink water from fountains marked "colored," and need a pass to be on Miami Beach after five o'clock?

Why at 15 or 16 didn't I doubt the fairness of these social values? Why couldn't I feel the discrimination placed upon a person of color? Why, as a Jew hearing about Jews who spent centuries being persecuted, couldn't I identify with these injustices?

I remember the day I felt the injustice. Our English teacher assigned us to interview someone who represented our chosen profession. Acting had always been my first choice, so I decided to interview the closest thing to it—an entertainer. It so happened that Sammy Davis, Jr. was appearing at the Copa City nightclub in Miami Beach. I was a senior in high school and I took the liberty to call upon him at the club one afternoon while he was rehearsing. He greeted me warmly and invited me to watch the rehearsal while he had someone bring me a Coke. I was thrilled. There I sat, Coke in hand, my eyes glued to one of the world's most popular entertainers. After practice, he walked over to me wiping his brow and neck, somewhat out of breath, and said, "What can I do for you, young lady?"

"You can give me an interview, Mr. Davis. I need it for my English class assignment."

After the interview, I asked if he would be willing to come to our high school to sing for us, never in a million years expecting his answer.

"What high school do you go to?" he asked.

"Beach High," I said proudly.

"Sure I'll come to your school. But only if you introduce me yourself, personally!"

I thought I would collapse. "You got a deal, Mr. Davis!" I said in disbelief. "You got a deal."

I practically ran the whole way back to school—a distance of over a mile. I reached the school before dismissal and ran to the dean's office, knowing Mr. Kessner needed to sanction all coming events.

"Mr. Kessner," I blurted out. "Mr. Kessner, I can get Sammy Davis, Jr. to come to our school and sing for the student body."

"Isn't he that colored singer?" he asked with a look of disdain.

"Yes, he's colored. You must have seen him or at least heard of him. He's wonderful. He's been on the Ed Sullivan show. He's a tap dancer, a singer and he plays the drums."

"I'm sorry. But this is something that the PTA would find most objectionable. You'll have to forget the whole idea."

"Why? What's the problem?" I asked.

"Well you know . . . colored and all. There would be a brouha-ha and it just wouldn't work. I'm sorry. You'll just have to make up an excuse."

I didn't even know what brouhaha meant, but I knew its implications. It was wrong. Very wrong. I understood the meaning of prejudice for the first time. Not even an ounce of self-doubt. I now had a feeling that matched a conviction, but that feeling came too few times. It didn't appear again until I heard my father's foreboding words when I decided to divorce Jack. "You're making the biggest mistake of your life. You will regret it for the rest of your life. You're nothing without him."

"Wrong," I said to myself. "You're wrong." But meekly, because under that feeling of truth lived the memory of an older feeling that was even more familiar—self-doubt. "Maybe, he's right. Maybe I am nothing without him and I'll live to regret it for the rest of my life."

The conditioning of self-doubt in women by their fathers, husbands and even sons has impaired the growth in selfhood for women probably more than any other single factor. Women need to borrow cocksureness from men, and men need to borrow self-doubt from women.

When I divorced Jack after 13 years of marriage, I was left with five kids and a six-bedroom home in Miami Beach that I couldn't afford, an Oldsmobile station wagon with ten more payments, and a Golden Retriever. There was nothing that could rescue me faster than another marriage.

In preparing for the impending divorce, I had already lined up my third husband, Tom. When that marriage began to fade, I did it again. After nine years of psychotherapy, six which included group, three years of graduate school, and a psychotherapy practice, I did it again.

When was I going to get it? I didn't need a man to feel worthy as a woman.

Sam Keen said that the best advice he ever got as a man was to ask himself these two questions: "Where am I going?" and "Who will go with me?" Never reverse the two or you're in big trouble. I always had someone to go with me, but I never knew where the hell I was going. I only knew I didn't feel safe going alone. Even when it wasn't safe to be with a man, I made it feel safe. When I had major evidence to prove otherwise, I rejected it. When I was alone, I was frantic. By 40 I had achieved professional success, loved my work and maintained a reasonable level of motherhood, but felt lost without a man. I still had the notion that only a man could take care of me. I went to great lengths to reinforce this myth.

I was suffering the wounds of a seven-week love affair that ended on a Tuesday morning. By Tuesday evening, I met my fourth husband, Mervyn. I unloaded my life's history on him somewhere between US 1 and A1A going over the Sunny Isles Causeway, a ten-minute drive. My grief over my broken love affair landed me in the arms of a man 17 years my senior, who gently said the magic words, "The trouble with you Joni, is that you never picked a man who really knew how to love you and take care of you." Once spoken, those words, were his portentous mistake. He got the job.

Just as men turn inward toward the unknown territory of their soul and discover the desert, so do women. Just as men had the injunction of "Men don't cry," women had the injunction of "Nice girls don't get angry." So our culture has produced a generation of women who cry when they get angry, and men who get angry when they really want to cry, but can't. We each developed a racket to cover up our authentic feelings for acceptance. And acceptance of whom? A society that doesn't know who they are and keeps producing more of them, until families become so dysfunctional that people go to their graves never knowing who they were.

I grew up in a society that genuinely admired youth and beauty.

Women were exalted and sexually objectified, especially if they had large breasts, small waists and flat tummies. Bathing suits were designed to reveal tits and asses. Even now, after years of feminism and women's lib, the bathing suits are briefer and the breasts are bigger. Look at the cover of any issue of *Cosmopolitan* and the first thing staring back at you are large breasts. We resent it on an intellectual level, but at a deeper level, we buy into it. Our belief system really controls our behavior, even when our values disdain it. I suspect that if I asked five young women randomly who they would rather be, Eleanor Roosevelt or Christie Brinkley, if they could come back in another lifetime, the majority would choose the latter.

Even as men fear aging and mortality, so do women. The myth of womanhood has been that better bodies, bigger boobs, tighter asses, pinchier noses and fuller lips can create self-esteem, romance, love and fulfillment. We now know the truths about these myths. Silicone can be life threatening, collagen can cause allergies, liposuction can be dangerous, and anytime you go under the knife, you are taking a large risk. I work with women who have had several face lifts, where the space between their lips and ears grows smaller with each surgery. Some can hardly speak, their mouths are so stiff. I see women who have had four or five nose jobs, and one who has had her breasts enlarged and adjusted six times. I have a client who increased her breast size only to have it decreased after she recalled being molested as a child.

My first analyst called me "Barbie doll." He had a flock of Barbie dolls as patients, most of whom I referred to his practice. He used to scare us by telling us that one day we would be like used tires, worn and old. "Uh-oh." I'd say over and over. "Uh-oh. I'd better find myself fast."

And not unlike men who don't understand the phrase, "You're not in touch with your feelings," guess what? Neither are women who haven't traveled the road to recovery and spirituality. Women may have a greater predisposition for getting "in touch" with their inner selves, but men have the same capacity. It's just that women, in general, have been given greater permissions to do so all their lives. Men have not.

From Anger and Resentment to Hope and Forgiveness

By the time Aaron was ready for his second leg operation, Jack and I had been divorced for 15 years, and I had had two other husbands. I was now 50; Jack was 54. He had a quiet, passive girlfriend. She was perfect for him. She never had an opinion, spoke only when spoken to and never complained. I had been married to Mervyn, my fourth husband for two years. He was 67. I was his third wife.

I hadn't been happy with the results of Aaron's first surgery, the operation he had on his leg after the accident three years previously. There was a length differential of over an inch, leaving him with a marked limp.

I couldn't find a physician in Miami who would operate on him again, so I had to take him to the Chief of Orthopedics at Mount Sinai Hospital in New York. Due to the nature of the surgery and the rehabilitative therapy necessary for a complete recovery, we had to stay in New York for two weeks.

Two cousins of mine lived in the city. One lived on East 44th, the other on West 44th. I stayed with the East-side cousin, and Jack stayed with the West. We met each morning on the corner of 45th and Madison and would walk the entire way to the hospital. For two weeks everyday, we would meet, walk and argue all the way up to Madison and 99th. We would stop either at Jackson Hole for a hamburger and an iced cappuccino, or at a Greek coffee house for omelets. The arguments would usually begin somewhere between Valentino's and Bloomingdale's. Something about those two stores would set him off. By the time we reached Jackson Hole or the Greek coffee house, we were too tired to argue anymore, so the break revived us enough to spend the rest of the day with our son. The fights were always about the past: Leftovers. He was bitter. I couldn't make a comment without it sparking an old issue from the past. It could have been a Woody Allen movie. All we needed were the cameras and the music to "I Like New York in June."

Jack accused me of being an unfit mother. Not the sort of unfit mother that you read about in the newspapers, but rather the kind who thinks of herself before the kids. The type that remarries and compromises the welfare of the children for her own selfish causes. The type that doesn't want to contribute to the support of her children. Everyday, we would pick up from where we left off the day before. We could have called this movie "Scenes From a Divorce: Fifteen Years Later."

I knew I hadn't sufficiently grieved the loss of this marriage yet.

This man, this 54-year-old ex-husband of mine for 13 years, and father of my five children, hadn't grieved enough either. There hadn't been time. I was busy trying to find husbands and boyfriends to rescue me; Jack was too busy trying to rescue himself from bankruptcy, his lifestyle and professional annihilation. Walking, talking, yelling, screaming, ranting and raving, gesticulating, crying and sobbing, five miles a day with an occasional interruption from a homeless person waving a cup in front of our faces, or Jack suddenly stopping in front of a window at one of Madison Avenue's well-known designer shops to encourage me to try on something he liked. Each evening was the payback for staying in the ring and going for resolution each day. We would dress, dine in fashionable restaurants and perhaps see a movie or Broadway show. Some nights we would go to a nightclub or just listen to Michael Feinstein at the Algonquin or Bobby Short at the Carlyle. We would cap the night off by finding an all-night cafe and sit there over coffee and baklava or galatobouriko, continuing where we left off earlier. For 14 days and 14 nights we fought, cried, cursed and argued until there was nothing left to say except honor and accept our feelings, pain, sorrow, grief and apologies. We moved on. 15 years later.

From Compulsivity to Befriending Our Disowned Parts

The following is a true story written by one of my clients. It is illustrative of the importance of embracing our shadow side for healing and growth.

Each of us has a shadow. Our shadow lurks in our unconscious waiting to be acknowledged and embraced. The more we deny our shadow the larger it becomes.

The purpose of all compulsive behaviors is to manage feelings and avoid our shadow. As long as the behavior is used as a resource to manage feelings, it acts much like a goalie in a hockey game, preventing the puck's entry. The longer we use the behavior, the more we deny our feelings. The repression of our feelings is what makes us sick; not the traumas that occurred.

Facing the shadow and embracing our disowned parts allows us to become more integrated. Once we feel our feelings and use them as inalienable powers to get our needs met, our energy is available to enhance our lives. The road to spiritual healing is through our shadow.

Ellen was overfed, overdressed and underloved. Poverty gripped her tiny family of tenant farmers in Southern Ohio. They lived in a mean little house across from railroad tracks that wound precipitously around the mountainous terrain. Her mother would walk along these tracks while Ellen watched fearfully from the window. One day, contrary to her promise never to leave Ellen's sight, her mother disappeared around the curve of the mountain.

Ellen was catapulted into the most abject terror at the apparent loss of her mother. She pressed her face to the glass, afraid to move lest the monsters behind her back would eat her up. After all, a four-year-old has no way of understanding the concept of "I'll be home soon." Ellen became critically ill with pneumonia shortly thereafter. Her grandmother soon drove by to see if a funeral wreath had been affixed to the door. Ellen recovered.

Ellen was an only child left alone to amuse herself with pornographic magazines, the home brew that her father made—whatever was at hand.

On weekends, groups of party goers descended on the little house. During these times, Ellen heard about abortions performed with coat hangers and watched as these people were given preferential treatment; overnight stays, big country breakfasts, anything they wanted. She watched the proceedings from behind a sofa. At other times she was treated to a night in a beer garden, or a visit to a neighboring farm inhabited by drunken men and their foul-smelling, slovenly wives. Other times were spent going on trips to Cincinnati with her mother. While there, they stayed with an older man who fondled her mother in the dark. Ellen was told to sleep in the dining room in a grotesque bed that folded down from the wall. Again, she was convinced that ogres were ready to kill her.

One evening, five-year-old Ellen stood in the yard, looked toward the disappearing sun and felt a thrill of excitement as she knew there was more to life than this hovel. She saw a carved stone bridge with flickering yellow gas lights, obviously a return to a rendezvous spot from another life.

The one glorious memory of Ellen's youth was her dog, Prince. With him, she knew love, devotion, companionship and the deepest heartbreak. Money was tight and the family moved. Ellen had been promised that Prince would soon follow them to their new home. He was temporarily staying with neighbors. Weeks went by without him and lonely dread filled her little heart. She mustered up the courage to ask her father when Prince would come. "Never," he coldly told her.

As for most people, this was one of the most difficult belief systems to change later in her life: the realization that she was deserving and her needs were legitimate.

The farm that they had left was situated in an area known as "Sunshine." It was really the complete opposite for Ellen. She spent her childhood suffering as an adult and most of her adulthood suffering as a child. The nightmares began . . . the garishly painted cars coming off the wall, the pounding drums, and always her playmate, Terror, was at her side.

Time for school came and she was sent off with neighborhood children, while her mother worked and her father went to the racetrack. After school Ellen would make her way through the bar to the betting parlor in the back. Facing his wrath was less terrible than being alone.

Bright and accomplished in school, Ellen was ahead of her classmates, which was probably due to experience more than inherent brain power. If she did not get perfect marks her mother stopped speaking to her. By age seven, she realized that her parents were ineffectual not only as parents, but as people. They were embarrassing, crude and tasteless.

To save themselves the bother of putting an effort into their child's development, Ellen was told that she was sickly. She was forbidden to participate in sports, music or social intercourse of any sort. Because of her love of books and thirst for a better life, she educated herself about the grace of living with beauty and refinement. She also learned to lie about her few friends, her whereabouts and her activities.

In her middle teens she met the first man her parents approved of, which should have been a shrieking alarm in itself. Eventually, they married—he to own an indentured servant; she to escape the hell of her family. The marriage was of the times: breadwinner, housewife, nights out for him, nights alone for her, then a son, two years later another son, three years later a terrible miscarriage and two years later another son.

Ten years into the marriage, denied real companionship, subjected to humiliating financial problems and lacking intimacy of any sort, she began looking for love in all the wrong places, as it is euphemistically described.

Separations, moves, reconciliations, more moves and the morass of co-dependence deepened. She was rearing the children alone and occasionally a heart day occurred. The first son playing the piano for her, the second son coming out of his shell with a surfboard, indications that the baby had an IQ larger than his father's weight . . .

About this time, her mother committed suicide—violently, with a gun. Ellen has never felt grief for losing this woman, only a grudging pity for such waste and self-absorption.

Ellen had been raised and baptized a Methodist, which necessitated a conversion to Judaism when she married her husband. This faith had been a source of comfort to her, albeit seldom. During her mother's funeral, her father told her that her mother had been an Orthodox Jew who was disowned by her widowed mother when she married outside of her religion. The monumental deceit perpetrated by her parents was ludicrous to Ellen. After all, who would give a damn?

The positive element in this fiasco was that Ellen formed her own faith, the Church of Ellen, dedicated to hedonistic pursuits.

Life dragged on. She lost and regained fortunes, lost and didn't regain lovers. The latest debacle to assault Ellen was the collapse of the family business. When this latest round of trouble began, the gauge on the tolerance tank in Ellen's brain hit empty. A creeping malaise, the kind preceding death, overwhelmed her. There was a core meltdown of her life force.

However, she watched a John Bradshaw workshop on TV one afternoon. His admonition to seek group therapy if one felt any or all of the symptoms of depression was as if he had spoken directly to her. She followed through and began to find her lost self. She became that most coveted of states, a child of light.

The positives are slowly, but resolutely taking over the negatives. She is no longer shopping for unnecessary items.

Ellen is able to look at herself, warts and all, and love her failings as well as her gifts.

Part III

Chapter 5

RESURRECTION, GROWTH AND EMPOWERMENT: THE PHOENIX AS A FEMALE

There is in every true woman's heart a spark of heavenly fire, which lies dormant in the broad daylight of prosperity, but which kindles up and beams and blazes in the dark hours of adversity.

—Washington Irving (1783-1859)

We don't know what it is that makes the human spirit so resilient. Some may attribute it to the way things are. It always amazed me to hear how so many of my clients who came from the most depraved and abusive families, could, in spite of their adversities, make it to the top. I often wished I could model this energy that gave new hope to their spirit and self-actualization. When we look at the histories of Oprah Winfrey, Whoopie Goldberg, Gloria Steinem, Tina Turner and so many other women, who have suffered inequities in their formative years, we wonder what they had that allowed them to not only overcome their suffering and trauma, but rise again, like the Phoenix. When we read about the atrocities committed against the millions of Jews and non-Jews in Nazi concentration camps, we have to wonder how? How did they not only recover, but raise themselves like the Phoenix and transcend beyond simple "recovering." So many expanded to beyond what ever would have been expected and even believable. How? What was this power that empowered their souls? Was it in fact their traumatic histories that gave rise to a new creative force? Or was it destiny that drove them to selfhood, no matter what obstacles they endured?

Sarah is 38 years old. She has been in therapy with me for a few months. During group, each member is asked to write and read their story. This is hers:

My mother and father had been married five years when my brother Duane was born. 13 months later, I came along. My parents probably appeared to have everything. Mama was young, intelligent and pretty, always referred to as the "Jackie K" of Huntsville. She was an artist with a Master's Degree in art history. My father was 11 years her senior, and a leader in the community. He was a prominent banker and his family was well known. Their new home was the largest and most elegant anywhere within 50 miles of Huntsville. It was completed the year I was born. For my father, it was too much. For Mama, not enough.

Mama ran a kindergarten in the house for the first ten years of my life. Nurturing and physical contact were provided by Annie Mae, the live-in housekeeper. I think I was always nervous, uptight and afraid around my mother. I don't ever remember her touching or kissing me. I never remember her changing my little sister's diapers, but I do remember Daddy and Annie Mae doing these things.

Mama was so stern, formal and serious. She wanted me to be like a doll—quiet, well-behaved, well-dressed and act like a grown-up. Duane and I fussed a lot, so Mama would always tell us to pack our suitcases as we were being sent away. I would pack and stand in the hall with my suitcase without uttering a sound, ready to go. Then Mama and Daddy would fight. She would scream and yell. She would often hit him. Then she would tell us to unpack and go to bed. This was what it was like from the time I was two or three until whenever.

Daddy was always drunk in the evenings. He would always deny that anything was wrong, never admitting to having had anything to drink. He would urinate all over himself, stumble all over the house, then eventually pass out. Mama would fuss and throw things. This was the way it was every night.

I saw Daddy as weak and helpless. I felt so sorry for him. Sometimes in his inebriated state, he would try to touch Mama. She would reject him with both emotional and physical abuse. He was too drunk to fight back. I never saw them kiss or touch each other. She acted like she hated him, and hated that she was financially dependent on him. I'm not sure what she hated more, him or the dependency.

One evening Duane and I were playing cards in the den. Daddy came home drunk. Mama got mad and threw a large pot of vegetable soup at him. The soup went everywhere, on the cards, on us and mostly on him. The vegetable soup and the cards stuck to the wall. We were sent to bed. When I woke up the next morning, everything was still that way. I had hoped that it was just a bad dream.

Mama would stand in front of the window and pull her hair out. She would scream and shake. She would look down at me, and then back at the window, and begin banging on it. I used to think it was all my fault. I knew she was unhappy. I was so afraid, but didn't know what I was supposed to do. She would pull our pants down and spank us with a hair brush or spatula so it wouldn't hurt her hand.

"If you cry, I'll do it harder," she would scream.

Mama was prone to temper tantrums. I always tried to keep her from having them, but no matter how hard I tried, I always seemed to make her have them. In my mother's eyes, I felt like I peaked by age two. I learned how to tie the bows in the back of my dresses and tie my shoe laces. I potty-trained before my brother. After that I could never look, say or do anything right.

Mama had average-size breasts, but her nipples were very large. One day, when I was four or five, while I was taking a bath, I took her razor and shaved my nipples off. I don't think I wanted to be like her. I wanted to be free. I wanted to be happy.

I had to sit in the beauty shop every single Saturday for what seemed like all day. I had to wear expensive frilly dresses. I hated them. I hated it all. I never felt relaxed around my mother. I felt best with Annie Mae or the baby sitters. They laughed and played with me.

I was in kindergarten when my mother first explained sex to us. She told us how babies were born. What I understood was that the man planted a seed in the woman and something about the navel. I was in kindergarten class the next day when I picked a piece of dirt or lint out of my navel. I thought this was my seed and that I would never be able to have a baby. I thought that I had done something terribly wrong and bad. I cried and tried to explain this to my teacher, but she didn't understand. I finally told my parents with shame, remorse and guilt—feelings I didn't even know had a name.

Duane and I always had wonderful birthday parties together.

Mama always wanted us to have the very best. She would only let us keep a few of the gifts, however, and the others went into the "gift" drawer. We always received so many nice Christmas presents from Mama and Daddy. Mama was very generous. Daddy was always drunk and would spoil everything. Mama would fuss and make us quickly put our things away.

We would all go to my father's homeplace every year. There were so many relatives. The women would be in one room, the men in another. I could never find a place to sit, and always felt so uncomfortable and so embarrassed about Daddy being drunk and trying to act sober—always believing he was "fine." My mother would bitterly complain about his family and how he thought they were more important than us.

We were always trying to get Daddy not to drink. He knew that he wasn't supposed to, so he always tried to hide it. He would drink straight out of the bottle, and quickly try to hide it. I would see him and I could smell it. He would always deny having had anything. This was the way he drank, and I never saw him drink out of a glass or in front of people.

We always presented ourselves as the perfect family to the world. Inside our house, Mama was always in a rage, throwing everything out of our closets and drawers into the middle of the room. Then she would make us pick it up. She would often put our toys in the garbage if the room was not cleaned up to her satisfaction. She would throw everything out of the refrigerator and demand that we clean it up. Often, she would take her arm and rake the kitchen counters clean, throwing everything off, breaking dishes, throwing food, appliances and anything else that was in the way onto the floor. She would say, "Now I have cleaned!" We would be left standing in all this stuff and would have to clean it up.

If we were in the presence of others, she was so pleasant wearing her Southern smile. I could always predict her responses. I calibrated her like a heart monitor. I didn't like being at home with her.

Daddy would try doing things with us, like throwing the ball, but he would always be in a suit and tie, and drunk. He took us fishing a couple of times, and of course ended up drunk. We would have to search the yard for him at night because he would have passed out somewhere. His glasses would be in one place and he in another. We usually had to bring him in so no one would see him. Often, we would have to drive around with my mother looking for him. His clothes would be torn, his glasses broken and his trousers wet, but he would always deny having had anything to drink or being drunk. I remember so many times begging him not to drink. I would cry and plead, "Don't drink Daddy. Please don't drink. You promised you wouldn't."

"Sugar," he would say, "I haven't had a thing to drink. Honest sugar."

I was in the first grade when my sister Dina was born. Mama and Daddy participated in a lot of social affairs. They traveled often, leaving us with sitters. These were the most relaxed times.

In the third grade I learned multiplication and division. My teacher sent a note home saying I needed some help. Mama was the president of the PTA, and I had always made A's. She was furious and probably embarrassed. Mama would use flash cards to drill me. She would be so angry and impatient. She would shake and throw the cards at me and say she didn't know what was wrong with me. I was so afraid. I couldn't think and would just go blank with fear. This same year I had to do a drawing of a human figure for a science class. Mama saw it and said it was horrible. "No one looked that way," she scolded. She drew one for me to take to class. I really thought mine was quite good. I had always drawn well and could draw better than anyone in the class. I just couldn't do things right or well enough to please mama. She didn't even like the way I brushed my hair. She would just yank the brush away from me, and pull it through my hair. I surely could not cry or complain.

Duane and I fought a lot. I seemed to get into fights with other classmates too. My mother had a tutor for me after school off and on because she didn't have the patience to help me.

Usually men I knew would drive Daddy home with one following in another car. They would see us, leave the car at the end of the driveway, and Duane and I would drive it in. We would drag him inside. This was pretty much routine.

By the time I was in the fourth grade, Daddy lost his job at the bank. I did not know exactly what had happened. I came home and saw him on his bed crying like a baby. He wouldn't stop. I felt so sad, and didn't like seeing him this way. This was a sad and confusing time. Mama was working day and night by now. Daddy would leave us at home and come back drunk. He would just disappear or say that he was coming right back, but wouldn't. Then

Mama would get home about 11 in the evening and go on a rampage.

I was about ten years old when Daddy was sent away for shock treatments. I was told that he would be gone for a while and would come back better and never drink again. We had tried Antabuse and everything else up to this point. Daddy was supposed to take the Antabuse. Duane and I would search his mouth with our fingers to make sure he swallowed it. There was constant fighting.

While he was in the hospital, I saw the movie "Shock Treatment," and was horrified. Daddy was gone for what seemed like a long, long time. When he came back, he was a different person. He didn't really know us and had no idea who Dina was. She would have been about three or four. This all happened in the 1960s and the number of shock treatments administered to him I don't think would be given today. He was always asking who Dina was. "Who is that little girl?"

We had to teach him how to eat again. He no longer knew his way around the house. Someone had to be with him all the time.

That summer Duane was working on a Moped and caught his leg in the fly wheel. I wrapped his leg and he was taken to the hospital. My mother had started the first "Head Start" program in the county. It was held at a black school. She put me in the school to show that it was a program for everyone. I was the only white child. I wasn't allowed to tell the neighbors or friends that I was in it. Some of the children in the program started calling me, and I was then sent to my grandparents. I really didn't know them well. Up to that point, I had really only seen them once a year.

My mother disliked my grandfather very much. He was her stepfather. She always called him by his first name. I had to do the same. She had nothing good to say about him. The day I was to leave, Mama and I went to the hospital so I could say goodbye to Duane. In the process, she got mad at a staff nurse. She was always getting mad at shoe salesmen, clerks, waiters or anyone she considered beneath her. She got angry about something, and said she was taking Duane out of the hospital. The nurse said she couldn't do that. This enraged my mother even more. She took Duane out of his bed, put him in a straight metal chair, turned it on its back legs, and pushed Duane out into the hallway, and onto the elevator. All the stitches were ripped out and he was screaming. She took me to the bus station, and I left for Kentucky to see my grandparents.

My grandparents worked in a carnival, so I spent the summer traveling around the country. I did this for several consecutive summers. We would be in one place for a week, then travel to another.

My grandmother was tense, just like my mother. I was always afraid and nervous around her. Sometimes she seemed to like me, but most of the time she didn't. I think she wondered why Mama had sent me to them. I tried real hard to please her, and to say and do the right things. She tended to be rather critical of the way I spoke and dressed. My grandfather liked me and I liked him. He was big and strong, and would hold my hand when we walked together. I felt proud. He was strong and sober. He began having sex with me. I was nine years old. I knew this was our secret and that I was special. He told me so. He said he loved me. I knew that he would never do anything to hurt me.

There was a man in the carnival show who would take his penis out and masturbate every time he saw me. This happened at least twice a day... everyday, for the entire summer. At the end of that summer, I went home and found out that my parents had divorced and my father was living across the street.

It seemed I had changed. Everything had changed. Time and the sequence of events get a bit blurry here.

In the seventh grade, I acted up a lot in school and forced my teacher to resign. I started fires, and burned charts and calendars. I was like the class clown. I did horrible things to the teachers. It was about this time that I went to an inexpensive dress store with a friend. I bought what I thought was a beautiful and stylish dress with my own money. My mother screamed and chastised me for having such cheap taste. She said as punishment I would have to wear it.

Mama seemed to hate me as an adolescent. I had trouble with math. I would just freeze up at the sight of numbers. I think I was 12 when I started having sex with my math teacher in order to make passing grades. He was disgusting and ugly and looked like a bull dog. I didn't think I had a choice. I hated myself by now. I couldn't make it home sometimes without wetting my pants. I would sit and draw for hours. I would draw faces and give them names and lives. It was like playing dolls. They could be whom I wanted, and I could too. I could make my dreams. But then I would tear them up into little pieces—I thought I was doing something wrong.

I had to care for Dina a lot. I would hit her. Duane and I would hit each other. Mama had been teaching night school for several years now. She didn't get home until 10:30 or 11:00 at night. We could pretty much do what we wanted. My mother had gone back to school and did so on and on for years after the divorce. For a rather long time Duane, Dina and I slept in my mother's bedroom in order to cut down on the electric bill. The lucky person was able to sleep in the closet. The other two got her bed.

I was caught shoplifting one night. I had never done this before. By the time I was 13, my mother was convinced that I was on drugs. She would take me into the bathroom, push my face into the mirror and make me look at myself.

"No one would look or act this way if they were not on drugs," she would scream. "Look at your eyes."

This went on and on. I would just start shaking in front of her. I would be so nervous. Finally, I said what the heck, and by age 14, I had done everything from pot to LSD and opium and everything in between. If I ate mushrooms, Dina did too. By the time she was eight she had done LSD and cocaine with me.

The first time I did cocaine, I felt everything that I was not. Confident, smart, talkative, carefree, tall, pretty, free—just like a palm tree.

I transferred to a different school in 11th grade. It was 1972, and the public schools were really changing. I was suspended. I got high everyday. Mama spent her summer in Asia that year and we were left on our own. She bought expensive clothes for herself, art work and rugs, and took trips everywhere, but wouldn't turn the heat on in our part of the house. She would scream and yell at me because she didn't like the way I drove. She would say I acted like I was retarded. I wasn't much for wearing make-up and that kind of thing, but sometimes I would try and Mama would tell me I looked like a clown or prostitute. She would just get mad and rub it off my face.

I spent my senior year at a different school. She took the three of us to Europe that summer. She bought me a new car. So there were really good things that she did do.

In 1973 I went to a small private liberal arts school in Louisiana. I graduated with a major in art. I trained in karate and worked extremely hard at my art classes. My mother married a prominent lawyer who was also a dwarf. They had not been married long when he got drunk and broke her finger. And, of course my father was right there to save the day, since he was still in love with her and living across the street. She blamed us for the divorce from the dwarf. She said Duane and I chased him away by smoking pot in the house, and that Dina treated him like a playmate.

I liked college and being away from home. I continued to do drugs throughout school, but I worked very hard and received honors and awards in art. I became pregnant during my senior year and had an abortion. No one knew except for Mike, the guy I had been dating. He would become so jealous and smothering. He would cry and put loaded guns to his head, and my head, break into my windows at night, and threaten me with knives.

By the time I graduated, Mike and I had stopped seeing each other and I was seeing Jeff, whom I had always liked during high school. Jeff had been serving time in a federal minimum security prison for possession and conspiracy to sell cocaine. I would visit him on weekends, take him drugs, and was there when he was released.

I did my postgraduate work overseas. When I returned home, I had gained a little weight. Perhaps five or six pounds. My mother cried and thought I was pregnant. She said I could either get an abortion or, she would send me away or pay someone to marry me. I do not think that having the baby was one of her options. I knew that I was not pregnant. She took me to a diet doctor the next morning and he gave me bags of speed and downers. I lost a lot of weight. I weighed about 90 pounds.

I went to graduate school at Louisiana Tech University, and received a Master's Degree in fine arts. I worked incredibly hard and rather obsessively. I continued to go through periods of shaving my hair off. I would fast for two or three weeks at a time and always drank to get drunk. But I managed to finish with honors and at the top of my class. I received a lot of recognition as an artist and by the time I graduated, I had already been in over a hundred juried, one-person shows.

My stepfather Hal died, and I flew home for the funeral. My mother called me in the middle of the night. I was still hallucinating from having taken drugs. That evening I felt my head and realized I was bald. I had to wait until that evening to go home because I was still so high. I had always liked Hal and his daughter had always been my good friend. Duane was released from prison for the day to attend the funeral. He was serving time for possession and selling cocaine. My mother told her mother and the out-of-town relatives that he was home from school. We certainly did not talk about his time in prison. Not ever.

Hal and Mama had not been getting along at all. They were both miserable. Hal was an alcoholic who didn't work and my mother would dress him up and take him places. There was not room for me to ride in the family car to the service, so Mama had me drive my father and grandparents.

I returned to Huntsville, and set up a studio with Jeff, freebasing everyday. I totaled my car in a black out. After three months, I left for New York. I had a couple of grants through the state, and lived there alone, rather isolated for a couple of years. I returned to Huntsville for about six months with a hundred-dollar-a-day cocaine habit, then I moved overseas, and then back to Huntsville. I resumed my use of cocaine, became pregnant and miscarried. I was selling to support my several-hundred-dollar-a-day habit. I was using morphine and just staying high. My car was under surveillance, and I was ready to be arrested. Instead, I went into treatment. Upon discharge, I was sent to a state-funded halfway house for about seven or eight months. My life was really at rock bottom.

I went to work in a frame shop. By this time I had started cutting my body. It became a compulsion. I would cut myself with razor blades, and then cover the wounds so they couldn't be seen.

I moved into an office in the downtown area where I had a studio. About a year later I started working in a treatment center with addicts. I worked a lot of hours and ended up in the hospital with bleeding ulcers and a high fever.

It was after I saw the movie "Amadeus," that I realized I should be doing art. I resigned and went to Spain. When I returned, I started doing art therapy for a couple of hospitals in Huntsville.

My mother gave me the money for a down payment on a house. It was an older home in the historical district, and I always had a couple of housemates to help make the payments. I was once again under my mother's control. She would give me expensive art work, antique furniture and oriental rugs.

I began dating a man my own age, which for me, was very unusual. I tried to be someone I wasn't. I tried to be what I thought he wanted. I hid the fact that I was in AA from him. He had a girlfriend in his home state. It turned out they were engaged and he was trying to decide which one of us he preferred. He chose her.

I went into a treatment facility for bulimia and anorexia. Upon discharge, I resigned from my job at the hospital, and started doing art full time again. A few months later, I started seeing George. I had met him at the same hospital where I had been previously employed. It was like that hospital gave me my life back: a job and an administrator.

George and I had a few dates when he was transferred to another hospital in another state. We continued to see each other, maintaining a relationship nine hours away by car. It was fine for me. I could visit for a few days, then get back to my own space. George accepted all my gay friends, strange hours and lifestyle. My mother thought George was good for me. She liked him more than anyone I had ever dated. Perhaps, it was his stability.

I had been sober six years by this time. Our wedding date was set. I was really confused about what I wanted. My mother was furious and refused to speak to me. I didn't know what to do, so I drank. I only drank for one evening, but it felt like a thousand. We married, and had a big wedding. We went overseas for our honeymoon, and we moved to Arkansas, where George worked. It all looked so picture perfect.

We moved to Houston. By now I had quit smoking, and was training again in martial arts. We bought a new house. We joined the country club. I joined the junior women's league and was on the art council. George and I were often featured in the social column in the newspaper. I gave numerous cocktail parties and was the perfect hostess. We traveled and in many ways it looked like I had it all.

I spent more and more time with my martial arts training. I was working out compulsively. George was transferred to Charleston. I remained in Houston for six months until the house was sold. I regained some of my independence and did not want to leave. I eventually went to Charleston, but felt like a prisoner. I became pregnant, but soon miscarried.

We bought a home close to the beach. I found a karate school and things seemed to get better. Then George took a job in Orlando. I didn't want to move, but it seemed I had no choice. After settling in Florida, I continued my training in martial arts, went to Korea and trained with the teams in Seoul. I left George a few months later. I became pregnant and had another miscarriage. I was in great despair and very confused. It was at this time I began therapy.

Not unlike Sarah, the journey for women as a whole has really just begun. Suffrage may have been the most significant turn of events for women thus far. Men have had much more time to get their acts together. However, since the theory that women mature faster than men may still prove to be true, perhaps both genders have arrived at the same stage but at different times. Two million years for men, and 75 years for women. The important thing is they have reached maturity simultaneously. At last, a chance for healthy relationships.

Virtues of women have remained constant throughout civilization, unlike the virtues of men. Ours is an old tape, which due to the social evolution of mankind and womankind has finally had an opportunity to reveal itself. Men have finally come to exemplify many of the same virtues. Women are beginning to embrace their animus. Some are more in touch than others. Men tend to be a bit anxious about accepting their anima. I suppose if men consider their anima as their "feminine side," and look for only typical "feminine" qualities, which may be projections of vulnerability, weakness, sensitivity, or in others seen as cunning, manipulative and engulfing, their hesitation can be readily appreciated.

I recently heard about a man who was sharing his life's work with a dear friend. He told him that all the energy and effort he put into his work was a labor of love. He identified this "labor of love" as his masculine side, illustrating that only his masculine side could have given of himself so unselfishly, thereby inducing that women aren't capable of laboring for love. His belief system, based on his personal history with the women in his life, produced this distorted perception of the anima. This, of course, reflects many men who have had engulfing, dominating and castrating mothers and/or wives. It's no wonder they would want to reject this powerful part of themselves. They view it like a vulture. The need to split off from that part is an act of self-protection. But, in doing so, they miss out on an opportunity to endow themselves with the most important part of their wholeness—their anima. The wild woman—that 40-thousand-year-old woman who maintains residence in men as well as in women—can start a fire in the belly of both.

The Search for Empathy and Truth

I keep my ideals, because in spite of everything, I still believe that people are really good at heart.

—Anne Frank (1929-1945)

And it would be so easy, I wonder sometimes, if the faces of good and evil could be so distinctly black and white, ugly and beautiful, shiny and scorned as described by the priest and rabbi in their morning sermons. Decisions in life become more difficult when the best faces of beauty have a shimmering shadow of ugliness and the worst embodiments of ugliness in moments burst out into a phenomenal glow of humanity and empowerment. I observe this dilemma as a therapist every day and am getting more acutely aware of it as I look back on my life as a wife and a mother.

I had divorced Jack and had passed the sentence of not holding him in my good books. I had judged and decided that despite the fact that he was the father of my five children I could not stay married to him. In my perception there emerged a seamy side of him that forced me to choose to separate from him. Yet he, at one time, was and for a long time remained, the most wonderful companion of my life. Despite the fact that I was ridden with the guilt of separating my children from their father, who by all standards was and remains a very caring and loving father, I had no choice left but to separate myself for the preservation of my sanity and the well-being of my family. But the story does not end here. This juggling of the competing loyalties continued as I brought up my children and still kept them connected to their father. It is the irony of being decisive that we have to look only at the black and can't be weakened in our resolve by the little grey that invariably breaks through. The moments of weakness are, perhaps, the moments of truth, but one has to delete all the redeeming impressions to go forward with the decision to break a relationship. Right at the moment of walking away there is that lurking thought that it might be all wrong.

I was the average girl growing up in the 1950s. I don't know why but the fact is that I was never much for social causes, such as banning the bomb, or stopping the war in Vietnam. Maybe somewhere I thought that these were the issues for men. I never protested in any walk or event and never wore a button on my shirt. It is not that I was numb about social injustice and moral outrage, but that at any such moment of desire or passion I could hear my father's voice asking me if I was in my senses doing those kinds of crazy things. I didn't know that I didn't know what I didn't know. I liken it to floating somewhere out in the middle of the ocean. I felt on top of things, but never knew the depth of what was underneath. I was living in a circumscribed world. I am not saying that I was following some clearly prescribed injunctions from my father, but that those were the unwritten and sometimes unspoken words that were the law for me. I accepted them at such deep levels, that I suffered from no conflict and lived in a beautiful la-la land. Yes, for the psychodynamically analytical audience I must confess that I had no ability to reflect. No, perhaps, it would be correct to say that I felt no need to reflect. It was a wonderful world. So wonderful that I envy it in my clients when I see it today. I was a child of innocence and after all this awakening, I still feel nostalgic about parts of it.

I had no opinions. And if I had, they were not really well-considered or thought out. It was a time devoid of knowing me. There was no fire in my belly, only water on my brain. I only knew what I was told. Told by my father. Told by Jack.

When you are used to knowing through someone else's brain and learning through someone else's mouth, you mostly do not learn the whole truth. It might have started as a way of not telling me the full truth, but over the years Jack had become a master of concealing the truth from me. Yet, deep within my unconscious, truth seemed to summon me. It seemed I always knew what I didn't know. This was the knowledge I acted upon. The truth was there in the dream stuff, and Dr. McKinley helped deliver the goods.

In May 1977, when I was married to Tom, Jack's trial began. The allegations were five counts for aiding and abetting insurance fraud and one count of conspiracy. He was found guilty on five counts of aiding and abetting and acquitted on the conspiracy charges. Sentencing was to be the Friday before the Fourth of July weekend.

Jack wanted the children present during the trial. At the time they were fourteen, thirteen, eleven, nine and five. The three eldest attended the trial everyday for five days. I was there too.

Each night we could review the horrors of the day by watching any six or eleven o'clock news cast. So could every other child in school. So could everyone else in the neighborhood and Dade, Broward and Palm Beach counties. Every night, his face, framed in a box at the upper right hand corner of the screen, would appear while commentary was delivered. Victoria would shout, "There's Daddy! Look! There's Daddy! Mommy is Daddy going to jail?" For five days and five nights they were confronted with the sight of their father fighting for his honor, his dignity and his truth.

Prior to the trial there had been other secrets. So many secrets. So many half truths, with hidden meanings and obscure content, imposed upon my senses. Those secrets, although well-concealed deliberately, so often materialized in symbolism and ominous feelings during disturbed and interrupted slumber. They were trying to tell me what my conscious mind could not. I was never sure of their meaning or impact, but they were the ones that surfaced in my dreams.

One of the truths Jack kept hidden from me during our marriage was that he had been faced with manslaughter charges. I learned that a woman had died after he performed an abortion. Ten doctors, expert witnesses, were going to testify against him. It was their professional opinion that he had used the wrong procedure. The woman had been $15\frac{1}{2}$ weeks pregnant, and according to Jack's training, there was an appropriate procedure to employ during this specific trimester.

Despite Jack's confidence that his friends, colleagues and mentors would support him, none did. Not even the doctors who trained him. Jack was looking at 15 years in prison. It appeared hopeless. Then, much to his surprise, he received a call from an OB/GYN epidemiologist from the Centers for Disease Control in Atlanta. The physician had been advised of the charges so they could be documented in the official national records. This was common practice with all legal medical matters. During this conversation Jack learned he had indeed used the correct procedure. The CDC doctor substantiated this fact by writing a letter of support. The state's attorney never filed the charges. It was determined, however, that malpractice had occurred. His case was reviewed by the Department of Professional Regulation and they decided that Jack had fallen below the standard of care. In view of these findings, coupled with the manslaughter allegations, Jack lost his license.

Jack had managed over the years to bring the lightning to himself on numerous occasions. He was known as an abortionist, often boasting that he could do up to 60 abortions a day. One of my fears was that he was performing abortions on women who were in their last trimester of pregnancy, which he denied whenever I questioned him.

During this time I was in analysis, and many of my dreams were being used as roadmaps to my unconscious. A recurring dream gave me another truth. I was always in a butcher shop, standing by the counter, looking at the butcher facing me. He was wearing a blood-stained apron holding a meat cleaver in his hand. I would glance to my right. There was a fish tank against the wall. The fish were small. They looked like babies. They were all dead, floating to the surface. The filtering system was breaking away from the pump, leaving the tank with little or no supply of oxygen. I would frantically run to rescue them, but I didn't know how to fix the aquarium. I always woke up crying, as if it were my fault that they died.

This is when I began to trust my unconscious. This was when I could no longer deny the truth. Jack was doing procedures which I could not tolerate. When I confronted him, he always promised never to perform abortions on women who were advanced in their pregnancy anymore than three months.

Gambling made it difficult for Jack to be truthful. Gambling, like so many other compulsive behaviors, alters one's mood, making it impossible to know the real self. When Jack was his real self he was the best. It was the gambling that was bad. Not Jack. It was the gambling that made Jack lie. It was the gambling that made him do things he later regretted. It was the gambling that destroyed our marriage. Not Jack. Unfortunately, you can't have one without the other.

Jack was a heavy roller in the casinos. He partied with the big boys and wheeler dealers of that particular genre. He wore Italian silk suits made for him by the Hong Kong tailor. He had a Patek Philippe watch—something he wanted since medical school. His ties were expensive. He bought a new Cadillac every two years. He loved Cuban cigars, particularly Romeo and Juliet Churchill. His favorite cologne was Aramis. You could smell him from a mile away. He had a distinct odor of Cuban tobacco and sweet perfume. It permeated everywhere he went—the car, the office, the hospital corridors and the house. In other words, he was hard to miss. He was never lost in the crowd. He usually traveled with an entourage, picked up all the tabs, and always spoke louder and faster than anyone else. One person called him the "human run-on sentence." There was always a response from the crowd. He always made an impression. He was loved and revered by some and despised by others. Nobody was ever nonchalant about a review of Jack.

Now he had come into the courtroom wearing a different expensive Italian designer suit with a different coordinated shirt and tie each day. He sported a well-groomed mustache and beard. His hair was coiffed and blown out each morning to perfection. The courtroom reeked with his trademark smell. The children sat together on the bench. I sat alongside. Each day we heard testimony that supported both his guilt or innocence, depending on who was litigating at the time—the state attorney or his defending lawyer. Television cameras from all three major networks were out in the corridors, hovering like vultures. The state attorney called Jack a "Mickey Mouse doctor who behaved like Donald Duck." It was a mockery of justice and law. He was found guilty on five charges of insurance fraud.

Sentencing was the Friday, just before the Fourth of July holiday. A reasonable bail was anticipated by all. Despite Jack's ostensible pull in the judicial system, the judge refused bail. Instead, he surprised the entire courtroom by holding the bail hearing until the following Wednesday, forcing Jack to spend the holiday weekend and more in the Dade County jail. We were horrified; shocked beyond belief. Even hardcore criminals were given bail upon sentencing. Why had the judge been so harsh? What caused him to be so unfair and blatantly punitive? The children were devastated. Jack's parents nearly collapsed. I was stunned. What provoked the judge to be so unyielding? Why this miscarriage of justice?

I was outraged. I knew for years that one day Jack would have to pay the price for his flamboyance and ostentatiousness. But this was irrational. It felt like there was something missing in the puzzle. What vendetta could this judge possibly have against Jack?

Two uniformed officers escorted him out of the courtroom before we could embrace him. He took off his watch, handed it to his attorney, and with a bowed head departed from the courtroom. I could hardly believe my eyes. My ex-husband, the father of my five children, physician and healer, loving son and decent human being, was being transported to the county jail. Nowhere in my life had I been prepared for this horrific event. The television stations all announced the verdict as if a murderer had been sentenced. In fact, during the same week a murderer had been sentenced, and Jack had preferential showing over him. Something smelled real fishy to me.

I was allowed to see Jack for a few minutes after he was taken to the county jail. He looked so pale and for the first time since I had known him, afraid. His color was drained. His Johnson and Murphy shoes were still shiny from the morning polish. His eyes were red and teary. His face was flushed. There were no words spoken, but I knew his thoughts.

"I'll come to see you tomorrow," I whispered through the small opening in the glass enclosure. He nodded. I was crying. I can still taste the tears that rolled down my cheeks. We both touched hands with the glass separating us.

"Don't worry," I said, not knowing what the hell I was talking about. But I needed to say something assuring. "It will be OK. Everything will be alright."

I left the jail in disbelief. How could this have happened? The next morning I told Tom I wanted to go back. He offered to drive me. I gratefully accepted. I baked a chocolate cake and carried it in my lap, thinking that's what would be expected. My only frame of reference to prisons were of course what I saw in the movies, and I had always seen wives or sweethearts bringing a cake. They wouldn't let me take it in. I had to leave it with an officer. I felt so foolish standing in line with all the other visitors holding this cake. No one else had one, so I knew I made a mistake. We all stood in line for what seemed nearly an hour, waiting to go upstairs in large caged elevators. I viewed the crowd. I stood out like a sore thumb. There wasn't a single human being that I felt I could relate to. Nobody looked like me. I felt like I was from another planet. There I stood in high-heels, wearing an Anne Klein linen dress, holding a chocolate cake.

The waiting area smelled of urine. The walls were dirty and needed paint. The overhead ceiling tiles were stained with rust and dirt. I was appalled by the lack of concern and consideration for human dwelling. My naivete and insulation from this environment made me ill. I felt nauseated and worried I might vomit holding the damn cake.

We were escorted in, just a few at a time. When I saw Jack he looked as if he had been there for a month. He had a scruffy beard, yet it was only a day later. He was so frightened that it became almost unbearable for me to look at him. He was always so self-assured. Now he wept. As he cried, he said over and over, "I just want to get out of here."

"I know. I know. It must be awful for you."

"Please bring the children. I want to see my children," he pleaded.

"No. Absolutely no. I will not. I never want them to have memories of you like this. It will haunt them forever."

"Please. I need to see them."

"Jack," I asserted. "You feel this way now, but I can assure you, that when this is all over, and it will be over soon, you will be grateful that I didn't bring them. Though you need their support, they must be spared."

He understood. He was in so much pain.

Tom was waiting for me downstairs. The car was parked just outside the jailhouse. I came to the car crying. I needed to do something. I called Jack's attorney and asked permission to write a letter to the judge. Jack was already in a precarious position and I didn't need to make matters worse. He approved, but only after he reviewed the letter.

Wednesday came, and went. Bond was set. Jack was not released on his own recognizance, as his attorney requested. The bond was paid and then Jack was released. He appealed and was acquitted.

One evening, just prior to writing this chapter, Jack, my daughter Victoria and I sat out on the terrace of my apartment. Jack smoked his cigar and I asked him what had happened. This is what he said:

In 1975 it had been legal to be covered by more than one insurance company. The Hispanic family he had treated for what turned out to be a staged accident (which Jack had no knowledge of) had over 20 insurance policies. It appeared they were in collusion with an insurance agent and a middle man, who was the mastermind of this scam. Jack knew nothing about the scam, nor did he sign any of the insurance claims submitted for reimbursement. He had a stamp with his signature that was used for all insurance claims, as did most physicians. The fee for the treatment he provided was $1740.00. The patient paid by check. This amount was collected over 20 times by the middle man, who then reimbursed the patients. In addition, this middle man would pay the premiums to the carriers, and provide a bonus to the patient which usually consisted of a paid vacation. The patients had nothing to lose (so they thought), and an opportunity to travel. The insurance agent received a percentage for the sale of all the insurance policies, and the middle man made out like a bandit. An accident was staged, and reported to the Florida Highway Patrol. The patients complained of pain, required hospitalization, received physical therapy and were discharged. No lawsuits were ever filed. The insurance companies paid the same claim over 20 times.

The patients were told that if they testified against Jack, the court would be lenient with them. Each member of the family told a different story and all three admitted under oath that leniency was offered if they testified against him. Jack was told if he testified against certain lawyers, which he would not name to me, then the case would be dropped. Believing that the truth would prevail and he would be found innocent, he refused to cooperate—and was subsequently thrown into the Dade County jail that terrible week in July.

For months I was haunted with thoughts of why the judge was so unreasonable. Why the bashing? It came to me from the Wild Woman in a dream, as do all my truths. She came and told me. I'll never really know of course, but this is what I believe happened:

Two years prior to this ludicrous trial, Jack and I were divorced. Our divorce was nothing short of a nightmare. Jack was determined to go all the way to court. Originally, he agreed on a settlement with my attorney on a handshake. This would have been far more generous and equitable for him than the court's final disposition, but he rescinded his original offer anyway. He decided to take his chances by using adultery as a leverage to avoid paying alimony. Although Florida law provided for no-fault divorce at that time, adultery could be used in consideration of settlement issues. We went to trial.

I knew I needed a heavyweight for a lawyer because Jack knew almost everyone in the judicial system. As a matter of fact, the judge who presided over our divorce case often frequented the same casinos with Jack. Many years later, he was indicted for illegal trans-actions, which eventually cost him the seat on the bench.

My lawyer was a tall, heavy-set, lumbering ex-judge who spoke softly, with full-bodied tonality. His heavy southern Georgia drawl gave one the impression that the South may very well rise again. He had Tip O'Neill's stature and Will Rogers' smile. Although he prepared me well for court, neither of us ever anticipated what was to come.

Jack was stacking evidence against me with adultery charges. Six in all. This really surprised me because I could only account for five.

The results could have been the plot for a modern-day Shakespearean tragi-comedy. To avoid dragging these men, (includ-ing the one I didn't know) into a courtroom trial that would become public record, I decided to admit to all six accounts only after my attorney told me he received a personal call from one man's (a rabbi) lawyer. The nature of the call was to inform him that the rabbi had been served a subpoena at the synagogue just prior to address-ing his congregation Friday night. The rabbi's attorney vehemently protested and demanded that we stop this ridiculous action at once. I was so ashamed that the rabbi should be subjected to such humil-iation, that I took the blame. I felt the only decent thing to do would be to admit all the charges rather than have a string of men dragged through my divorce trial. The letter "A" was now branded into every cell, atom and molecule in my body. Even my psychiatrist told me I should get on my knees and thank God that Jack wanted me back after I had been so compulsively promiscuous. This, of course, was prior to my decision to divorce him. Jack diagnosed me as "sick" and in need of psychiatric help. So, I was shuffled off to the first psychiatrist referred to him by another male physician.

Now my divorce would become public record. This spectacle was more than I could tolerate. It never even occurred to me that the rabbi might have been partly to blame, and that this could be a natural consequence of his philandering behavior. (Now you may understand why I wanted to originally title this book, "Water On The Brain.")

My divorce trial was my first encounter with the judicial system. We sat in a room somewhere in the old Miami Courthouse on Flagler Street. The room might have been any room in any courthouse in the United States built in the late 1920s. It was drab, in need of refurbishing, decorated with U.S. and Florida flags. I got the distinct impression that the judge was bored with his job and he did not think it right that this kind of information be used in his courtroom. He felt some concern for protecting our children and felt this information could be detrimental to their well-being. Florida law didn't give a damn about anything except alimony, child support and custody, and the judge didn't want to preside over a kangaroo court. Every time Jack insisted on stacking the adultery charges against me, his child support payment was increased another hundred dollars a month. Jack was so angry and so determined to get even, that he played his hand in court much like he did in the casinos. He steamed. He steamed away reason. He steamed away a reasonable and equitable property settlement, and made a mockery of our marriage and divorce.

But he was like a German tank—relentless, plowing over the advice of everyone in the courtroom, including his counsel and the judge. By law the judge had to allow his testimony, but this annoyed him to no end. He refused to let Jack use names, so this necessitated using numbers for identifying purposes. A chart was made on my behalf by my lawyer. Each name corresponded to a number between one and six. The rabbi was number one; number two was to another lover, and so on. Questions were directed at me by Jack's attorney asking me to recall dates and places of where and when I had encounters with these numbers. "Is it true, that on September 4, 1973, you and number three spent the weekend in Sanibel Island?" I had to search down the list and see, first of all, who was number three, and try to recall if in fact the answer was yes or no. My attorney sat to my immediate right, and as soon as the question was asked, we would quickly join heads together, glance down the list, look for the corresponding number, and after a moment's discussion between us, I would respond. I was never good with dates, so it might have been Sanibel Island on the date in question, but with another number, so I would have to explain. The judge grew more impatient, but Jack hung in there and went for the kill. I was a nervous wreck. I had no idea of what the outcome might be.

My parents were still not speaking to me for getting the divorce, so they weren't there for moral support. I was too embarrassed to ask any friends to help. I knew my analyst didn't want to get involved. I couldn't ask my brother to take a day off from work. It wasn't in my nature. So, except for my attorney, I was all alone. Tom wanted to be there for support, but I knew that would go over like a lead balloon. So there I was, all by myself, 35 years old, and feeling like five.

Now, what does all this have to do with the judge's decision not to hear bond and keep Jack in the county jail? Actually, I have no real evidence, but I had the dream soon after Jack's sentencing. The Wild Woman came again. She told me she suspected that Jack's judge had been a mighty good friend of the rabbi, and that whenever an opportunity presented itself for retaliation, seize that moment. I tend to wonder . . . and justice for all?

There are those moments in time when the patterns of circumstance and coincidence send a clear message, as if they were written in the wind. Proof or evidence is not needed. This was one of those times.

The Search for Wonder, Enjoyment, Wildness and Solitude

A person will be called upon to account on Judgement Day for every permissible thing he might have enjoyed but did not.

—Talmud

In his book, *Between God and Man,* Abraham Heschel writes, "The awareness of wonder is often overtaken by the mind's tendency to dichotomize, which makes us look at the ineffable as if it were a thing or an aspect of things apart from our own selves; as if only the stars were surrounded with a halo of enigma and not our own existence."[15]

I really don't know what it was that possessed me to listen to my daughter Emily when she said I should visit Banner Elk, North Carolina. There had been so many times when my children made suggestions that went in one ear and out the other. After all, raising five children often presented a variety of requests which I couldn't possibly take seriously all the time, but, for whatever reason, something clicked inside me when she made this suggestion. Mervyn and I had long considered the idea of buying a mountain cabin, but never seemed to find the time or energy to pursue it. It was one of those things that hung in the "well maybe next year" file. But, this time it was almost as if I didn't even have a choice.

I had heard about the Blue Ridge Mountains from Emily several times before. She had been invited to visit a friend in Banner Elk, a small mountain resort town in northwestern North Carolina. She came back quite enthusiastic and suggested Mervyn and I visit the area.

We speak so often about letting go that it has become a cliché. According to the way I was raised, and Mervyn's map of reality, things are supposed to happen with a considered evaluation of all details, especially when they entail an investment of a considerable percentage of one's life savings. With my austere upbringing and my husband's sense of caution, I wonder how I ended up on the Blue Ridge Parkway, making such a large commitment for simple joy and deeper feelings of happiness.

Twenty minutes onto the parkway it began to rain and get dark. A dense fog set in. Sometimes it appeared as if ghosts were floating in front of the car. There would be clear moments, but as we drove on, the fog became opaque, obscuring our vision. Suddenly, I was near hysteria.

"Stop! Just Stop! I can't take another minute of this. We'll all be killed," I shrieked over and over. "I knew I shouldn't have listened to Emily. Why did I have to listen to her now" I thought, cursing as the tension and anxiety grew.

"Do you want to drive?" Mervyn shouted back. "Just quiet down and relax. You're making me a nervous wreck!" I could sense that Mervyn was terrified too, but as usual, he stayed in control, but still frozen to the wheel.

Except for eating and evacuating, Emily had not shifted her position in the back seat since we left Miami. She still had her Walkman on, and the rain and fog didn't concern her at all. We could hear the muted beat of rock and roll.

"Emily! For God's sake, turn that thing off already, and get us the hell out of this place!" I snapped.

Emily bolted up and looked around, dazed. "Where are we? Are we there yet?"

"That's exactly what we want to know. Where the hell are we?" Mervyn asked. "Do you know how and where to get off this parkway?"

"I've never been on the parkway before. Why did you go on the parkway? You should have just stayed on 321. Why don't we ask someone?"

"Who? Tell me who, Emily? We haven't seen a soul for over an hour. Who are we going to ask?" I said, gritting my teeth. I was scared to death, and even more afraid to express it, fearing Mervyn would make me drive. So I swallowed it, but it fell like a lead balloon into my stomach.

We drove on, unable to see more than one yellow line at a time ahead on the curving road. I promised God anything. Just get us out of here alive. We spotted a forest ranger station. By now I was in a frenzy. Emily went back to sleep with her Walkman.

I shouted to the ranger, "Can you help? Please get us out of here. Can you take us to Banner Elk? We'll pay you whatever you want, but please drive us out of here."

"I'm sorry ma'am," he said in a restrained southern drawl. "Can't leave my post. Just take the next exit to Linville. Follow the signs to 105 North, hang a left, and it'll take ya' right inter Banner Elk."

"Please. You don't understand sir," I literally begged. "We can't see the road. I'll pay you whatever you want. Just drive us in."

I thought Mervyn was going to kill me.

"What's the matter with you? He told you he can't leave his post. Leave the man alone."

I had to urinate so badly by now, I couldn't contain it any longer. Afraid of bears and the dark woods, I couldn't believe I could do what I did. But I did it. I went behind the forest ranger's station and relieved myself. I swore if I got out of this place alive, I'd never, ever come back.

We followed his directions and saw a Holiday Inn. I stopped to use the phone to call Archer's Inn, the bed and breakfast where we had reserved a room. Now it was nearly midnight. I pleaded with the owner, Joe Archer, who answered without leaving any doubt that I had awakened him, to come and get us. I went off on a tirade of how we had gotten lost on the parkway, and how I feared for our lives. He sounded too exhausted or sleepy to argue, so instead, he responded politely and agreed. He must have been accustomed to Miami tourists and their panic attacks with their first encounter with North Carolina mountain roads.

The next morning we headed down Beech Mountain to look at property. Mervyn and I agreed we wouldn't buy anything this trip. Just look. "Remember. We're just going to look. Not buy," he reminded me at least ten times.

We drove around the area, just to see what was available. It was August. The foliage was full, rich and green. The mountains were covered with trees. Hemlock, North Carolina pine, locust, poplar and evergreens were everywhere. Rapid streams and rivulets ran alongside much of the highway. Once off Beech Mountain, we continued down Highway 194, not knowing where we were going. The car seemed to make its own decisions. We simply followed the road.

"Blueberry Farm. Pick your own berries," a sign read. The road twisted, winding down narrow hair pin curves with sudden drop offs, protected by nothing more than short wooden or concrete pegs along the curb. There were deliberate road bumps that were cautious reminders to be careful.

I had never seen so many trees. Thousands of native trees and thick underbrush framed one side of the road. Ground cover with an assortment of spectacular bright-colored North Carolina wildflowers framed the other. In some areas the trees were so full that they formed giant arches across the two-lane road. I felt as though I was driving through a Monet landscape.

We passed an old tobacco barn, with hanging tobacco leaves. We sideswiped an opossum, the first I had ever seen, scamping across the road.

Then the road began to straighten out for a few yards. We saw the sign. "The Glen at Crab Orchid. Cabin for sale."

"Look, a for-sale sign. Let's go look," I said.

We turned onto a dirt road filled with stones that ran past a small pond on the left, and two more on the right. There, set back about one hundred yards off the little winding dirt road sat a piece of sculpture in space. Mervyn stopped and we both got out at the same time. We thought it was a mirage. Could anything be so beautiful? It looked like a picture of something never to be found in my lifetime. "How lovely. How simply lovely," I whispered. "I can't believe it. My God, it's beautiful."

Thick old logs, perhaps 30 or more inches wide, filled with mortar, hand-hewn, duck-tailed and devoid of nails composed this 125-year-old log cabin. A shanty, sloped roof line covered with weathered shingles was supported by old vertical logs that framed the porch, which was surrounded by rolled old hand-hewn locust logs, still partly covered with original bark. There were no front windows, only an old pine door with a solid glass window, covered by another screen door, its wooden frame painted red and green, like Gucci colors. Attached to the door was a miniature broomstick with a calico bow wrapped around it. There, leaning against the front of the house on the porch was an old wheel from a long-forgotten water mill that had once been painted red. Dahlias at least four or maybe even five feet high with giant blooms in bright assorted colors covered the bark logs along the porch. Weathered half barrels, filled with pink and bright red geraniums sat on the porch. Swollen ferns hung from the rafters, next to twisting and clanging wind chimes. A hummingbird took a drink from a glass feeder suspended from a dogwood tree. A Golden finch darted across the front lawn toward a feeder hanging from an adjacent dogwood. It was enchanting, something from a fairy tale or some faraway land in another century. Had I fallen into a wonderland? Suddenly the world looked different.

I felt a shift in my mood as I gazed at the cabin in its pastoral surroundings. Colors were brighter and more vibrant. My breathing changed. My heart actually raced, like I had made a special discovery. I acted like a child visiting Disney World for the first time.

The cabin sat on two acres of rolling green grass, with a few old apple trees, one of which had a hole near the center. As I walked in awe around one side of the cabin, I confronted huge evergreen and spruce trees that shared space with full-blossomed bushes brimming with blueberries waiting to be picked and eaten. Native pines lined the driveway which ran behind the cabin. A weathered, worn, wooden locust plank bridge ran over a babbling brook that came off the mountain behind the cabin and emptied into the adjacent pond. I walked over the narrow bridge and saw poplar, locust, walnut, chestnut and birch trees framing the other side of the property.

Robins sang, catbirds screeched, blue jays squealed and sparrows chirped. It sounded like a symphony of nature. Suddenly I could hear the refrains of Beethoven's Sixth Symphony, the "Pastoral," as if the North Carolina Symphony Orchestra were playing it on the lawn.

I was captivated. I had to have this place. My body knew it. My pulse felt it. I knew it would be mine, but how? Mervyn and I agreed we'd make no purchase, just look.

We both walked silently toward the car, each of us reflecting on what we were experiencing in the moment, yet not wanting to invade the other's thoughts. I spoke first. "Well, let's ask how much it is. That can't hurt."

Mervyn knew he was in trouble.

We drove up beyond the cabin and saw a large home nestled beneath the pines. A man greeted us.

"We're interested in the cabin. Are you the owner?" Mervyn asked.

"Yes. Why don't you come in. As a matter of fact, my wife and I are moving out of the cabin and into our new home today."

"You live in the cabin?" I asked.

"Well, not after today. We've lived there for nearly three years while we were building this house," he replied.

"I'm Dick Hauser. Please come in," he said. There was a coolness about him, a sort of illusive personal boundary that gave the impression that he was evasive or perhaps equivocal. As Dick led us in, his wife Patty shouted at him, not realizing we had entered. It seemed we interrupted a domestic quarrel. When she came down the stairs and realized she had company, she apologized. I told her I was a marriage counselor and we could settle the matter right now. We laughed, and their fight ended, at least for the time being.

Patty was a beautiful woman, somewhere around 50. She looked like the perennial homecoming queen. Blonde, blue-eyed and fair-skinned. She had the smile, the sweet Southern accent and the looks. Even in her gardening gear she exemplified class, style and most obviously, power. Dick was reserved, quiet and pleasant. There was never a doubt who would be the negotiator.

We spent several hours with them. They told us how they came upon the glen 13 years before. Patty had actually discovered it herself, traveling with their kids one summer just looking for property.

Dick was a dentist in South Florida, where he and Patty spent their time when they were not in the mountains. Patty had been born and raised in North Carolina. They had spent years developing the property, and now the cabin. Several other lots were for sale.

"How much do you want for the cabin?" Mervyn asked. I held my breath, praying it would be reasonable, but having no idea what reasonable would be.

"Ninety thousand." Patty didn't hesitate.

I wondered if $90,000 was reasonable. Having been raised in such a penurious fashion, $90 thousand seemed like quite a lot. Even if it wasn't, I automatically decided that it was.

We chatted a while longer, each sharing our enthusiasm about the area, and some other chit-chat. Mervyn said we would discuss it and get back to them in a day or so.

We drove back to Archer's Inn with our hearts in our mouths. Neither of us could contain our excitement.

"What do you think?" we both asked simultaneously.

"I've never seen anything like it, It's almost magical. It's the most beautiful cabin I've ever seen. I'm in love with it," I said. I can't remember Mervyn's words, but they were similar. We both agreed it was special. But we had also agreed we wouldn't buy. Just look.

"What do you think I should offer them?" he asked.

"Can we afford to buy it now? I thought you said we were just going to look?"

"Well, we always wanted something in the mountains. We both fell in love with it. I suppose we should look around and learn about the area. That would make more sense. Don't you think?"

I had no room for thinking. Only feeling. I couldn't imagine looking around the entire Blue Ridge mountain range and finding anything more enchanting or more beautiful than that cabin.

"I'll offer them 75 thousand," Mervyn said.

"Okay, 75 thousand. But, not a penny more." I said emphatically. "That's all we can afford." I said it with such conviction, as if I really knew about a budget. I also didn't want to give Mervyn the impression I was being too greedy or demanding.

We talked all night. But the one thing that remained constant was the $75 thousand offer. That was our limit.

The next day Mervyn went over to see the Hausers. I stayed at Archer's Inn for two reasons. One, I was too afraid of a negative response. The other, I felt Mervyn could negotiate better if I weren't around. My emotions were too difficult to contain and I was afraid that would compromise the negotiations.

While Mervyn was gone all I did was pray. I suddenly realized why I had listened to Emily. This had to have been the reason. Why else would I so willfully agree to drive up to the mountains. It was meant to be, I told myself. It was meant to be. I paced for hours, reading to pass the time. I couldn't concentrate. I tried to watch TV. That was no better. I fantasized about spending time in the mountains, decorating, gardening and perhaps even writing a book. Before I knew it, Mervyn had returned.

"Well?" I asked with my fingers crossed, hardly able to breathe. "Well?"

Mervyn just shook his head, pointing his right thumb down with his head hung.

"No? We didn't get it? You didn't make a deal?" I nearly cried.

"No. You told me not a penny over 75 thousand. They turned it down," he said.

My chest felt like it had caved in. I was so disappointed. How could it get away from me so easily?. "Shit," I said. "Shit, shit, shit, shit, shit!"

I sulked for the rest of the day. We went to dinner at Archer's Inn, and I said nothing. I just stared out the window at the view, with the lights flickering over the mountain range I said nothing. My fork automatically lifted the food to my mouth. Mervyn said nothing either. We ate in silence. Finally I spoke.

"Why didn't you offer them 80 thousand?"

"You told me not a penny over 75. Remember?"

"You should have offered them 80. We might have gotten it," I said.

"Say that again," Mervyn said.

"You should have offered them 80 thousand."

"Do you hear what you're telling me? You specifically told me not a penny over 75 thousand. Now you're telling me I should have offered them 80 thousand?"

"Right. That's what I'm saying," thinking, *What an ass. I can't believe he didn't have the brains to offer five thousand more.*

Mervyn looked at me and said, "I want you to remember this. I want you to hear exactly what you said," he replied.

"Why?"

"Because, I did. And we own the cabin. I got it for 80 thousand."

I screamed. The people in the dining room all stared at me. I began hitting Mervyn on his arm, cursing him for letting me go hours in grief over the loss of my dream cabin. I cried and cried.

"Why are you crying? We own the cabin."

My emotions were so polarized I didn't know what to do with myself. So I cried, laughed, hit him and hugged him.

Every season the cabin at the glen wears a different face, each with its own beauty. I went there this winter in January to write. I was all alone. Snowbound. It was below zero everyday. So cold in fact, that three times the pipes froze. I couldn't get out for a week.

I can remember a time not too long ago when the thought of driving alone through the mountains would have never been an option. Or the idea of being alone for a week would have been sheer torment. Now it was January 1994. I was alone driving north from the Hickory airport where I had taken a small twin-engine prop jet, something that would have terrified me just a few years ago. Here I was, driving in the snow with enthusiasm toward the cabin. I thought about the times I couldn't drive on the Florida Turnpike, even on a sunny day. I recalled the fear I experienced before getting on any airplane, and how I had to say a silent ritual prayer each time I boarded. I had to touch the plane as I entered, ask God to get me there "safe and sound, smooth and secure." Those were my ritual words. I would have to hold my husband's hand on take-off and landing, and God forbid if I had to travel alone. I needed 10 milligrams of Valium 20 minutes before every flight. If the flight was delayed, I was an embarrassment.

And now I was driving alone toward the cabin in the middle of winter, with snow beginning to fall. Lots of snow. I had never been in a snowstorm, and I was about to confront one head on.

By the time I reached Blowing Rock, about 35 miles from the cabin, the snow came down intensely. The wind howled as I crossed the mountain range. The car seemed to shiver. I thought I might be in some danger. Yet, there was a strange delight in experiencing danger alone. I could make a choice. To spend the night in Blowing Rock or continue. I had rented a compact car. I had asked for a four wheel drive, but they had none. I asked about snow tires, but they assured me, none were necessary. So, I trusted I was safe. And I felt safe. There were some times when I felt concerned, but not once did I feel the terror that used to be my familiar companion.

I continued. As I drove north, the snow fell harder. Cars were moving no more than ten or fifteen miles per hour. By the time I reached Boone, I began to reconsider my decision about staying overnight. Should I continue? Was I being foolish? What if the visibility continued to worsen? The road up the mountain could be treacherous. Perhaps, I should go the longer way through Banner Elk. At least I wouldn't have the incline to manage up the mountain. I considered all the options, and somewhere deep inside I heard the voice again, "Just keep going." Suddenly, I felt autonomous and independent. Not just in thought, but in my body. I followed my intuition wondering all along if I had gone crazy. I remembered the incident in Cancun. No. That was different. I knew not to go diving then, but gave my choice away to others. This time it was purely my decision, and I felt I could go on. The snowfall was heavier. My vision was obscured. There was hardly a car on the road. I had no one to follow. No lights to lead me anymore. Day shifted swiftly into night. But I intuitively knew I would find my way. And I did.

The ground was pure white. The sky matched so perfectly that you couldn't tell where the ground ended and the sky began. The bare trees were draped in snow, with icicles suspended from their branches. As I watched from my window, deer pranced across the snow-covered meadow beside the cabin. Two were on hind legs playing with each other.

I put on my coat, wrapped a muffler around my neck, donned wool mittens and pulled my cap down snugly. I put on my fur-lined boots and went for a walk on the soft white ground. My boots sank down until the snow reached my calves. I heard a crunch each time I took a step. I looked up and felt the falling gentle snow touching my face. I heard nothing. Absolutely nothing. The world was white, still, silent day, holy day. I made circles in the snow, stretching my arms out and up. Such beauty. Such glorious beauty. And I was here. Here, in the middle of it all.

It is not necessary to climb Mount Everest to experience growth and change. More often, it is the subtle nuances that move us on our path. Oftentimes, we are not even aware of them. They just happen, and suddenly, there is change. It was hard for me to account for these changes. Even in this story, I hardly recognized it as change until I began to write it. We need only to be willing. When we decide to commit, the universe seems to cooperate.

The Search for Spirituality

Our Father, which art in heaven, Hallowed be thy name.

—Matt. 6:9

The Lord's Prayer left an impression on me that not only is He a he, but He has all the power. It is He that giveth; and He that taketh away. It is He that created me, delegating my mother as the vehicle that transported me to this earth. Furthermore, it was a he, my father, who determined my sex.

"The Lord is my shepherd; I shall not want. He maketh me to lie down in green pastures; He leadeth me beside the still waters. He restoreth my soul."

In my deepest moments of despair, whenever I have felt an ill faith upon myself and have fallen to my knees in desperation; when I am consumed with catastrophic fantasies and fear I cannot seem to manage or resolve, it is the 23rd Psalm I recite to give me comfort and peace. I use it as a mantra for meditation. Even today I sometimes talk to God as if He were old, wise and personal.

There are many stories about God and creation. I have read American Indian folklore about creation whereby God had been determined to be female. There have been other religions based on goddess worship in which she is revered and even reigns as a divine spiritual ruler. These religions were often viewed as mysterious and for the most part, the followers were scorned for their beliefs. They were considered anti-Christian or pagan. I have also read literature that describes God as androgynous, both male and female.

However, most come to embrace the supposition handed down

by the Bible, Michelangelo, *A Course in Miracles,* and Cecil B. DeMille that God is male, creating Adam (and all other males) in the image of Himself.

Eve has always been considered an afterthought. A very good one, but nevertheless, an afterthought. Her contribution, although equal to Adam's, followed his creation. In other words, she came second. Even God's closest kin, best friends and most messengers are men. Abraham, Moses, Mohammed, Buddha, Jesus Christ, the twelve apostles, Allah, Hare Krishna and Catholic priests are all male. On rare occasion, women have been designated with the title of Saint but only after they died and performed at least three non-medical miracles, sanctified by a quorum of men. Most prophets, divine spiritual masters and enlightened beings have been men.

Perhaps the future holds the promise that one day women can teach the divine truth on a more regular basis. Women have never really tried to play it up, and until recently they abdicated their pos-sible reign without protest and too much fuss. They've always had the intuition. They may just need more time. Their divine images that have been cast in stone highlighting their large breasts and prominent vulvas are qualifications for Playboy centerfolds, not nec-essarily spiritual leaders. I've never once seen a statue of God or a male spiritual leader that accentuates their testicles or buttocks. The only gods sporting divine bodies were those in Greek and Roman mythology. Any artistic projection of the God I've known referred to as the Holy Spirit never resembled a sex symbol. Charlton Heston came closest.

As Keen says there is a sense that woman was, is and always will be "goddess and creatrix." The men who awe and revere her can be viewed as few, sensitive, enlightened and spiritual. Unfortunately, most modern men don't. If they did, statistics would not reflect what is described in some of the following chapters. In her present exile woman remains overworked, underpaid, battered, unequal and rightfully annoyed with her present imprisonment. Things are changing, however.

The only assurance I have ever known from my biological des-tiny was having to get up every four hours for feedings, change every diaper, attend PTA meetings, Brownies, Cub Scouts, soccer, baseball and football practice; carpool to Hebrew school, ballet and piano lessons; make birthday parties, bar and bat mitzvahs, and be as present as possible while getting divorced, going for a master's degree and fighting for my economic and psychological life. What may appear to be "womb worship" may also be considered the miracle of life, coupled with interminable responsibilities that change your life forever. My ability to conceive, deliver and raise children was a gift I graciously accepted without conscious thought or consideration. I was under the influence of Demeter, the goddess of grain and motherhood, along with Hera, the goddess of marriage. I was also under the influence of my mother, who said repeatedly, "Have at least five children. Your father only let me have two. I always wanted more. Have four for yourself, and one for me." So I obliged both my parents. I married a Jewish doctor for my father and had five children for my mother, without ever giving a thought to the implications of parenting. I know now that every child needs at least a father and a mother.

The seed was planted by a man. The baby was delivered by a man, and the bill was paid for by a man. I carried, labored and learned how to be a loving mother only after making many mistakes while trying to survive and become whole. For perhaps the most important task of my life, I was the least prepared and trained than any other.

There was no father present at my children's deliveries to hold his child to his breast, singing welcome to the world. Two out of five times he was either shooting craps or delayed at the dog track. The abandonment was very real to me. My birthing ability was never given any reverence. "Peasant's work" is what I heard. Just hours before my first delivery we were delayed at a drug store on the way to the hospital while Jack received instructions on how to load film in the Polaroid.

"Make me a bowl of oatmeal" is what I was ordered to do before he would drive me to the hospital when I went into labor with my fifth child. It isn't his fault. His father treated his mother like "peasant stock." You can only know what you know.

Throughout life we all experience the intense pain of misfortune. Suddenly out-of-the-blue, everything begins to go wrong. Dodging the onslaught of one bad experience after another, we just want to shut our minds to the pain that no amount of rationalization or self-hypnosis can divert. I have experienced this sort of pain in my life and have seen it in the lives of my friends and clients. But it hurts the most when the bad times are perpetrated by the betrayal of a trusted and respected friend and associate.

As a therapist and as a supervisor for the work of other therapists, I have never doubted the supreme importance of the patient/client's interest. By definition, the patient/client of a psychotherapist is vulnerable and places his or her trust in the benign care of a healer who takes him or her to a state of greater strength and effectiveness. Unfortunately, sometimes the position of power assumed by therapists tempts them to take advantage of their clients either physically or mentally.

I've always been repulsed by such actions and never hesitated to voice my outrage and indignation at such exploitation. Despite the fact that guidelines have been established to prevent therapists from using their power to fulfill their lustful desires, the practice continues behind closed doors.

Equally repulsive is the power that therapists have to satisfy their need to control and win reverence from others through their clients. The phenomena of groupies and cults in psychotherapy are as damaging as sexual violations and I regard them as a form of emotional incest. A therapist's objective is to help the client gain autonomy out of his or her state of co-dependence. The transfer of the client's co-dependency from existing parent figures to the therapist is a perpetuation of the problem in a new form. In his book, *Hymns to an Unknown God,* Sam Keen warns us: "Be wary of anyone who fascinates, captivates, overwhelms. When you can't tear your eyes away from someone, you probably have begun to look at your life through their eyes rather than your own . . . These practices may be hazardous to your spiritual health."

I have had the opportunity of working very closely with John Bradshaw, who has the remarkable ability of creating a powerful transference in very large audiences in a matter of hours. He very well could have used this phenomenal power to become a cult guru. But he has carefully respected the boundaries of the therapeutic contract, and never lost focus of his objective to create autonomy in his clients and reduce their co-dependency. My views on this subject are not unique. I just subscribe to the generally held views of the practitioners of this healing and caring profession of psychotherapy.

Sometimes my firm commitment to my clients has conflicted with the supervision of my associates. I'm always sensitive to my associates feelings and respect their authority to treat clients, yet I must balance this with concern for the clients. The clients' needs, of course, always come first and sometimes disagreements result. On occasion disagreements have been perceived as personal attacks. The therapists sometimes expressed their feelings of hurt through defensive maneuvers, but the problems were usually resolved in a few days. There was one incident, however, when the conflict erupted into a blistering, vituperative attack. I tried to protect myself from the stress by ignoring the situation, hoping it would pass away. My position, however, demanded an ethical stand.

I consulted with all my colleagues as to what I should do, and there was a consensus as to the appropriate action. There were inherent dangers in the confrontation of this particular therapist, and the little girl in me was scared. In some of my regressive moments, I longed for the security of my co-dependent days with Jack. I'd conveniently forgotten all the pain and humiliation that motivated me to move on to the path of selfhood. As an escape, I fantasized about looking for some powerful male figure to take over the responsibility of the decision process. Deep down I knew this was not possible. I was an adult with adult responsibilities. Instead I prayed for guidance and objectively tried to assess what was right. It was a clear choice despite all the dangers and certain repercussions.

My prayers paid off. I got the strength to act and the moral courage to support what I believed was right. With full awareness of the likely dangers, and facing a group consciousness with a demonic force, my conscience had made the unflinching choice supporting the principle. That for me was the only path.

As expected, I was hailed with a barrage of insults and abuse and was forced to fight off a systematic campaign of vilification.

I wondered about what other women in history and fictional characters in novels had done to protect themselves from similar situations. I remembered reading somewhere that more than nine million women had been burned during the Inquisition. I thought about Hester Prynne *(The Scarlet Letter)* and the humiliation and shame she endured from self-righteous neighbors and spiritually-minded brethren. I thought about Ayla, from *Clan of the Cave Bear,* who was cast out by the clan and abused by many of its members. I thought of Mary Magdalene, Joan of Arc and other righteous females who suffered anguish, disdain and even death from ridicule and scorn. I remembered hearing how Harriet Beecher Stowe was castigated and admonished for her advocacy of women's rights, and I thought too of the men who had suffered the same inequities. I cried for them and for myself. I had a new companion—fear was her name and I needed to make her my friend.

I went to my cabin in North Carolina to heal my spirit. Often in the morning mist, you can see a blue heron sunning herself on a tree stump near the edge of the pond there. There are twin birch trees, where light beams from the sun's rays seep through and shed their silvery reflections upon the water. But, I was having a very difficult time, even in this spiritual space I had come to call my own.

It was Sunday morning, quite early, around seven o'clock. For some unknown reason, I turned on the television. The reception in the mountains is terrible, unless you have a satellite dish, and we don't. An unfamiliar face appeared on the screen. I later learned it was Robert Schuller. He was interviewing Victor Frankl. They were discussing their most trying moments in life, each sharing how they turned to their own beliefs in God. Although not of Reverend Schuller's faith, I was able to relate to his experience. His story touched me and I was able to see great parallels to my own sense of despair, frustration and even panic. He candidly disclosed how he had failed at what he thought to be a personal calling from God. He was given a calling to build a great cathedral, one that would come to be known as the Crystal Cathedral. During the course of his mission, not unlike myself, he had been faced with one obstacle after another, each weakening his sense of self-worth, causing self-doubt and disillusion. He took up a relationship with his wounded part, trying unsuccessfully to nurture his own soul. Finally when he felt hopeless and suicidal, he asked Jesus to heal him. He described himself as having fallen into bed, arms outstretched, overwhelmed with shame and sorrow. Once he heard himself ask for help, he felt a finger pressing on the top of his head, releasing negative forces and energy that he described as toxins from his body. The next morning when he awoke his depression was gone. He felt he had been cleansed. After that, life took on new meaning. He felt renewed, ready to meet new challenges with a sense of trust and faith. The story had a happy ending of course. I watched him deliver his sermon from a grand pulpit to a huge congregation in the most beautiful cathedral I had ever seen.

I reached for my afghan and set out for the pond. I spread out the afghan and laid down, arms outstretched, facing west so I could look toward the twin birch trees. I usually sit in the lotus position with my palms facing upward. But on this particular morning I chose to lie down on my back. I looked up at the twin trees as if they could provide the answer. "Please help me."

Then, as if another voice came from within, I began to recite, "The Lord is my Shepherd I shall not want. He maketh me to lie down in green pastures." (I looked around. There I was, in green pastures.) "He leadeth me beside the still waters." (I looked to my right and saw the clear still pond.) A sudden chill passed through me. "He restoreth my soul."

Another voice within asked, "What did you say?" Then another replied, "What's the difference, keep going."

I began a dialogue with myself, answering and responding, anecdoting and analyzing, all the while continuing a poem I did not know that I knew, nor what it was named. Obviously somewhere stored deep within the unconscious was memory for knowledge that I consciously did not know existed. "He leadeth me in the paths of righteousness for his name's sake."

"I hope I did the right thing," I said.

"Yea, though I walk through the valley of the shadow of death, I shall fear no evil; for thou art with me. Thy rod and thy staff, they comfort me."

"I wonder what rod and staff mean?"

"What's the difference?" another voice responded. "Keep going."

Confused and unable to even guess what I was quoting, I guessed it was "The Lord's Prayer." Not being religious or even knowledgeable about Judaism, I couldn't identify what I was later to discover as the 23rd Psalm.

"It can't be the Lord's Prayer." My inner voice argued.

"The Lord's Prayer begins with, 'Our Father, who art in heaven'."

"Right!" I said, "Then what am I saying?"

Pressured to continue from one of my inner voices, I proceeded as if someone was saying it for me.

"Wonder what a rod and staff are for?" I asked myself again.

"Stop analyzing!" My inner voice challenged. "Just go on!"

"Thou preparest a table before me in the presence of mine enemies."

"Boy! Did you give me enemies!" I nearly shouted out loud.

"Why? Why did you do that?"

"Surely goodness and mercy shall follow me all the days of my life and I shall dwell in the house of the Lord forever."

"What did you just recite?" I asked myself again.

"I don't know, but whatever I said, I didn't say it. Something or someone said it for me."

"Then do it again," demanded the inner voice.

I did it again. And again. I did it three times, each time getting stuck on the "rod and staff," wondering what it meant.

After about an hour that seemed like ten minutes, I stood up, stunned and confused from the experience. I felt much better. I folded the afghan, walked to the cabin and continued to walk up the mountain; something I developed the habit of doing whenever I visited here. Walking along the road, a quarter of a mile up the mountain, is a wonderful aerobic exercise I do while I'm there. As I approached the top and the end of the road, somewhat breathless, I noticed a white round light cast against the embankment. Looking for the source and unable to locate it, I approached cautiously. As I came closer, the light grew brighter, almost translucent. It seemed to move and change shape slightly and continuously. There, in the middle of this round lightness, as if in a radiance of its own energy, were a rod and staff. Two branches had fallen from the chestnut tree. One, the shape and size of a rod with a natural resting place for the thumb of my right hand; the other a staff, nearly seven feet high, with a fully rounded hook. There they were; two branches illuminated by the light just waiting for me to find them. Taken back by the symbolism, I looked toward heaven waiting for some kind of permission to take the rod and staff. No answer. I reached into the light with both hands grasping both the rod and staff. I again looked up and heard my inner voice say, "Who are you God?"

Another voice within answered, "I am that I am."

I walked away almost spellbound, wondering if Moses experienced this same sort of profound humility. I had often felt inferior in my life, but never so humble. I walked a few more steps down the mountain road trying to make sense out of my experience. Suddenly from out of nowhere, without warning, a beautiful doe jumped in front of me, and pranced upward as if I had been invisible. Startled by the unexpected visit, I pulled back in a jolt, holding both the rod and staff to brace myself. I had owned the cabin for nearly two years, and not once had a deer presented itself. I knew something profound had occurred. Being a well-grounded reality-based psychotherapist, owning an apartment and the cabin, holding leases on several offices and having many mailboxes, things of this nature did not happen. Afraid that others would think I had lost it, I was careful not to tell too many about this experience.

I've come to believe however, that it is in our darkest moments, when the soul deeply grieves and seeks within to find the answers that we find our God, inside ourselves. It is when we are ready to surrender our egos, and genuinely ask for what we need that our answer comes in ways that somehow find meaning to our needs and restore our soul.

When I returned to Miami, I told a friend of my experience. I wanted to know the significance of the rod and staff.

"You know what a rod and staff were used for, don't you?" he asked.

"Not really," I explained with some embarrassment. I hadn't even known what I had recited until I called my daughter, Linda, in California. She was able to identify the psalm. She said she had a copy of it on her refrigerator. She wasn't sure whether it came from the Old or New Testament. She called me back after she spoke to her rabbi, telling me it's one of David's Psalms. Once she told me, of course I recognized it.

"Well, a rod and staff were used by shepherds. The rod was for protection and the staff was for keeping the flock together and to cull the herd," my friend said.

"What does 'cull the herd' mean?" I asked.

"That's when an undesirable sheep is removed from the herd by the shepherd's staff." Sometimes the shepherd has to kill it for the safety of the other sheep," he replied.

Suddenly, without a moment's hesitation I had my affirmation. The answer I had been seeking was revealed clearer than if it had been typed and sent to me on parchment paper, certified mailed and with a presidential seal. God had let me know I had done the right thing. Was this a God outside myself? Did this divine experience come from within my soul? Or perhaps both? Had I manifested this experience through need and desperation? Did my soul speak to me or did it transcend somewhere beyond my mind's comprehension of space and time, my beingness suspended into some eternal connection with all things? I don't know if it is even important to know. What is important is that it was my experience, my healing and my resolution, reached by my need and willingness to allow it to happen.

We all have the power if we open our hearts to our own God; our own beingness. The fact that much of the world uses He to describe the Lord is purely academic.

The Search for Self

There are places in the heart that do not yet exist. Pain must be in order that they be.

—Leon Bouy

My daughter, Linda, once told me that we need to lose ourselves before we can find ourselves. Soren Kierkegaard, the Danish philosopher, said, "And this is the simple truth: that to live is to feel oneself lost." Before one can have a loving relationship with another, one must have a loving relationship with oneself. Having a relationship with oneself means having to finish our business with our source relationships. Discovering ourselves is a long, arduous journey that requires a great deal of courage. Most people never take the journey, and consequently, they die never knowing who they are.

Not unlike Dorothy in *The Wizard of Oz*, we go through life looking for our hearts, our wisdom and our courage. We travel our own yellow brick road looking for answers, hoping to find a wizard along the way who will show us the way home. It's only when we let go and face our greatest fears, as Dorothy did, do we become empowered. Vulnerability is the seed of empowerment which gives rise to the genius in each of us. Out of this genius comes our phoenix, unfolding a plethora of resources that were always there but shielded by our defense mechanisms and guarded by our fears. This is when our higher power seeks to guide us to the way home. And, this is when Glenda the Good Witch of the East appears to help Dorothy return home to Kansas. "Just click your heels together, my dear," she says.

"Well, why didn't you tell me that in the first place?" asks Dorothy.

"Because if I had, you wouldn't have believed me anyway."

Saying good-bye to Mom and Dad, grieving the past and having faith in the process is essential for one's growth. Saying good-bye to men means saying good-bye to our fathers, boyfriends, lovers and husbands temporarily to discover, heal and reparent ourselves. It does not mean going it alone. It means knowing who we are, accepting responsibility for ourselves and becoming the person we were meant to be.

And there is that search for selfhood. The state when you can look at the outside reality and decide what it is; you make decisions and feel sure of yourself when you have an inner self that validates all your actions. There is a sense of finality about the process and a feeling that this is where you need to go. It is a movement toward a goal, an affirmation of a sense of destiny.

And as I move toward my integration, I get rid of those debilitating regrets, and I get more clarity as to what is really worthwhile. Whatever could not be is, at best, a perpetual possibility. I see a positive vision, that of my own. I might for once genuinely have personal priorities. I live as a person who can have a self, a sense of integration that helps me see others as they are and myself as I am.

And there would be a sense of mission, a personal sense of being, a drive of self which is empowered by the innate energy of my self. When life has no beginning and no end, and life and death have no differences, just different states, there is no fear. There is no fear and there is no striving. There is movement and joy of living. And yes, there is no fear for me and no fear of the inability to take care of others. When there is a contact with the essence of being, the joy of living is characterized by looking into the life of things.

Each of us finds our own path into the discovery of self. My path took me in many directions. My search came in many different ways; partly unconscious and without deliberation. Psychotherapy was one path. Being open and willing was another. Being in the moment was most significant in experiencing my I-amness. Time is irrelevant in the exploration. The important thing is the recognition of self. Who am I? What is my purpose? What are my wants, needs, likes, dislikes and where do I want to go?

Let me share with you one of the most significant events in my personal quest for self-discovery.

It seemed as though I had never been alone. Now I was 45. I had been married three times for a total of 20 years, and had lived with a man for five. I had been either married or living with a man for more than half my life. The last ten years were spent with men not of my faith. One had been Episcopalian, the other Roman Catholic. My Judaism, as with my self, somehow got lost in the romantic shuffle, and I slipped further away into the abyss of no-man's land. Who was I? I had forgotten. Who was the woman who's Hebrew name had been Yochevet? Where had she gone?

"Do you want to go to Israel?" my girlfriend, Ellen, asked.

"What are you talking about? What do you mean 'Do I want to go to Israel?' Are you crazy? I have bills up the wazoo, a full case-load and responsibilities. You're asking me if I want to go to Israel? Why would I even give it a thought?"

"Because there is a mission sponsored by the Jewish Federation, and you'll never believe the cost," she exclaimed.

"How much?" I asked for the hell of it.

"A thousand. One thousand dollars!"

"I don't believe it. One thousand dollars?"

"You heard me. One thousand dollars. And it's for ten days."

"Let's do it. When do we leave?"

Before I knew what I had agreed to, I was on an El Al flight to Tel Aviv. Maybe it was impulsive. Maybe not. But there was no way I could not have gone.

I really don't know what it is when I write about the calling. For some it can be a deep drive or compelling force which pushes or pulls in a direction without conscious awareness, as if one is being called to their destiny, divinely guided. For others, it feels like a path carved out to follow. For me, it's like a wave that lifts me to where I need to be. I have no real conscious awareness of this wave.

Often, not even a clue. It's a state of suspension, an act of submission, of letting go. I let it take me where it calls, and never give it a thought until I receive the final message. This can take weeks, months and more often years. Clarity usually arrives after the fact.

This is how my search for self was reclaimed. This was part of my journey.

I'm sure that this mission was probably no different than any other sponsored by the Jewish Federation. There's no doubt that they know how to sell Israel to their American brothers and sisters. American Jews are essentially born with a sense of responsibility, pride and eternal guilt about Israel—even those of us who had little or no religious upbringing. I think it's in our DNA too.

The very first question asked to us by our guide Moshe upon arrival at Ben Gurion Airport was, "Are you Jewish Americans, or American Jews?" Those of us that answered the latter were wholeheartedly converted upon our return with a new commitment, and a pledge to donate at least $1,500. The Federation never fails to raise the conscious awareness, heighten the spirit and soul, and double the level of guilt to get what it needs—money. The amount I pledged soon ballooned to $2,500 before I returned to the states. What I received from them, however, money couldn't buy. Perhaps it was the magic of Israel, its people, her history, or maybe the salesmanship of the seductive blue-eyed, dark-skinned Moshe, coupled with my vulnerability and lost soul. Whatever it was doesn't matter. The trip changed my life.

I remember exactly and precisely where it happened. It had been happening all along, from the moment the 747 lifted off the ground at Kennedy. I knew something was happening even before take-off. It was in my pulse. I knew it was going to be a special trip.

Each day I spiritually went to the well. Each day I felt the shift in its depth. Miracles began to happen. The changes were so subtle they obfuscated the obvious. I was coming home. I was coming home at last. Each day brought a new light and insight. Each experience opened me more. The more I opened, the more I received. Israel was taking me on a wavelength to a place and a dimension I had never known. Yochevet was there, waiting for me.

It happened in Tel Aviv, but not immediately. I had already been to the kibbutzim and the Moshav Netiv Ha-Asara, two distinctive living communities in Israel. I went to Jerusalem, saw the excavations and visited the home of David and Bathsheba. I drank a cup of wine after the precisely calculated timed entrance into the city of Jerusalem with my fellow American Jews, just moments before sunset, on the eve of the Sabbath. Moshe lifted his cup toward heaven and said, "Shalom. Welcome home everyone."

I went to the synagogue in Tel Aviv on Simchat Tora, watching in awe and delight the children on the shoulders of their fathers, parading gleefully, waving Israeli flags in celebration of this joyous holiday. I went to the reconstructed 1948 battlefield of Yad Mordechai. I saw the leper's caves and Yad Vashem, the museum and memorial of the holocaust. I saw the Kfar Saba absorption center and met with Ethiopian Olim, where thousands of Ethiopian Jews had been airlifted more than a thousand years into the future. I saw the hunger and wounded souls in the eyes of the dark-skinned children. Their faces spoke to me of pain and suffering.

I went to Beit Hatefutsoth, the museum of the Jewish diaspora, the Golan Heights, and floated in the Dead Sea. I danced the hora in the streets of Yaffa, saw the walls of Jericho, attended the Kabbalat Shabbat—the Friday night Sabbath services—and prayed and placed my written prayer in a crevice of the Western Wall in Jerusalem. I planted a tree in Hod Hadsharon, the Jewish memorial garden, and had even played the accordion for the residents of a Jewish congregate living community for the aged in Rishon-le-Zion. I climbed Masada, the mountain and fortress of the Zealots, where thousands of Jews chose mass suicide rather than surrender and be captured by the Romans. I climbed Mount Carmel to the Carmelite Monastery Mukhrakah to view the Jezreel Valley, the breadbasket of Israel. I traveled along the Lebanon border and lunched at a border moshav. I visited the Mitzpeh to study a "Populating the Galilee" project for the Jewish agency. I went to Caesaria, Tiberias and visited the Qumran Caves, where the Dead Sea scrolls were found. All of this and more was moving and inspirational but nothing like the experience I had at the Museum of Jewish History.

There had been two museums: One painted white, the other black. The black museum symbolized night, the white day. The white one, the one with the scrolls, changed me forever. It might have been the seventh or eighth day of our journey. We all gathered around the exhibit. Inside the glass structure was the skeleton of a woman covered in a shroud. Her arms were crossed. Moshe asked, "Who knows what is a bubba?" I raised my hand. "It's a grand-mother."

"Yes," he said. "Bubba is the Yiddish word for grandmother. This was someone's grandmother. In her dress, next to her tsistkilas (breasts), like all bubbas, she held many precious possessions she feared were at risk."

I suddenly thought of my bubba. This was so typical. She would gather up articles during the day, collecting them with the intention of putting them in their proper place before she would retire. I always thought her breasts were so large, but in fact, they were not large at all. They were sharing space with the items she collected during the day, just like the one Moshe described in the exhibit.

This memory unleashed my emotions. The moment the memory hit my soul, my barren spirit and body gave way to the grief. The tears started slowly, just giving warning to what was to follow. Years of repression, abandonment of self, denial, loss and redemption poured out of my mouth, my eyes, down my face, while sobs echoed through the museum with a force I had no resistance or ability to control. They came relentlessly. The years had finally caught up to the present. There was no turning back. I had come home. The response terrified me. I felt overwhelmed with emotions I could not compute nor contain. My weeping could be heard throughout the museum. Moshe had the good sense to ask our American tour guide to escort me from the museum and take me back to the bus.

My state of grief and homecoming frightened and confused me. I felt lost, as if I had regressed to a child. Everything appeared larg-er than life. The interior of the museum resembled mirrors in a fun house. Images were distorted. The corridors appeared twisted and convoluted, like a maze. I thought I might be hallucinating. But no. This was no hallucination. I was in a process of integration. Wherever I walked, I would see oversized reminders of my heritage: a mural by Chagall, a Menorah sculpture by Agam. I would go for-ward in a direction that I thought would lead me to the exit, only to be confronted by another exhibit or piece of Judaic art work. Then another, and another. I was bombarded with symbols of my faith, my heritage and my people. My collective unconscious burned its light into my soul. These were my roots. Not just the people of Israel, but of the diaspora and of all time. Not just the holocaust, but the Inquisition, the pogroms and the eternal struggle for survival. I had been there through all the wars, the bondage, the Exodus, with all the memories, through all time. This was me. I had found Yochevet. I had come home.

To get where you need to go, you must remember who you are and where you came from.

Part IV

Chapter 6

LESSONS I LEARNED ABOUT:

Living in a Man's World

It's a man's world, and you men can have it.

—*Katherine Anne Porter*

There is no doubt that women have an extraordinary influence on men. Those goddesses, the Madonna, and Mother Earth creatures, creators of life, loving and nurturing, play powerful forces on the Eros and psyches of men. Let us not forget poor Ulysses, how he had to restrain himself, stuffing cloth in his ears, so he wouldn't hear the muse of the Sirens as his ship passed by their islands. Or Samson, who lost his strength and power to the whims and aphrodisia of Delilah. And in the beginning, there was Adam, smitten by Eve, unable to resist sharing the forbidden fruit she coaxed him to eat. Ah women, look what havoc you have played on men, those weak-kneed, insufferable first-chosen creatures of God, waiting to be engulfed and seduced.

What would David have without Bathsheba? George without Martha? Franklin without Eleanor? Muhammad without Khadija? Marcos without Imelda? (Probably more closet space.) Bill without Hillary? (He'd have to run the country himself.) John without Jackie? (Maybe a White House that reflected more of America, rather than France.) Desi without Lucy? (Boring.) Ike without Tina? (Nothing.) Or Sonny without Cher? (No political career.) In reality, it's those

weak-kneed, first-come-first-serve men who become kings, states-
men and prime ministers.

I keep wondering why most Nobel prizes go to men; why
Barbra Streisand didn't even get nominated as best director for
"Prince of Tides." Why women can't become priests. If this is truly
a woman's world, why do we have wars? What is this myth, that
men have about women, that it's really a woman's world? Just look
around you and see who controls the economy, politics, governments and corporations of the world.

If women ran the country, America would be a better place than
it is now. The following are the results of a Gallup survey reported
in the June 1993 issue of *Life* magazine:

- America would be kinder and gentler. Nearly half, 44 percent, of women surveyed said the problem of poverty and
  homelessness should be an "extremely important" government priority. Among men, 29 percent offered a similar view.
- America would be less armed and dangerous. *Life* reported
  that about 70 percent of all women in their survey said they
  favored making firearms more difficult to buy; 50 percent of
  all men questioned agreed.
- America would be tougher on crime. More women than men
  believed government should make the war on crime a top
  priority. Women also were more likely to support stronger
  action on drunken driving, drug dealing, rape and sexual
  assault.
- America would be more family-friendly. Large majorities of
  both sexes agree that more should be done for America's
  working families. But women were somewhat more likely
  than men to favor government action on a variety of programs to help working parents, including paid maternity
  leave and child-care programs.
- America would pay men and women equally for equal work.
  "Unequal pay for equal work, sexual harassment, discrimination in hiring and promotions, child care—all are rated by
  more women than men to be 'very serious' problems."
- Juxtaposed to all this data, the study suggests that women
  remain less interested in politics and civic affairs than men.

- If you're wondering what the chances are that women will run the country in the near future, forget it. Presently, only about six percent of all members of Congress are women.

Women, however, make excellent politicians in everyday life. The second definition for "politic" in the *New Merriam-Webster* dictionary is "shrewdly tactful." By definition, there isn't any doubt about women's contributions and achievements in the home, family and community. Although most women have not achieved the political status of Indira Gandhi, Benazir Bhutto, Margaret Thatcher and Golda Meir, there are thousands more who in their own inimitable fashions mold, shape, support and bring about social change worldwide.

Most women haven't yet had the privilege and honor of sitting on the 15th floor of some glass-enclosed electric monolith skyscraper or fashionable Fortune 500 office building executive suite with panoramic views of the skyline overlooking the water.

Unless you happen to be an executive secretary or part of the exceptionally few five percent of female executives, you won't know about the chefs that are hired to prepare daytime meals in the executive suites, or personal trainers who arrive daily. Most women aren't aware of the private foreign language lessons taught in the comfort of the office. Few of us ever know about the daily visits from chiropractors, massage therapists, hair stylists and even psychotherapists. Nor do we know about the expense accounts, first-class airline tickets, corporate homes or yachts for weekend retreats, chauffeur-driven limos, expensive cars and mobile telephones. But I'm not sure we're really missing anything. How many people who work on the first 14 floors of those glass and concrete tombs really know how miserable those masters of the universe are anyway? Let's take a peek at the illusion of the 15th floor for a moment.

Do you know how many really know who they are? How many of them have hypertension, ulcers or burn-out? How many are unfaithful to their wives or have unfaithful wives? How many are alcoholics, rageaholics and workaholics? How many take tranquilizers and sleeping pills? How many are clinically depressed and lonely? How many have said, "I'm going to throw myself out of this window"? How many have attended at least ten or more workshops on empowerment, stress management and leadership and haven't effectively implemented one solid change? They've become so accustomed to the rat race, they don't even know they're in it; that they're dying in it. Each day they die a little more. If it's a man's world, then you guys can have it. In a recent article in the *Wall Street Journal*, Rochelle Sharpe writes about female gains in corporate management, "You've come a long way—maybe."

Women have moved into nonclerical white-collar jobs in droves. They held 46 percent of all such positions at the companies reporting to the U.S. Equal Employment Opportunity Commission in 1992, up from 22 percent in the late 1960s.

But women aren't matching these gains in management. A *Wall Street Journal* analysis shows that women still held less than a third of the managerial jobs in the 38,059 companies analyzed. They held just one-fourth of the jobs classified by the EEOC as "officials and managers"—a broad category that includes a wide variety of supervisory posts, from the manager of the janitorial service to the CEO of the company.

She paints a dim view of what's ahead too. " . . . in spite of the men's losses and women's gains, men continue to hold the bulk of management jobs and, unless growth rates change considerably, will continue to hold them for a long time. At the current pace, women will not achieve parity with male managers for another 20 to 30 years." Don't sweat it gals, at least you'll be alive.

Even though man emerges from woman (with the exception of Adam), it is man who puts man there in the first place. This perennial struggle of dependency, whether it be men on women, or women on men is not really a problem. Menachem Begin once said, "With every problem there is a solution. Here we have no solution. Therefore we have no problem. We have a condition."

We're "people who need people." What's wrong with that? It all depends on who you need and how much. Women are just as bonded to men as men are to women. It takes two to tango. So let's give up the idea that bondage to the opposite gender is a problem. The real problem is the who (not the what), and how much. Men need women. Women need men. Yin and yang; anima and animus. Every male needs to claim his feminine side. Every woman needs to claim her masculine side. When the search is over within the self, then the need for another outside self is transformed into choice. Love out of need is very different than need out of love.

Bondage, as we know and understand it, can serve as fodder to fuel emancipation and separation. Emancipation can be useful self-exploration. Exploring one's self can give rise to developing a relationship outside ourselves. For until we can have a relationship with our self, we cannot effectively have a relationship outside ourself. Without full knowledge and acceptance of self and all of our self, especially our disowned self, we cannot be free to choose others. The goal is for two autonomous individuals to merge for the enrichment of each other.

If one perceives and maintains bondage as a form of slavery and servitude, then undoubtedly there is no redemption. Every journey begins with a first step. And just as I have heard many alcoholics say they were grateful for the disease of alcoholism as their first step to recovery, I too feel grateful for the "bondage" I have endured as a preliminary requisite to personal freedom.

Since the beginning of time, women needed men to hunt. It is quite probable that women could have hunted if need be. Men needed women to tend the hearth. It is also possible that men could have cooked. But they shared each other's powers for the greater good of all. Physiology perhaps gave rise to domination, but not for all. There are always exceptions, as with David and Goliath, Samson and Delilah, and Ulysses. Domination can have many sources. Physiology isn't the only one. Usually one bestows power. It is not received. The assumption that power is received is a result of unawareness, passivity and an unwillingness to explore one's self.

As we are waking up, opening our eyes and mouths and developing heightened awareness, we can make choices to give, to take and to share. The tragedy is to carry the anger, the sorrow and the images throughout our one and only life. Women who have been adversely affected by men and who have grown bitter from those experiences have been left to focus on their persecution and victimization, wasting precious energy on undeserving disturbed creatures of their own woundedness.

In ongoing groups I facilitate, I can't help but concern myself with some of the women who harbor deep resentment toward men. Most of them are now in their early 1930s. They unwittingly project their historical experiences on men as a whole, further alienating themselves from potentially gratifying relationships, intimacy and personal happiness. Their history of abuse and subjugation has understandably made them hypervigilant and mistrustful. When stories from their pasts resonate through their filtering systems during group interaction, their response is quick and inflammatory. The whole reaps the anger for the few which were the cause.

It is essential to realize that retaliatory responses are self-defeating. They preserve injustice and breed contempt rather than liberate the soul. They keep us stuck in the same dysfunctional and abusive system we came from.

Recently, during a three-day training course, the myth of men and women revealed itself on the last day. One of the trainees, an Asian male, was unable to attend the first day due to an unavoidable delay overseas. He anxiously arrived at the end of the second day directly from the airport, thinking "better late than never." His intention was positive, but the results were disastrous. His unexpected entrance was like a stone hitting still water, creating a silent rippling effect. The four female participants, coupled with my daughter and I, had genuinely bonded and enjoyed the female unity we had experienced over the previous two days. The absence of male participants was consciously noted and spoken about in terms of advantage and intimacy. Both Linda and I warmly greeted Meehar. Meehar carried in Baci chocolates, hugging only me—he had never met the others.

I introduced him to the group, unaware of the unconscious impact of his late entrance. We spoke briefly and continued with Linda's didactic presentation on "Integrated Models for Group Psychotherapy."

The next morning we all began the training session as usual with a brief "feeling" check-in. The first woman to speak, Anne, felt anger and mistrust due to the unexpected late arrival of Meehar. She explained that the group was already bonded and had gone through the various and contiguous stages of group process. She stated that she felt "violated" and reluctant to work as a client at this juncture. (The training required each therapist to become a client in order to fully understand the techniques and process.) She also articulated that this was not about Meehar, but rather about the timing, feeling that the group had regressed to a lower level of intimacy. She described his entrance as a "penis coming into the room." The other female members joined her assessment, expressing more of the same feelings. One women said that she feared she would be "punished" by the presence of the "penis." Another said that she was angry—not at him, but by the interruption, also reciting the metaphor of the penis penetration into the womb or vagina.

Meehar, trying desperately to contain his feelings, said somewhat nervously that he understood the feelings of the members and would be willing to do whatever the group decided. When asked what he felt about the process, he anxiously said, "No feeling."

Linda, realizing that he was using a defense against his feeling, probed more.

"I feel fine. I have a feminine side and don't see the difference. I'm very comfortable with my feminine side," he replied.

"Say more about your feminine side," Linda probed.

"I feel scared."

The group had attempted through their projections to "castrate" Meehar as he entered the "womb." Overcompensating, he castrated himself, denying any "difference" between femininity and masculinity. As an attempt to feel feminine and to align himself with his new "wombmates," he projected femininity, aligning it with fear, while the women projected masculinity with punishment. The myth emerged even in a training session with highly developed, well-trained psychotherapists. The intention now was to process the feelings as he was being scapegoated, extrapolating the myths as the basis for the processing. Once done, by externalizing the feelings and retrieving the projections, we were able to move on.

There was indeed a boundary violation issue. Had we known he would arrive late, we might have been able to avoid the problem, but once he entered, however, all we could do was to confront the issue and deal with it through role modeling, conflict resolution and retrieving projections.

Men and Power

Women have served all these centuries as looking-glasses possessing the magic and delicious power of reflecting the figure of man at twice its natural size.

—Virginia Woolf (1882-1941)

Robin Givens, the ex-Mrs. Mike Tyson, poignantly relates in *Details* magazine that the trouble with men is their concern with power. "Look at Wilt Chamberlain. He says that he slept with 20,000 women and everyone thinks that it is funny. If a woman had done that . . . I mean, why didn't someone just say to him, 'you're a disgusting pig'? And there are men who say they were only giving women what they wanted, that women are conspirators hanging around hotel lobbies waiting to trap men—excuse me, six-foot nine, 280-pound man, maybe you have some responsibility in this."

In a recent column, journalist Ellen Goodman wrote: "The Patriarch of the Year Award goes to the real thing. Cecil Jacobson, a fertility doctor who meant it when he told one patient, 'God doesn't give you babies—I do.' He artificially inseminated at least 50 women patients with his own sperm. To Jacobson, convicted of fraud, we send the traditional cigar. The exploding kind."

For too long, a man's sense of power has been attached to his penis and his pocketbook. The bigger they are, the more powerful men feel. These external symbols of self-worth are really a coverup for shame. A man's need to be "worth more" is quite often because he feels worthless.

Power is a cover-up for feeling powerless. The more things that a man can accrue, the more he can prove his worth. The more he can "lord it over," the more powerful he feels. Unfortunately one never really knows the power of power until it's too late.

In 17 years of private practice I've observed that many of the most financially successful men, particularly those involved in the corporate hierarchy, seem to have many of the same psychologically induced manifestations in both their minds and bodies—that being panic attacks and "the incredible shrinking penis" syndrome. In some cases, a few of these men have reported that they actually felt like their penises were being sucked up into their lower intestines.

In exploring these feelings I discovered they were metaphors for how the men felt about their lives. Quite often the panic attacks were centered on a fear of flying, which they identified as a fear of "going up too high too fast" in their career or business. The feeling pertaining to their penis shrinking or disappearing, metaphorically described their impending sense of impotence, mutilation and even castration in their corporate or professional careers. I also discovered that the more sensitive and defended the men were, the more somatic they became. These men tended to be more neurotic and assumed personal responsibility for everything. The men who had anti-social personality character disorders had little or no reaction. They blamed everyone for any misfortune. They seemed to have arteries of steel.

Perhaps what best illustrates this concept is the O.J. Simpson tragedy. On Friday, June 17, 1994, everyone in Los Angeles and the rest of America froze in their tracks to watch "the chase of the century." Football's greatest runner conceivably ran his last mile while his fans and the entire nation watched.

One of America's most loved and respected athletes had a dark side and the media gave us the opportunity to get a glimpse of our own as we stayed glued to the television that Friday night waiting to see if O.J. would commit suicide. And if for some reason we denied our own shadow, we then projected it onto a man who had been unofficially sainted by this country. These projections must be retrieved.

A hero, a great athlete, a tribute to American football, a man with a smile that stole the hearts of both men and women, was also a wife beater, fugitive and possible murderer facing life in prison. Icon or iconoclast? Can one man be both? The answer is yes.

Each of us is capable of being both. Nixon, who was castigated as a thief, megalomaniac, and except for Andrew Johnson, the only president ever to be considered for impeachment, died a political hero, revered and exalted for his foreign policy genius. John F. Kennedy, one of America's favorite presidents, was also apparently a sex addict. While Cuban missiles sat 90 miles offshore, ready for deployment at any moment, our beloved president was smuggled out of the White House wrapped in a carpet to go get laid.

The trouble with me, and perhaps many women, is that we give our power away as if we never owned it. Even this evening, while reading this chapter to my husband, he corrected my spelling on the word, "poignantly," which I had actually spelled correctly. It looked right to me, but if he said it, it must be true. I automatically assumed that he knew more than me. Without hesitation, I deleted it and spelled it his way, with the g following the n. It looked wrong, but it must be right, I thought. As he was proving it to me by rummaging through the New Webster's Dictionary, he accidentally leaned on the computer and erased 12 pages of text which could not be retrieved. Besides, he was wrong. So, even as I am writing a book on the metamorphosis of women, I still get suckered into the old belief that men are smarter and wiser.

I don't know if these are the injunctions of the fathers, or modeling of the little girls on their powerless mothers many of us grow up with . . . that awe of the men. I observe in therapy everyday, that despite all the empowerment of the women's movement it is still so hard for women to feel themselves as equals of men. Logically, the point of independence has been made, but at the emotional level we have that need to be sanctified by a man. I many times define it as the "father wound," which pathologically expresses itself in the form of a compulsive need to please and win the father.

I lost my power one time to a person of power—religious power. It was not a relationship. It was a state of daze. I was not a child. I was 27 years old, and the mother of three. I had seen him since my youth. I had heard the stories of his piety and religious knowledge from my parents and members of his congregation. As a teenager, I had so many times heard him deliver his sermon from the pulpit, as if it were being delivered as the Sermon on the Mount. It was sometimes difficult for me to make the distinction between God and this messenger of God. I had seen thousands shake his hand with reverence. And then one day he put his hands on my shoulder and I could not pull them off. He put his lips on my lips and I could not push him away. I had regressed to the age and strength of a little girl. It was like the incest of a girl by her father who creeps into her bed with authority, and absolves the relationship of all sinfulness through his sublimity and power. I felt I had been incested by a spiritual father.

Nervous and shaken by his unexpected behavior, I froze. My mind raced with contradicting thoughts and overloaded on double messages. Raised to believe that men of the cloth were incapable of such illicit behavior, it was inconceivable that this could be happening. It must have been my fault. He could not be culpable. So I took on the blame, even after he came to my home uninvited and unexpected, carrying religious books under his arm on a rainy afternoon. He had known Jack was hospitalized. I had told him that afternoon when I met him at a wedding he was officiating just a few days before.

I was seduced by his aura of holiness. It was so difficult to say no. His power and the many years dividing us made me feel powerless, like a little girl falling helpless into the arms of a holy man. It was an act of submission to divinity.

Jeopardizing his professional responsibility, personal life and reputation, using his power and position for his own needs and getting away with it, is illustrative of man as power seeker. God only knows how many other women in or out of his congregation and other congregations have been seduced by this power disguised as a man of God.

I can't absolve myself of the responsibility because in the end, all our behaviors are our acts. Everyday I help women take back their inalienable right of respect and dignity, but I know that it takes a lot of effort to throw out those multi-generational, almost archetypal, demons of submissiveness and loss of power.

When I decided to divorce Jack, terrified of what the future would hold for me and my five children, I went to my parents for emotional support and understanding. What I got instead was shame.

"You are making the biggest mistake of your life!" my father shouted, as the veins in his neck turned into ropes. "You are going to live to regret this for the rest of your life. You're nothing without him!"

My mother added, "Any father is better than no father. If you want a divorce, at least wait until Aaron (who was then two-and-a-half) grows up."

This conversation ended in nine months of self-imposed silence between my patents and me. When I needed my parents the most,

I was instead shamed the most. I had sabotaged their dreams. I had discarded their illusions. My needs for personal happiness didn't equate with theirs.

This familial behavior, coupled with social conditioning, religious bias and cultural influence allowed this to brew to contentious levels. Even today as I write this story, there is a weak voice inside me that says, "Be careful. This is too dangerous to write about, don't rock the boat."

I, too, have been responsible for not taking a stand. Instead, I have protected the powerful for fear of betraying the poisonous pedagogy, which has been my legacy. This semi-conscious fear was the mortar which held me hostage to my own limitations and fostered my dependency. It kept me a prisoner to my belief system, feelings and behaviors. Empowerment and self-actualization seemed a million miles away.

The victimization and exploitation of women perpetrated by the violence and domination of men became the cannon fodder for feminism and radicalism. Not unlike the reaction to any oppression or persecution, whether it be toward gender, race, religion or country, a revolution is inevitable. History tells us so. Once a level of conscious awareness occurs and someone cries out for justice and equality, the momentum begins. The passion resonates in the hearts and minds of other kindred spirits, some of whom may not yet have clarity nor understanding, or even feel the implications of suppression. Don't forget. It's in our DNA. Women are the agents of nurturing, set up in society to become the caretakers, the givers and the mediators. It's hard to change the blueprint.

Until today, I don't define myself as a "feminist." I don't relate to the sound of the word. It has always characterized an oppositional stance against men. And I love men. That's part of my problem. If anything, I relate more to the definition of a femme fatale. I do, however, espouse the theory that defines "feminism" as political, economic and social equality of the sexes.

Radicalism and/or supremism is just the pendulum swinging too far to the left—which is common when a revolution occurs. The system needs to test its power before it can stabilize. Polarities are existential. They are part of the human condition.

Recently, I was asked to speak to a gay women's group who take the "men" out of "women" on their official stationary, so it is spelled womyn. Never having seen that done before, I was afraid of what the evening would hold for me. Unaware of my apprehension, I found myself dressed up like a life-sized Barbie doll, wearing a silk dress with four slits up the thigh and a neckline down to the solar plexus. Talk about a reaction formation. I invited one of my therapists, Laura, who happens to be a lesbian, to accompany me. I was terrified and felt I needed support. As we left the car to go inside, I asked Laura if she thought they might think I'm a lesbian.

"Not after they see you in that dress!" she said.

The first member to greet me was wearing a black tee shirt that said FEMINIST, TERRORIST, WARRIOR. Most of the 16 women attending had been sexually abused by a man sometime in their childhood or adolescence. Their histories with men in their life had been appalling. It was evident that they couldn't and wouldn't ever trust a man again. To me, their radicalism and supremism/elitism was just another form of fanaticism. This is what scared me. Not their sexual preference, but the obvious expulsion of their feminine side. These women disowned their genetic essence. As a balancing act, I overcompensated by carrying it for them. In looking back, that's probably why they invited me to speak. I mirrored what they needed to see.

Keen postulates a startling idea that "until women are willing to weep for and accept equal responsibility for the systematic violence done to the male body and spirit by the war system, it is not likely that men will lose enough of their guilt and regain enough of their sensitivity to weep and accept responsibility for women who are raped and made to suffer the indignity of economic inequality."

I wholeheartedly agree that society has expected men to be warriors. But which came first? The chicken or the egg? Is it possible that the warrior instinct in men created a society that fostered this behavior? When didn't women protest the war system? When didn't they weep for their fathers, friends, husbands, sons, grandsons and brothers? And since when have they been perpetrators for systematic violence upon the male body? Women have been wanting to share and take responsibility for human rights and equality since time began. Women are now and have been willing to fight in wars they've never been responsible for causing. They were just never allowed to.

What women in history can be equated with the tyrannical rule of Hitler, Mussolini, Stalin or Saddam Hussein? What injustices and atrocities to human rights have been matched by women leaders? That women have exalted, sexualized and worshipped men in uniform is true. And that war heroes have affirmed and perpetuated the myth of "saving damsels in distress" is true also.

In what way can women take equal responsibility and weep more for men and mankind? If apologizing to men for not taking that responsibility, or weeping for the violence perpetrated upon them by the war system would alleviate their guilt and engender more sensitivity toward women, then let me be the first to apologize. If this is what it takes, then so be it.

Battered Women

It costs me a lot, but there's one thing that I've got. It's my man.

—M. Yvain

In her book, *The War Against Women*, Marilyn French claims that women are mistreated worldwide and that this is a war against women perpetrated by men:

- In Quito, Ecuador, 80 percent of all women report having been beaten.
- Statistics presented at the United Nations Conference on Women in 1980 show that women do two-thirds to three-fourths of the world's work, produce 45 percent of the world's food, but have only 10 percent of the world's income and 1 percent of the world's property.
- Women often are denied historical recognition. Poland's Solidarity Movement for example, was begun not by Lech Walesa, but by two female workers.
- An estimated 100 million females have been killed in the developing world, either by neglect or violence, and 20 million have been genitally mutilated.
- In the United States, women are still paid less than men and are not equally represented in our political system.

"The climate of violence against women harms all women. To be female is to walk the world in fear," French writes, adding that "men seem unable to feel equal to women. They must be superior or they are inferior."

No fundamental change will occur, she says, until men are forced to admit that sexual violence is their problem. We already know that one out of every four women are sexually violated by the time they are 13, and 80 percent of them know their offenders.

As Sandy Hill, a deputy features editor of the *Charlotte Observer* says, "If only half of what she writes is true, it is a damning indictment of all of us."

Author, Alice Walker writes, "I feel safe with women. No woman has ever beaten me up. No woman has ever made me afraid on the street. I think that the culture that women put out into the world is safer for everyone. They don't put out the guns, they don't encourage the shooting. If you value your life, whether you're a man or woman, if you had a choice, you would choose the culture that lets you live rather than the culture that is killing you."

Roughly 2,500 women die each year in this country at the hands of their romantic partners. A few days after O.J. Simpson was arrested, the *Miami Herald* published the following statistics compiled in 1993 by the National Clearinghouse for the Defense of Battered Women:

- Nearly 30 percent of women murdered in the United States die at the hands of a husband or boyfriend, and a woman is beaten every 15 seconds.
- The American Medical Association estimates that four million women a year are victims of severe assaults by boyfriends and husbands, and about one in four women is likely to be abused by a partner in her lifetime.
- An estimated 35 percent of women who visit hospital emergency rooms are there for symptoms of ongoing abuse.
- About 75 percent of calls to law enforcement over domestic violence matters occur after the couple has separated.

In 1993, 234 murders in Florida were the result of domestic violence. There were 1,636 rapes and more than 100,000 assaults, according to Florida Department of Law Enforcement figures.

Thankfully, never having been raped, physically beaten, genitally mutilated or passed over in lieu of a man, I cannot speak from any personal experience with regard to male dominance, aggression or violence. However, having been witness to nearly 16 years of hearing horror stories about such abuse, I can readily appreciate the collective fear and rage women are carrying.

My personal history of abuse by males has been limited to what we have come to know as emotional abuse. What I endured was not even definable nor recognizable at the time. It took four marriages, three divorces, five children, eight years of psychotherapy and the women's movement for me to be able to view my history with men as emotional abuse. It is easy to recognize a black eye, torn undies, burns, bruises and lacerations as acts of violence. My scars were hidden, minimized by this culture that had grown to accept female subjugation as normal.

Battered women produce battered children who become either the next generation of battered men and women or their offenders. Each generation begets the next, each with greater damage than the one before.

Then we wonder how an O.J. Simpson story can happen. I am sure by the time this book is published, we will have heard that O.J. was a product of abuse, compounded by the projections that our society placed upon him. What concerns me is that unless we retrieve these projections, we reinforce their power, giving them permission to do whatever they will. They begin to believe they are omnipotent. The tragedy of these projections is that these athletes are rewarded with astronomical salaries and the teachers who mold the minds of athletes, scientists, artists and all of the world's future leaders, are economically deprived. Something's rotten in the U.S.

In her book *Waverly Place*, Susan Brownmiller exquisitely illustrates the portrait of a battered woman using the Joel Steinberg/Nedda Nussbaum case which tragically resulted in the murder of their six-year-old child, Lisa Steinberg. Although fictionalized, she captures the torment, torture and perrenial tragedies so often endured by women. What's the answer? I'm not sure. But one thing is for sure. Without a sense of self, there's no hope. For the women and children who lost their lives through violence and abuse, your voices from heaven can be heard.

Fathers and Daughters

How sad that man would base an entire civilization on the principle of paternity, upon legal ownership and presumed responsibility for children, and then never really get to know their sons and daughters very well.

—Phyllis Chesler

In his book, *Fire in the Belly,* Sam Keen exquisitely cites the struggle of the resolution of the oedipal stage of development; that stage which Freud postulated was the most crucial for sexual identity, that part of child development when little boys take leave of their mothers to identify with their fathers, and when little girls, never having to leave their mothers, want their daddy's love to ostensibly validate their identity and self-esteem. Not an easy task for any child. Not unlike any other stage of child development, this one too depends largely on family, culture and societal influences. In families where moms and dads have not yet completed their maturation process, the children suffer the consequences of their parent's unmet needs, often becoming surrogate spouses for each parent and in many cases, the parent of the parent. The parent's needs often supersede the needs of the child. This adaptation fuels the fire for co-dependency.

Cultural and social backdrops can also complicate matters. The Industrial Revolution resulted in either the emotional and/or physical abandonment of "father" in the family system, leaving both sexes paternally deprived and virtually fatherless. The loss of, and the wounding from fathers has caused interminable abandonment issues for both sexes.

The great dilemmas and ambivalence experienced by boys with regard to their mothers are not unlike the struggle girls experience with their fathers.

Daughters grow up needing their father's love, attention and approval. All children need to feel they matter. One of the ways in which girls learn to matter is how their fathers respond to them. Without this validation, girls may never develop a truly actualized self. They're forever looking for love in all the wrong places. This does not mean that without fathers girls don't stand a chance to actualize. It means that as long as a father is physically present and emotionally absent, the personal growth and development of girls will likely be affected. Keep in mind, this is a generalization and not an absolute. I have known women who grew up abandoned by their fathers who maintain a self-loving image.

The opposite of father abandonment is enmeshment. This can happen with either parent. Fathers who have forsaken or lost their wives can often unwittingly use their daughters in the service of their own ego to alleviate their abandonment issues. A father out of touch with his own feelings or powerless to affect change in his relationship often takes his daughter to become his "unlawful wedded wife." This cross-generational bonding can be manifested both in overt or covert emotional, physical and sexual abuse. In any case, boundaries are obliterated, causing serious wounding and even permanent scars. Even in the most seemingly innocuous cases, where enmeshment is disguised by love, generosity and protection, it can be self-serving and confusing with serious implications. Fathers, as well as mothers, who live out their unrealized lives through their children quite often manipulate them to become what was either unattainable or lost in their own life. When a father makes his daughter "Daddy's little girl" he leaves her with unrealistic expectations and a hard act to follow.

When I turned eight, my father took me to Macy's in New York to purchase an accordion. He was a frustrated musician with unfulfilled dreams from his impoverished childhood. Growing up in the early 1900s, the second son of Russian Jews, he and his older brother and two sisters barely had enough to wear or eat. Life meant surviving. Art, music and academic pursuits were unthinkable. Although the desire was there, the means were not. Music was something to dream about. He wanted to be a pianist or physician, but became a hotel clerk instead. Children sometimes inherit their parent's dreams, whether they want them or not.

My own dreams revolved around becoming an actress or a dancer. Growing up in poverty like my father, the movies were my escape. I wanted to dance like Yvonne DeCarlo or Rita Hayworth. By the time I was 13, I could recite everyone's part in "Gone with the Wind." I had seen it at least a dozen times. But according to my father's map for my life, acting wasn't an option. His plans included a chartreuse green, 80-base accordion (80 buttons on the left side of the instrument). So I grew up suppressing my own dream, carrying his strapped to my chest. In spite of my resistance to learning the instrument, the talent was there. By the time I was ten, I was playing "Lady of Spain" (with the bellow shakes) and "Hava Nagelah" for the residents of South Beach. At 16, I was invited to join the musician's union as its youngest member. This thrilled my father. I now realized two of his unfulfilled dreams. The union provided me with "club dates" at some of Miami's most depraved night spots. My father reacted with joy and nachus (the Yiddish word for pride in one's children's accomplishments). He was impressed with my ability to earn $50 plus tips for a four-hour club date. In 1956 he earned $100 for a 60-hour week. He told me that playing the accordion wasn't work. I was simply "practicing and getting paid." Somehow I never saw it that way. My friends were at parties and football games while I was playing songs from the 1930s and getting hit on by drunks.

My father would faithfully attend every club date with the expressed intention of protecting me by sitting toward the back of the lounge so as not to appear conspicuous. He carried my now 120-base, full-size, black Excelsior accordion along with two 1,000-song fake books that contained every imaginable song ever written in the history of music.

"Play 'Melancholy Baby'," a staggering, foul-smelling sweaty drunk would request.

"After my break," I would say.

When I didn't know a request, my father would be prepared to hand me the sheet during my 20-minute break. I would rush off to the toilet stall in the women's bathroom to rehearse and memorize the piece so I could play it as if I knew it all my life. That is how I learned "Melancholy Baby," "It Had To Be You," and at least two dozen more.

I'd be tipped with a ten or twenty dollar bill stuffed down my backless dress. Then I'd stroll over to my father while playing another song and ask him to extract the bill so he could tell me the dollar value as he squealed with excitement.

This, I was to discover 30 years later, was nonphysical sexual abuse. My father unwittingly used me to get his needs met. He didn't mean to hurt me. I'm not blaming him nor do I harbor any hostility toward him. It's simply a fact that I must acknowledge. It's quite true that I profited personally and financially from my musical background. Nevertheless, the message was also clear that I had to please my father. In doing so, I subjugated my will in order to please his. I learned how to say yes when I wanted to say no. My father's happiness was more important than my own. This setup breeds co-dependency and when you perform to the beat of someone else's drum over the years, you learn to abandon yourself.

When I was 13, my parents sent me to the University of Miami summer band camp to learn the flute (another instrument of their choosing). In spite of my disinterest and protests, I managed to receive the award for the camper who made the most progress. Unfortunately, my parents were not present at the closing banquet to see me accept it. They were in Mexico. One year later, they sent me to the same camp. That year I chose to play the field. Boys were far more exciting than the flute. The consequence was no award the year my parents attended the closing banquet.

My father sat still, expecting that I would receive many awards. But alas, I received nothing—not even the booby prize. As the evening progressed I watched his face turn from its normal olive color to a glowing red. His fingers tapped the table. When it was clear that no award was forthcoming, he gave me the silent treat-ment. Much to my misfortune, the banquet was on the evening prior to our annual vacation to Gloversville, New York, my mother's hometown. Ever since we had moved to South Beach we made this horrendously hot car trip yearly.

The trip was traditional. So was the way we packed our 1954 Ford Sedan. The suitcases went into the trunk with the accordion and my music on top toward the back so as not to interfere with unloading each night as we stopped between Miami and New York. Four to six watermelons were lined up on the back seat floor, which my brother and I used as footrests. It was also traditional to pack the night before we left. This evening had been no exception. All sys-tems were ready to go. The car was loaded. We had the AAA Triptik and the family was expecting us . . . except I didn't get an award.

Instead of leaving as scheduled, my father went on a four-day personal protest, punishing everyone by going to bed, getting up only to eat and evacuate. My mother sobbed the whole time. The watermelons began to rot.

So desperate was I that I wrote a letter describing the consequences of my not receiving an award to the camp's musical director, adding that my parents weren't speaking, my father went into bed and silence, and our trip was ruined. Added to this travesty was a probable divorce. I mailed the letter with my mother's encouragement and approval.

As I could have predicted, my father soon returned to his normal behavior, which mind you, was never jovial, but at least tolerable. Our trip was uneventful with the exception of occasional threats to toss either my brother or me out of the car for not behaving properly. In fact, he had actually done this once before when my brother was seven. So we took his threats rather seriously.

When we returned two months later the mailbox was stuffed with so much mail that the letter carrier had to leave the surplus on the floor in the mail hall. Most of the mail had a University of Miami official stamp marked on the upper left corner. Amongst the dozen awards was a letter that read:

> Dear Joan,
> After cleaning out our band camp office, we came across these awards we neglected to present to you at the closing banquet.
> For this oversight, we are truly sorry and hope you will forgive our negligence. We are certain this will make your family very proud of your efforts.
> With sincere apologies,
> Fred McCall, Band Director

I was 14 when this incident occurred. 40 years later, my father's behavior was unchanged. When the colleague I wrote about earlier in the book filed a lawsuit against me as I had suspected and feared he would, I went to my father. I told him about the lawsuit and asked if he could help me with the legal fees. He turned me down.

"Just like you got into this mess, you'll find a way out of it," were his encouraging words. I was in a state of disbelief. I still had the hopes and expectations of a little girl that he would take care of me. This happened every Yom Kippur, the night before the holiest day in the Jewish religion, the day of atonement. He was so angry I had asked for his help, that he refused to come to the traditional breaking of the fast meal the following evening. Once again, he punished everyone, my children, my brother and his wife, my husband and other family members. Once again, 40 years later, he went on a personal protest—this time because I had asked him for money I needed and didn't have. If he had been a poor man, unable to afford the loan, I would never have asked. That he had an abundance and I had no where else to turn, I thought surely he would respond. His belief system is such (and I'm sure it's a carryover from his impoverished childhood and the Great Depression) that he thinks the money will run out before he does. Whenever I needed my father the most, is when I felt the most shame. And here again, I make no judgment. I hold no grudges, ill feeling or hostility. Yes, I am angry with my father for his abandonment in a time of genuine need. However, it was not my father, but his process that once again wounded my spirit. This distinction, although easy to recognize and intellectualize, still has emotional side effects. Sometimes even after years of psychotherapy, it's still so hard to separate the person from the behavior.

My family was one of those that didn't show any of the outward signs of abuse. There was never any alcohol in the house except for Manischewitz wine, which was used only on the high holy days and Passover. With the exception of my mother's weekly mahjongg games, there was never any gambling. My parents never raised a hand to us. Nor was there ever a curse word spoken. My parents were married for 56 years. My home was consistent, secure and loving. And yet it was dysfunctional, giving rise to my compulsivities and idiosyncratic behavior. I married four men and lived with one, all who carried the same traits as my father. Each were different, but in the end, they all had a common denominator: "My way or the highway."

My fourth and present husband, Mervyn, the only benevolent father figure I've had, controls with loving kindness. It was difficult to see at first because it was so well disguised with genuine caring, probably the trait that made me want to marry him. He would be the father I never had. At times, he too, with all his benevolence, kindness and support, is another critical parent.

It's amazing how we keep trying to resolve our source relationships with our mates. What's even more amazing, is that we know how to find them. Even if these traits are not obvious in the beginning of relationships, we can trust that they will emerge and in some way we can claim some responsibility for that. Our need for resolution with our fathers is so strong that sometimes we turn our mates into replicas of our fathers. The filters from our history can sometimes make us see things that might not even be there.

So what's the answer? Finish your business with your father, otherwise you will reenact the same business with the significant men in your life.

My family system, coupled with the society I grew up in, fostered my dependency and helped to create another multigenerational accident. It is also true that the same dysfunctional family was also functional. I received many strengths and assets from the same parents who emotionally abused me.

When we are born we instinctively know the truth about ourselves. We learn how to abandon it by being and doing for others. Again, this was not my parent's fault. They are not to blame. No one is. But we need to know what has happened to break the denial. Breaking the denial will help us get in touch with the repressed or unconscious feelings which can help end the perpetual cycle. Then we are free to make the choices we had from the beginning.

So when I hear folks say, "my parents did the best they could do," I say, "Yes, I know, but they also did many things which caused great pain out of perhaps the best of intentions." As Bradshaw points out, intentions are irrelevant. We need to know what happened to us.

Sex

Tits and Ass and All That Jazz

My time had finally arrived. I was 19, married five hours and anticipating "magic." I bought a white nylon peignoir, similar to the one worn by Vivien Leigh in "Gone With The Wind."

I closed the door to the bathroom in our suite at the Fontainbleau Hotel, stepped out of my white lace wedding dress, and into the sheer nightgown. I left on the lace garter belt, leaving it to Carl's imagination on how to remove it. I looked at myself in the mirror. My make-up was still fresh from the wedding.

"Leave it on," I said to myself. "You'll wash it off after he falls asleep." I slid my arms into the sleeves of my robe, checking my breasts with the palms of my hands to raise them as high as the bust line would allow. How I envied girls with teardrop-shaped breasts. What mine lacked in shape, they made up for in fullness. One more mirror check. Turn to the side, face front, fingers on hair, breath check, another dab of Shalimar and out I went.

My heart was racing with anticipation. I approached our wedding bed. I saw it as a sanctimonious alter with hidden expectations beyond my wildest dreams. I would be taken into a rite of passage that would change my life forever. In the morning I would wear the smile Scarlett wore after Rhett had raptured her the night before.

Carl appeared to be asleep. I had so wanted him to see me in the translucent peignoir. I wanted him to gaze at me lustfully, lift me onto the hallowed alter, ravage my innocence then drift into sleep locked in my arms. I rehearsed it in my mind at least a hundred times.

I let the robe slip from my shoulders and drop to the floor. I gently cleared my throat to signal my presence. No response. I slipped under the sheets gliding next to the man I had married only five hours earlier. He was lying on his left side. I could feel my nipples harden as they brushed against the hairs on his back. I could feel the excitement between my legs and the passion escalate as I reached over to touch his back. I kissed it gently. I waited. A loud snore.

Then it was morning. The sun came through our picture window overlooking the Atlantic Ocean. I watched it come up. I waited all night for something to come up. All that presented itself was the sun. Another snore. A yawn, followed by a sigh.

"What's wrong?" I asked, afraid of the answer.

"Nothing. Why?"

"Nothing?"

"Yeh, nothing. What's your problem?"

"We were married last evening. I anticipated a bit more than I got. I thought you might have had the same expectation. Was it something I said or did?" I asked, assuming responsibility for his behavior.

"I was tired. The wedding and all. I must have fallen asleep. I was exhausted. Let's order breakfast. I'm starving."

I waited 19 years for the biggest disappointment of my life. All that hype. All that fanfare. The morning after and I was still a virgin. What was worse was that I felt unloved, cheated and abandoned. What a way to start a life together.

The rejection I felt that night, my wedding night, and the two years that followed, became the fuel for my sex and love addiction. The seeds were planted by my parents, fertilized by Carl and the soil provided by our compulsive culture. This rejection to my fragile, underdeveloped ego, ignited years of proving myself worthy as a woman. I don't have any recollections of the marriage having been consummated. The only things that stand out in my memory about those two years with Carl were the feelings of being unloved, unworthy and unimportant.

I had always defined myself as a sexpot. I knew I had it, even when I didn't know what it was. One of my earliest memories of myself was encapsulated in an act of innocent seduction. I was six, saying goodbye to the neighborhood boys on Sheridan Avenue in the Bronx. My family was heading to Miami Beach. It was 1945. As the car pulled away from the sidewalk curb, I remember blowing kisses in all four directions. At eight, I would delight myself by dressing up like a gypsy. Wearing my mother's black taffeta skirt and white peasant blouse, I would sense that when I pulled the blouse down off my shoulders, it revealed prominent shoulder bones which heightened my sexuality. I remember the local male merchants telling my mother to "Watch out. She's going to be something when she grows up." This puffed me up, reinforcing my already early prepubescent sex appeal. At 13, I memorized the lines to "Ruby Gentry." I became the local teenage Jennifer Jones, pretending to be in the arms of Charlton Heston. There were no wet dreams, but the feelings were there. My body responded like a bass drum to my fantasies of making love to Charlton Heston. My classmates called me "Ruby." Boys would flirt, whistle, be playful, stare and pass anonymous love notes. During high school I was voted the girl who most wanted to be photographed. I was everyone's wish when we played post office and spin the bottle. I would substitute the names of my boyfriends in songs, sneak into empty apartments in our apartment building to neck and pet, but never did I once consider "going all the way." Girls were expected to be virgins until marriage. Elvis fantasies could take us only so far.

My childhood dream was to become the high school homecoming queen; a dream highly unlikely for a girl from South Beach. The competition made it virtually impossible. I had to compete against better grades, school service club participation, popularity and the richest girls in town, some of whom even had nose jobs. My curriculum vitae included a B-minus average, Future Teachers of America and the Miami Beach High School Marching Band. I was a long shot; even if I looked like Gina Lollabrigida and acted like Jennifer Jones.

When I learned that I made it to the finals, I knew I had to push into fifth gear. I was one of 16 finalists to be presented to the student body before the final vote. I calculated that I needed the junior high vote. I knew the senior high vote would be split among the other 15 finalists, as they were all from the same clique. My hope was to secure the seventh and eighth grade vote.

We were all to be dressed in white prim, Bryn Mawr dresses, accentuating our innocence and minimizing any glamour. We were told to walk gracefully across the auditorium stage as we were presented individually to the student body, then, step back in our place in line. I covered my plunging neckline with a jacket to hide my large breasts which jutted out above the corset that pinched my already small waist to a mere 22 inches. The two or three horsehair crinolines under my dress suggested a fuller hip line than I really had, giving me a perfect hourglass figure. Somehow I managed to disappear and not alert the dean of girls, who in a heartbeat would have removed me from the line-up. As my name was called, I dropped the jacket, and sauntered across the stage like Jezebel. The response was electrifying. Every pimple-faced 13 and 14-year-old male jumped off his seat, whistling or howling for what seemed to be at least five minutes. Dean Tarror whisked me offstage waving a critical finger at me, but it was too late. The die was cast and a few days later they announced the two runners-up and the winner over the public address system. Delores had become the Homecoming Princess.

Getting Laid and Being Afraid

Men do not think of sons and daughters, when they fall in love.

—Elizabeth Barrett Browning (1806-1861)

Sex, career and motherhood, the triad of female initiation rites, form the pillars of female identity.

Glance through a collection of erotica and pornography from various countries and periods, and you will be looking at assorted sizes and shapes of breasts. Breast after breast, rising triumphantly. Pink nipples, brown nipples, small nipples, large nipples, pointed, rounded, soft, hard, real or artificial. Each, for at least ten thousand years, waiting to be caressed, fondled, nibbled, sucked and kissed. And let's not forget the buttocks, that over or underdeveloped, rounded or flat, high or low fleshy bulge. That part of the female anatomy sometimes referred to as butt, bottom, or tush, so often used to identify a woman as "a great piece of ass."

Why the emphasis on size? Why this continual worship of tits and ass? As Sam Keen so eloquently puts it, "men are horny to the core," and in addition to celebrating the phallus in its proud stance, these female anatomical parts help create that stance. Therefore, why not celebrate both?

Girls in the 1950s who got laid were called tramps by the girls who didn't, and easy lays by the boys who did. Getting laid was no bargain. It got you a "reputation," which could never be rescinded. For most girls, getting laid meant getting married first. The few that did it before marriage risked pregnancy, abandonment and a bad reputation. These consequences kept most of us in check, and the few that tasted of the forbidden fruit were not envied by those who didn't.

Social values, coupled with parental gobble-dee-gook, forced us to repress our sexuality, forfeiting our needs until we said, "I do." "Sex is dirty. Sex is bad. Only bad girls have sex before marriage. Only have sex with your husband." It's no wonder why most marriages have a disorder of desire. Sex was used many times by women as the secondary gain in securing a marriage proposal.

I remember that three months after my divorce from Carl, I had met Jack. Within hours of meeting me he wanted to take me to bed.

Even though I was delirious with sexual desire after my unconsummated marriage to Carl, I stalled Jack until he told me he loved me. It didn't take him long to realize all he had to do was say those magic words and bingo, I would submit. Somehow, "I love you" gave him license to have sex with me. In my view, getting laid meant getting married, so now Jack had to submit to marriage. The power of sex, or lack of it, drove us into a marriage neither of us were ready for.

In 1957 I was a freshman at the University of Alabama. I had been invited to spend the Thanksgiving holidays with my roommate, Harriet Goldstein, who lived in Memphis. She had also invited another roommate, Judy Gross, whom I had known since age 13. Judy and I had been confirmed together. Unable to afford returning to Miami for both Thanksgiving and the Christmas holidays, I accepted her invitation. I had just turned 18 years old.

We boarded a small twin-engine plane in Birmingham. This was my first flight. The plane encountered heavy turbulence and it felt like we were suspended from a large rubber band in the sky. Most of the passengers were either screaming or throwing up. I remember enjoying it.

Harriet had arranged a date for each of us to attend her temple's annual Thanksgiving Day dance. Judy and I were to meet our dates at the synagogue. My date was David, the son of a pharmacist who lived in Memphis. We arrived looking like we were from another planet. Dressed in several horse hair crinolines puffing out our low-cut organza dresses, we made our entrance. Stylish and theatrically made up, wearing white fox capes around our bare shoulders, we walked in like two Hollywood starlets. Memphis had never seen the likes of us before, especially in a synagogue. The room fell silent. The other young women stared, some with their mouths agape. The young men were speechless. We had definitely made an impression. But at the time, we didn't realize what kind or just how much.

Two young men, a little older than me, approached us. They introduced themselves.

"Hello. I'm Alan Fordyce, and this is George Klein. We couldn't help notice you both when you came into the room. Are you here alone?" Alan asked in a slow Southern manner.

"No. We have dates that have been prearranged," I replied.

"What about after the dance? Can we see you then?" Alan asked.

Judy and I looked at each other nodding our heads. "Yes. We'd love to meet you. It will have to be later, as we both have commitments," I eagerly responded.

"Can you break your dates?"

"No. I don't think that would be fair to our friend. She made the arrangements and we wouldn't want to get her in trouble. But we'll cut it short," I said.

"What time?" he asked.

"Midnight. Meet us at midnight. Come to Harriet's house after midnight. We should be back by then."

They agreed and wrote down Harriet's address. "Twelve midnight. See ya' then," they said in unison and slipped away. Later that evening, I had the task of getting ill so I could justify terminating my date early. My date was so conscientious, that he insisted on taking me to his father's drugstore for some stomachache concoction his father made up. I moaned and groaned before and after swallowing the stuff. I begged off and told him how sorry I was for having to end the evening early. He was so sympathetic. I felt sorry for him. Nevertheless, Alan and George held my interest much more than David.

It was 11:50 by the time David and Judy's date, Jerry, took us home. We jumped out of our party dresses. I threw on a pair of bright red corduroy pedal pushers and a black turtle neck jersey. I slipped my feet into my black Pappagallo flats, brushed out my long hair, applied more red lipstick and dabbed my cheeks with the same. The horn honked just as I dotted my cheeks.

"We'll be right down," Judy shouted from the upstairs bedroom window where we were dressing. We dashed down the stairs, and jumped into the car with the two strangers.

We drove around for what seemed to be over a half an hour.

"Where are we going?" I finally asked.

"You'll see. We'll be there soon enough."

George was a disc jockey on a local radio station. His trademark was that he spoke in rhyme. Everything he said to us was also in rhyme. At first it was cute, but then it became obnoxious. Alan told us that he had a construction company. That his father, in fact, owned the largest construction company in Memphis.

More time passed.

"Where are we going?" I demanded, this time with a tone that was not to be misunderstood.

"We'll be there soon, and then you'll know," he said in a whimsical way.

Judy and I were in the back seat of a 1957 Pontiac. We looked at each other. She took my hand, indicating she was frightened. I was too. Almost an hour had passed since we left Harriet's house, and neither of us knew where we were, where we were going, or who our two escorts were. Had this happened today, we would have assumed we were goners. But in 1957 all we had was our naivete and curiosity.

We finally arrived at an entrance to something. It was bordered by enormous wrought iron gates decorated with musical notes and instruments.

"Do you know where you are now?" asked Alan.

"No. Where are we?" I asked.

"You'll see."

Alan blinked his headlights on and off a few times. The gate opened. He drove in. We drove for at least another quarter of a mile until we arrived at a huge building, adorned with two stone lions and blue and green lights illuminating the pillars decorating the front entrance. There was a 1957 Cadillac limousine parked in the front.

"Do you know where you are now?" Alan and George asked almost simultaneously.

"The library?" I responded. I had never seen anything quite like it before.

We got out of the car and Alan and George opened the door to the limousine. The floor was covered in a lush royal blue carpet with the letters "EP" woven deep into the pile.

"Now? Now do you know?" they asked again.

Judy and I looked at each other, each puzzled as to our whereabouts. We had no clue.

The guys escorted us up the steps to a massive wooden double door. Alan rang the bell and a few moments later a large, obese man answered.

"Hello Lamar," Alan said. "These are the two girls I told you about. Judy and Joni. The ones from Miami Beach."

"Hi. Come in," he replied.

Then, he appeared, dressed in white ducks and a white tennis sweater bordered with a red and blue braided trim. Judy recognized him first. She squeezed my hand so hard, that she dug her nail into me, leaving me with a small scar until today.

"Come on in," he said with a smile that sent us swooning and nearly into a dead faint. "Is this really happening?" I asked myself. "Could this be real? How could this be?"

Alan and George were close friends of Elvis. They had been at the dance keeping an eye out for girls Elvis might like.

Elvis showed us through Graceland. He introduced us to his mother. There was a crucifix in every room, teddy bears throughout the kitchen and gold records wallpapered one of the recreation rooms in the finished basement. He took us upstairs to show us his bedroom. It was a royal blue and white showplace. His bed seemed large enough for at least five people. His bedspread was royal blue with his initials embroidered in white. He showed us his closets. There was one for show clothes and another for everyday wear. There, hanging in his show closet, was a gold lamé dress suit. I had seen it before on a poster. I was now in a state of near delirium.

Elvis played some of his recordings. He played his guitar and sang to us as I sat frozen to the sofa in a state of disbelief and mystification. I wanted to capture this moment in time, bottle it and replay it again and again, just like I played Elvis' records. We watched him and his friends shoot pool and play darts, and before we turned around, night became day. I felt I had made history. I would never—could never—be the same again. It felt as though this experience had an element of divine intervention. I can still feel it on my pulse. It was an epiphany!

It was morning before Judy and I reached Harriet's house. We slipped in so no one saw us and fell into a deep sleep. When we awoke neither of us could believe that it really happened. The phone rang. It was Lamar and he asked for me.

"Elvis wants to see you this evening," he said.

Nearly collapsing from joy, in a fearless bravado I responded, "Well, if Elvis wants to see me tonight, then have him call me."

Judy couldn't believe my response.

Five minutes later, he called.

We went back to Graceland. Elvis played his hit records, his guitar and served us Cokes and ice cream. We played pool, joked around and soon forgot we were with him, until he got down on his knees in front of me and sang "Till," interrupting the song with an occasional moist, light kiss in my ear. If one could fall off the planet, I would have.

I thought I was going to have a stroke. Imagine me, Joni Gilbert, being kissed by Elvis in his basement music room. Not long ago, I watched Elvis on the Ed Sullivan Show and screamed my head off. If anyone had told me then I would be with him now, getting kissed in the ear, I would never have believed it. I felt special and proud. Every girl in the country would have given her soul to have been there and there I was, in Graceland, with him! Overwhelmed, I shared the story with my mother in a 14-page letter, which I asked her to share with my best girlfriend, Marsha Horowitz, who was still a senior in high school. This letter, as one might imagine, received schoolwide attention, so that when I came home from college that Christmas I was an instant celebrity. My telephone didn't stop ringing and I was bombarded with endless questions and enthusiastic greetings from nearly every high school student in Miami Beach.

More exciting was that Elvis asked me to join him in New Orleans, where he was filming "King Creole." The invitation arrived in the form of a letter to the University of Alabama student union post office. The letterhead and envelope was decorated with various portraits of him. This nearly caused pandemonium in the student union. This evidence quieted any doubt that I might have been there.

This personal invitation threw me into a tizzy of joy and shock. It transcended becoming the Homecoming Princess.

It never occurred to me not to tell my parents about this once-in-a-lifetime opportunity. It never occurred to me that their response would be to forbid me to go.

"If you go on this ridiculous escapade, I will withdraw you from school, and cut off any further support for your education. Forget this preposterous idea, or you'll pay for this mistake forever!" I will never forget or forgive my father's response.

My parents, fearing I would lose my mind and my virginity, forced me to relinquish my ultimate fantasy. Imagine giving up a weekend with Elvis to maintain your virginity. But, alas, I did, and I've regretted it ever since. My sexless wedding night with Carl would be my next opportunity with a man—some consolation prize!

A year or so later, I received a letter from Elvis telling me that he would be doing a benefit with Sammy Davis, Jr. at the Fontainbleu Hotel in Miami Beach. He invited me to be his guest. By this time I had married Carl. I was tortured. Should I go? How would it appear? I'm married. I agonized over my response. Judy agonized with me. "You're married now, Joni. Do you think it would be right?"

The power of parental injunctions and conservatism had won. I didn't go. My second shot at Elvis, and I let it go.

In *Fire In The Belly* Sam Keen confessed that never once as a "budding man did you hear another man boast about the long, slow pleasure he experienced in sex, or speak of the beauty of the changing hues of a woman's eyes, of the sweet contentment of lying with a woman after love." As a woman, I can gratefully cherish lingering hours, and perhaps days, after the loving, mentally drawing upon the soulful content which permeated afterward. Often my heart and skin tingled with nearly the same magic that poured between my legs hours or days before. Just accessing mental pictures of that moment could kinesthetically resurrect the feeling of being there again. Being a woman certainly does have its rewards. Lingering pleasure is one.

That men think of women as paradise regained is not unique to men. Women often think that men are too. We have been conditioned to "Stand by Your Man," love, honor and obey, recreate, procreate, copulate and subjugate. So that without knowing why, women gradually come to resent men too. Both sexes become disappointed and disillusioned with each other, each thinking that perhaps there is another out there that can better meet their needs. And, perhaps sometimes there is, but not until we know ourselves intimately. Each gender sets up the other to be the savior who is supposed to make us whole and reconnect us to our severed feelings. Men don't corner the market on this projection. It belongs to us all as a product of our dysfunctional families, culture and human nature.

The sexual wounds I incurred were four marriages and a live-in boyfriend, each relationship designed to replace the previous one that had been unable to fulfill my fantasies and give me what I thought I deserved. Imagine expecting a man to stand and deliver. Four marriages in a lifetime is no disgrace. It's the expectations that are unrealistic which reinforce the fantasy that men are the saviors that then lead to resentment.

And if the penis is the straight and narrow pathway to paradise, imagine what the vagina can do! The fact is that neither of our pleasure organs can ever make us whole and reconnect us to our severed feelings. It is the soul that has the magic potion which can bring us to ourselves as whole and spiritual beings.

As women may be the promise of paradise for men, let it be known that men are often the promise of paradise for women. And not unlike men who receive their sense of self in the reflection they see in the eyes of women, it is also true that women wait for those same responses in the eyes of men. It's the blind leading the blind.

Thinking for so long that it was the penis and vagina that would bring us back to Eden, I cultivated Delores, my shadow, like a prized package. Only, I pretended not to even know her. Believing that my vagina was my passport to happiness, I kept her in the basement of my soul, unlocking the exitway only when I needed another conquest. I learned very early in life what mattered and how to win. I would bring her out when she served my purpose. But because I disowned her and used her only for my own aggrandizement, she turned against me. She haunted me when I was most vulnerable. Her choices were poor, but her influence was powerful. Her consequences destructive, I needed to befriend her, embrace her, make her part of me so she would never have to go underground and deceive me again. This was the part I had severed. The part I needed so desperately to reconnect with. But to own her was my shame. I learned that my shame was also the source of my spirituality. To name her was also to accept her. To accept her was to love myself. All of myself. And to love myself was to heal my wounds.

Love

Suzanne takes you down
to her place near the river,
you can hear the boats go by
you can stay the night beside her.
And you know she's half crazy
but that's why you want to be there
and she feeds you tea and oranges
that come all the way from China.
Just when you mean to tell her
that you have no gifts to give her,
she gets you on her wavelength
and she lets the river answer
that you've always been her lover.

—*Leonard Cohen*

It is so hard to attribute any causality to the way we meet other persons in this world. Some of them are good for us and some of them not so good, and some of them may be bad. They move into our lives in so many different ways. It is a bang, a whisper or just total lack of awareness and the clock has gone full cycle. They move in stealthily, almost on tiptoe and even before we become fully cognizant they have become parts of our being, a new set of eyes with which you see the world, a new set of ears to hear the outside world and an openness of our bodies when we unite with someone to feel the world as one. The autonomies of two selves merge to enrich each other and to reinforce the strength of each one.

It is a bond of unity with an unverbalized commitment. And it is perhaps not a commitment as it is characterized by absence of that sense of being constrained. It is like joining in a dance in which one leads the other, the other leads the one and really, nobody leads either. It is a floating through the air and the process is an end in itself. The sharing is at the level of things that are valued and real. The sense of connection is not in physical contiguity, but the contact that transcends the constraints of space. It is the archetypal fulfillment of that extension that has eternal yearnings in our souls, our bodies, our whole being.

It is hard to reflect on such relationships because they defy the objectivity and the limitations of verbal molds. But let me share with you what happened to me once.

And I don't know how I was attracted to him. Was it him or her? Did it really matter? It can be a story of a he or a she, but my preference would be to write it as he.

His name was given to me by a friend, or a friend of a friend. I seem to recall that it was a strange name, or just unfamiliar, or just strange to me; one of those that is hard to pronounce, or has a resonance which is different from the everyday John, Robert, Suzie or Liz. It had the resonance of the exotic and I was curious.

I arrived at his residence and the sense of mystery stayed. There were more questions rather than answers, but it was a gentle curiosity, not characterized by need to uncover someone's privacy but the childlike sense of wonder which just wants to feel, reflect and absorb.

This does not happen in all the relationships we develop. Most emanate from basic needs and their projections into other mother- and father-like figures. They all come disguised as love, the absoluteness of commitment that urges us to marry.

In 1792, Rabbi Mendel shed light on this issue when he said:
"If I am I, because I am I
And you are you, because you are you,
Then I am and you are.
But, if I am I because you are you,
And you are you because I am I,
Then I am not, and you are not."

Perhaps Rabbi Mendel understood the difference between love and co-dependence even before Melodie Beattie.

Susan Campbell once did a study comparing the first four stages of childhood development to four stages of the evolution of a relationship, assuming you make it that far. Most don't—the reason being that the second stage, which corresponds to the "terrible twos" in child development, becomes so stressful that nothing ever gets resolved. So most couples give up and divorce before they ever reach the third stage. She equated the first stage known to us as "falling in love" as the co-dependent stage of the relationship. It's the recapitulation of symbiosis, which is characterized by the collapsing of ego boundaries, heightened sexual intensity and chronic euphoria. It's, "I am you"—everybody's favorite part. Some of us even get addicted to it. The recovery movement has given it a name. It's called "love addiction." It's as powerful as any chemical substance on the market for those with a predisposition to obsession. M. Scott Peck says that "it is a potent misconception, because falling in love is subjectively experienced in a powerful fashion as an experience of love." Most importantly, it's "After the Lovin'" that counts, according to Englebert Humperdinck.

Social psychologist Erik Erikson referred to the first stage of development as "Trust vs. Mistrust." Can I trust that the universe is a safe place? How will I know? My mother will form the very first template. If I can trust her, then I can trust the universe. If I can trust her, then I can also trust myself because I am her too. I have introjected her. Therefore, I can trust you. I can look into your eyes, just as I gazed into my mother's eyes, and I can see me projected in your loving and accepting face. I can go into trance, regress and become a narcissistic infant getting all my needs met again. Now, that's mood altering! It's the development of the first ego strength; that of hope, and the power of being. Freud called it the "oral stage," that primordial stage of energy that he called the "id," ruled by the kingdom of "pain and pleasure," where pleasure always wins over pain. Eric Berne labeled it the "ego state" of the child. Sam Keen describes it as "being swept away, waves of pleasure; softening, streaming; orgasm; egos dissolving; two becoming one; the right chemistry that produces fusion." I like to think of it as the first season of the year, like Vivaldi did, "Spring," budding with romance.

A year or so later, perhaps even sooner, when things are going so well, you decide to move in together, or even worse, get married. The boundaries bounce back and spring turns to summer. Things get hot, but no longer in the sexual arena. That gets cool. The Hatfields meet the McCoys, and you begin to sweat it out. You argue. "We always opened the presents on Christmas Eve." "Well, we opened ours Christmas morning, and never before." This stage, Campbell suggests, is like the second stage of childhood development: Counterdependency. It represents the process of individuation, autonomy and separation. It suggests that the honeymoon is over. It is that stage of development which Erik Erikson described as "Autonomy vs. Shame and Doubt," the beginning of separating from mother (with each other in romantic relationships, and not necessarily unhealthy). It goes from "I am you," to "I am me." If you give me my space, but protect me from hurting myself, I can grow and feel excited about the things I am learning and exploring. But, if you, your fears and your own unfinished business get in the way of my development, and you inadvertently stunt my growth and cause me to become a case of arrested development, I'll become angry and resentful. I'll make you and everyone around me miserable, whichever way it feels most comfortable for me. I'll either become passive aggressive, and withdraw so you can't hurt me, but I can hurt you; or, I'll piss on you directly, so you'll have no doubts about where I am coming from.

It is the stage where holding on and letting go becomes the dynamic. The ego strength is the development of the will, and the power becomes "doing." Freud called it the "anal stage," holding it in until you explode. It's the terrible twos, toilet training and learning how to fight fair. And boy, does this ever get played out in relationships. It usually destroys them. It's the essence of all intimacy: conflict. And intimacy must be able to tolerate conflict. Only most people don't know how to negotiate the differences. They never learned how in their families of origin, therefore they never had any role models. No one has a set of rules to resolve anything. If you get through this stage, which can sometimes take 20 years, you may have it made.

Next comes autumn. Colors change, expectations fall and time bares the differences. Each has his or her own truth. Each stands his or her own ground. Each grows independently of the other. Campbell called this stage "independence," corresponding to the third stage of life. Erikson called it "Initiative vs. Guilt." The ego strength is to develop a sense of purpose, and the power is to develop an identity. "I am a man. I am a woman. We are a couple." Freud called it the "oedipal stage." If I know who I am and become the person I was intended to become, I can love myself. Therefore, I can love you, because I am now capable of extending myself. But if my life became one of adaptation in order to survive, and I never find out who I really am, then I project all my unmet needs and unresolved conflicts onto you and expect you to make me happy.

Therefore, I am not, and you are not. We are two halves trying to become whole. One half multiplied by another half never equals a whole.

Then comes winter, synonymous to the fourth stage of life, known as "interdependence," "I can be we," or what Sam Keen referred to as "the coming together." Erikson referred to this developmental stage as "Industry vs. Inferiority." Its ego strength is to develop a sense of competence, and its power is to acquire the basic survival skills. If I feel inadequate, inferior and defective, then how can I expect you to love me? I am an object of contempt to myself. Therefore, I will project myself upon you. If you don't reject me, I will find ways to make it happen to prove how bad I really am. But, if I have reached my goals, found my authenticity, followed my bliss and plowed the paths for my soulful quest, then what is it without someone to share it with? I love you, but not because I need you; I need you because I love you.

According to Pam Levin, when these developmental strengths and powers are satisfied, our needs get met. Until then, we look to others or things outside ourselves. You cannot fix an internal problem with an external solution. We each must heal our own wounds. The healing of our spiritual wounds stops the emotional hemorrhaging of the insatiable wounded child in us, and allows for giving as well as taking. The sharing and blending of two whole persons "coming together" to enrich each other's life. To give energy, not just take. To extend yourself, for the sake of nurturing your own and another's growth, as described by M. Scott Peck in *The Road Less Traveled.* "Real love," he writes, "is a permanently self-enlarging experience."

The question is, can one go through these stages in one lifetime with one relationship? I don't know. I didn't. I never made it to the last stage with anyone. It took me this long to do the repair work. Four husbands and a live-in boy friend. I'm not blaming my parents, the men in my life or myself. I'm not blaming anyone. I'm happy to have finally understood the obstacles. At this stage of my life, with my level of growth and understanding of human relationships, I can accept love on different terms.

Intimacy and Conflict

In a February 1994 feature story in *Time* magazine, Lance Morrow laments on the badness of men as viewed by women. He takes a serious look at the way men in general have been viewed by women and particularly, feminists, especially those militant feminists who spell women with a *y* instead of an *e*. It might be noted that this particular breed of feminists has good cause for their militancy. Not all, but a good many were physically, emotionally and sexually abused since early childhood. They have inadvertently over-identified with their offenders and have split off, disowning their feminine side as a defense for survival.

They, the enemy, or "Evil Empire," as Morrow sarcastically refers to men, have been under attack to the point of public bludgeoning, including a campaign of books, movies and television shows written by both men and women depicting men as monsters who have no positive place or intention in the universe. Implications were made that generalize men into a category of no-goods, here on earth simply to destroy, harass, intimidate, rape, violate, dominate, murder and psychologically, economically and politically annihilate women.

In her latest novel, *Foxfire: Confessions of a Girl Gang,* Joyce Carol Oates writes, "It's all of them: men. It's a state of undeclared war, them hating us, men hating us no matter our age or who the hell we are . . ."

In addition, Morrow quotes *The Women's Room,* by Marilyn French. "All men are rapists. They rape with their eyes, their laws and their codes." Allan Carlson, president of Rockford Institute, said, "We are at the tail end of the deconstruction of patriarchy, which has been going on since the turn of the century. The last acceptable villain is the prototypical white male . . . I think matriarchies are always a sign of social disintegration. In history there are no examples of sustained, vigorous matriarchal societies."

If this is the stuff which makes the centerfold of *Time,* then what are we saying about the attitude of our culture towards those pathetic, rundown, demoralized, angry, defiant, ruthless, fragile, confused, scapegoated, criticized, misunderstood males? How can we share our lives, our jobs, our country and our planet and make this place a better world to live in? All this pissin' and moanin' about how bad they are, and how bad we are, is just another way to avoid intimacy. Those of you who have found solutions like staying single, divorced, widowed or finding lovers of same and/or opposite sex, perhaps have one way of resolving the conflict. But what about you others? What are you going to do? Fight for the rest of your lives? Go to bed angry and resentful? Or not sleep at all? Use the kids as pawns? Buy more clothes? Find a boyfriend? Work out five times a week? Or get loaded? Spend half your life and money in court? Develop ulcers, colitis, breast cancer? Never learn how to say, "I'm sorry"? We've all been part of the problem. How can we effectively become part of the solution?

There have been so many changes and developments lately in our social, cultural and political infrastructure. Economics and technology have been a "Space Mountain" ride. In looking back at history over the last thousand years, it is easy to conclude that the most significant advances in civilization have been made in this century, and especially since the 1960s. I believe that my lifetime and the lifetimes of my contemporaries thus far has been a microcosm of more than one thousand years. What was once so easy to define as a "truth" has been broken down and built up again so many times that it no longer holds constant. Truth, values, insights, mores, norms and paradigms are in constant motion. Even religious traditions are being challenged. Nothing seems to be forever anymore.

Only one generation ago, all this was not true. My parents roles were defined. Marriage was forever. Men worked. Women for the most part stayed home and raised the children. Arguments were usually settled by one or the other in the marriage dyad. People agreed never to disagree. Compromise was more like an act of submission. One usually gave way to the other. Patterns of behavior were predictable and usually stayed constant. Life may not have been totally fulfilling or self-actualizing, but it was far less confusing.

Today, becoming together brings a whole new gestalt. We know so much more today than we knew even ten years ago. The field of psychology has catapulted itself at least one hundred times over. Freud would go into shock if he returned today. Can you imagine what he could have done had he known what we know today? Each of us brings to a relationship the old and the new patterns. There hasn't been enough time since the 1960s for things to really settle in; for us to examine our new lifestyles. Things are moving at such a rapid pace that what was new only a few years ago is already old. I spent a fortune on my computer four years ago and now it's practically obsolete. My video camera, which looks brand new and cost fifteen hundred dollars only five years ago, embarrasses me now. Compared to what's selling in the stores today it's like an antique.

The goals people bring to a relationship that seem to have been shared and embraced by each other in the beginning of a commitment, can, and often do, change at an independent rate of each person's separate growth. So many of us start out with the same intentions, hopes, dreams and interests, only to find out that what we both thought was important then, has shifted or changed in the course of time. Each of us brings a plethora of attitudes, traditions, behaviors, beliefs, customs, values and rules to our relationships. Each of us has our own histories colored and flavored by different realities.

How do we work out those differences without giving up our own specialness and uniqueness? How do we become together and stay together? How important is staying together? What price are we willing to pay to do so?

Will marriage and family have the same values it had only one generation ago? What are relationships in the 21st century going to look like? I don't have the answers. I don't even know if the answers to these esoteric questions are all that important. If change affects everything as it has, then even the answers are subject to change.

I recently saw "La Belle Epoque," a Spanish film that won the Academy Award for best foreign film. A delightful comedy that takes place in Spain in the late 1930s, it illustrates what may become a paradigm for relationships in the next century. It reflects a couple's total and unconditional acceptance of one another, barren of expectations, with minimal accountability. Is such a thing possible? I really don't know.

In a group that I co-facilitate with Meehar, the subject of friendship with the opposite sex came up for discussion as a result of two group members becoming close and meeting outside of group. One is married, the other is not. She is 59. He is 31. It raised so many issues that the group, which normally runs two hours, was extended another 15 minutes so we could have sufficient time for an appropriate closure.

The group responses to this issue varied from "I could never accept my husband having a friendship with a female and spending any recreational time with anyone other than me," to "It's not an issue for me at all. I can't expect to meet all his needs, nor can I expect him to meet all of mine. Therefore, as long as I can be included on any recreational activities, I have no objection. I do, however, expect him to give me the same consideration. What's good for the goose, is good for the gander." The second statement elicited a response of total disbelief from the first woman. "I can't believe you mean what you say. It doesn't sound real!" The feelings and responses this relationship provoked set off charges from each member which lasted the entire session.

The group is made up of a cross-section of religions and cultures; members reflect their own views regarding protocol for conducting their marriages and intimate relationships. Most members are married. Three are not. One has a part-time live-in boyfriend. One male is single and presently not in a relationship. One female is recently separated.

We had a smorgasbord of opinions, views, responses, projections and expressions, each sharing with their Muslim Pakistani male therapist and me what they thought to be their unequivocal truth.

The questions that arose during this heated discussion included: How close and honest can we really be in our intimate relationships? What are the standards and codes of behavior that will preserve and protect our relationships? How much space do we need? Can relationships outside the marriage with the opposite sex pose a threat to the marriage or relationship? How much are we willing to risk the relationship for autonomy? How much are we willing to risk autonomy for the relationship? How much can you really trust your partner . . . and yourself? How wide or narrow can you set your boundaries without jeopardizing the relationship? How can we get our needs met outside of our relationship that are not being met in the relationship? How much honesty can your partner tolerate?

The answers to these questions are not one-for-all-and-all-for-one. Obviously, each couple defines their own relationship based upon their own belief systems which generate their behaviors. These beliefs and values become the foundation of the relationship. The more aligned you are, the less conflict. That is why there is some wisdom in marrying your own kind, simply because the beliefs and values are usually more compatible.

Whatever and however you feel about the above questions, "happiness" is more likely to occur if you both agree on the design of your relationship. Some nonconventional relationships which seem to work and have maintained high levels of intimacy, joy and friendship are that of Jean Paul Sartre and Simone de Beauvoir, Katharine Hepburn and Spencer Tracy, and Goldie Hawn and Kurt Russell. Each partner in the relationship agreed on the terms which defined the relationship. Who are we to judge what works for others? What doesn't work is when one partner has a different map of the relationship than the other and wants him or her to change. Then you have a power struggle, which inevitably leads to dishonesty, acting out and the demise of the relationship.

Where people seem to get stuck in relationships is around the issue of disclosing their truth for fear of either hurting or angering the other. These anticipatory anxieties are based upon personal histories and serve to reinforce old belief systems. As I said before, intimacy must be able to tolerate conflict. If you can't be honest in your relationship, then you don't have intimacy.

There are certain instances where I believe complete disclosure of one's feelings, thoughts and behaviors can cause considerable and unnecessary damage to your partner. This may sound contradictory, but there are no absolutes. The ninth step in the twelve-step program highlights this concern when it says, "Make direct amends to such people wherever possible, EXCEPT WHEN TO DO SO WOULD INJURE THEM OR OTHERS." It's important to use good judgment and evaluate if the disclosure is more in the interest and service of oneself to absolve guilt or discharge anger, rather than in the interest of the relationship. If you're not sure, it's time to seek a therapist.

Fair Fighting and Resolution

We don't see things the way they are. We see them as we are.

—Anaïs Nin (1903-1977)

Fair fighting skills and effective communication are the way to resolution, but the results you may want are not always guaranteed. Sometimes nothing works. There are certain outcomes in behavior we can predict by using language in a way that sets up responses that lead to productive solutions and raise the level of intimacy between partners. This model of communication is used in group and couple therapy, communication and marital workshops, and organizational developmental seminars for corporations. It is also modeled by me when working with clients who need a healthy and effective way of communicating. The model honors the five freedoms described by Virginia Satir, one of the leading family therapists of our time. She identified certain inalienable freedoms, which include: the freedom to see what one sees (rather than what one should see); the freedom to hear what one hears (rather than what one should hear); the freedom to feel what one feels (rather than what one should feel); the freedom to think what one thinks (rather than what one should think); and the freedom to desire and want what one wants (rather than what one should want or desire).

Use "I" messages. They tend to diffuse defenses. When we use the word "you," "you always," or "you never," we are inviting a fight. "I" messages are self-responsible statements. They avoid judgment of the other person.

Since we each see and hear the world through our own filters, and operate out of our belief systems and values, it is not difficult to understand how our perceptions can become personalized based on our own histories. If shouting at your home was a precursor to someone getting hit, then you would tend to get triggered whenever you heard shouting, anticipating the same results. You would probably have a very negative reaction if someone shouted at you. If, however, shouting was the way your family members learned to get their needs met because everyone talked loud and often, and it was customary in your culture and tradition to shout when speaking, then shouting itself would not trigger that person the same way it might trigger someone else. Triggers tend to set off different responses with different receivers. Each of us has our own map of reality. We each perceive the world from our own map, based upon our own experiences. 99 percent of the time most highly reactive states have nothing to do with the here and now. They are more about one's history.

I believe the key to healthy relationships is communication. Communication is the key to understanding. Understanding means tolerance and support for one another. It helps maintain intimacy. Relationships deteriorate or end unnecessarily when communication breaks down. Of course, it's not the only reason, but healthy communication can often settle issues that would otherwise stay repressed and come at you from behind when you least expect it. Communication maximizes listening skills, strengthens the relationship and most of all, it produces positive results. Besides, it saves wear and tear on the colon.

I recall not too long ago, when my eldest daughter Linda and I were in a heated argument prior to a workshop we were both to facilitate. Driving through the Blue Ridge Mountains toward the cabin, I reminded her of a debt she owed me, including the latest addition, a transportation fee from the airport that I had paid. Under her breath she spewed, "Add that to the list too, Mom. God forbid you should pay for anything!"

Angrily I retorted, "Don't you intend to honor your obligations?"

"You're so cheap!" she said.

"Cheap! How can you even think that? That's the last thing I expected to hear from you. I feel as though you don't appreciate what I do for you!"

Having to take a leave of absence from her job due to her sudden illness, upon her recovery she decided to develop a private practice. Anxious and harboring fears of inadequacy she was not fully in touch with, she used anger to disguise her feelings and directed them outward (naturally toward me).

Worried that we would bring our unresolved conflict into the workshop, I insisted we work through this impasse. She agreed. Four hours later, having walked around a mountain on my property at least 20 times, doing "Post Cards From The Edge," peeling away layer after layer, we finally touched bottom as she began to weep like a frightened child.

"Mom," she cried, "What if I'm not as good as you?"

"Linda!" I replied, "You're only 27 years old for God's sake. I'm 51. When I was 27 I slept until noon everyday. I had three children that never saw my face until they returned from school, and sometimes not even then. I didn't know I had a brain until I was 35. You'll not only be as good, you'll be better!"

After four and a half hours of feuding, but fighting fair, and doing our very best to stay in the now and maintain rigorous honesty, a resolution came.

I thought of my own mother and her inability to work through any mother/daughter conflict. A scene like this would have ended abruptly, without any discussion, except for her saying, "I don't want to talk about it" and resulting in at least three days of the silent treatment.

Most people are terrified of arguments for a simple reason. They never saw any positive results from arguing in their homes, and it brings up unpleasant memories both cognitively and kinesthetically. They agree never to disagree, which is not intimacy. It's avoidance due to fear. Avoid fighting at any cost. Don't rock the boat. Leave well enough alone. It's only going to make matters worse. It's not worth losing sleep over. It's not going to matter anyway. I'm afraid she'll leave me. These are but a few of the rationalizations people have for not fighting, even not fighting fair. They are the injunctions from a childhood that taught them how to adapt in order to survive. By the time you grew up that's all you did—survive. Survival doesn't cut it.

We need tools to know how to run a relationship, like any other system. We learn it for everything else we do in life, except for having a relationship.

After dating Mervyn about three months, he invited me to Los Angeles to his cousin's 60th birthday party. I accepted. Coincidentally, his cousin's 32-year-old son was in Miami, and Mervyn invited him to dinner one evening. Josh and I hit it off so well that sight unseen he invited my daughter Linda, whom he had not even met, to his mother's birthday party in L.A. That evening, we called her in New York, where she lived at the time, and he invited her to attend. They were both excited about the event and looked forward to meeting each other.

Since this was my first social event with Mervyn's family, I wanted to make the right impression. I carefully chose the right clothes, not too flashy or ostentatious. Mervyn's relatives were lovely, and everyone looked alike. Conservative. Very, very conservative. They were transplants from both the Midwest and Philadelphia. Linda and I, even in our most conservative dresses, stood out like sore thumbs.

Unfortunately, Linda and Josh did not hit it off. Bad move. But what do you do when you're three thousand miles from home? To make matters worse, because of his disinterest in Linda, Josh ignored her. She knew no one. Neither did I.

There was only one musician providing music for the party, a Greek keyboard player. Linda has been dancing Greek folk dances and belly dancing since she was 12 years old. It was a favorite hobby of Jack's, so he taught her how to dance.

The musician played "Miserlou," a Greek folk song, which inspired Linda to move around in a most sensuous way . . . like a belly dancer who refrained from using her torso and hips. She used only her shoulders and moved rhythmically to the sounds of the keyboard, which sounded more like a Greek mandolin. I watched her out of the corner of my eye, reminding myself to speak with her some time when we were alone to suggest she be more selective in what company she chooses to dance in.

Mervyn went into a snit, totally ignoring me. Not understanding what the problem was, I asked, "What's wrong?"

"Nothing. Nothing's wrong," he responded in a sharp voice that sounded more like that of a sergeant.

"Are you angry? You seem angry," I said.

No reply.

"Mervyn," I said again. "You seem angry. What's wrong?"

This time he got up from the chair and simply walked away in a huff.

Not being a mind reader, I was perplexed. I felt stupid walking after him trying to understand his feelings and his behavior.

"You seem angry," I tried again.

"Angry? I'm not angry," he said, in a manner incongruent with his skin color and facial expressions. He gritted his teeth through a fake smile. "Why should I be angry?"

I thought it was senseless to keep interrogating him to complete dissatisfaction. I made a mental note to take a pass on this one. "Brain dead," I said to myself. "Brain dead."

I left the party with that sick feeling in the pit of my stomach. "Oh well, another miserable learning experience. Another guy that doesn't say what he means, or mean what he says. Tomorrow's another day, and I'll be back home soon enough. This guy's history."

Back at the house where we were guests of his cousin, he decided he was ready to discuss the matter.

"We can talk about what happened now!" he said in a "you better listen to me" voice. "You want to know what's wrong? I'll tell you what's wrong. But you don't talk. Don't say a word until I'm finished. Not one word. Do you understand?" he demanded, pointing his right index finger at me.

I simply nodded my head, afraid to speak and ready to bolt from the seat, but I had no place to go. The next plane out wasn't until tomorrow, and I had no choice but to sit there as his captive.

Mervyn went on for nearly a half hour, scolding me for not doing something about "her" behavior.

"How could you allow her to act like that in front of my family? What's the matter with you? Don't you have any common sense? How did you raise her? Don't you have any brains?"

I said nothing.

"You humiliated me. You embarrassed me. Her behavior was unacceptable. You ruined my evening."

I stared in disbelief. How could I ever get hooked up with such a retard? He's right. I have no brains, no common sense. I'm an asshole. I can't believe I'm three thousand miles from home with this brain dead senior citizen who's behaving like a first-class clown, scolding me, as if I were his child. "Oh my, God. Please let this night go quickly. Let it end. Just let it be over!" I prayed silently to myself.

"Now. You can reply if you choose," he stated seriously. "What do you have to say?"

I was dumbfounded. "He's giving me permission to speak?" I asked myself.

"So? Speak!" he demanded.

Suddenly, a flash entered my brainless head. "Use the change model. You know, the communication model. What the hell. You have nowhere to go to get away from this dickhead. Use it. See if it works. If it works on him, it'll work on anybody."

I assumed my professional therapist position. I sat tall and straight on the hassock he had appointed to me. My effect was cool, but appropriate. I managed to stay composed and steady. I began. Clearing my throat first, I honored his feelings, even though I wanted to rip his head off.

"I appreciated what you have shared. I can understand your anger. I am truly sorry that you were so upset by her actions," slightly accenting the word her, with guarded, but meaningful tonality. "I am also sorry that it ruined your evening. That wasn't my intention. I hope you can accept my apology." I continued to maintain eye contact with him. He was pacing the room like a tiger in a cage, still cooling down from his pontification.

"That's it? That's all you have to say?" he asked.

"No. I have more. Shall I continue?" I asked politely.

He gestured his hand as if to give permission. I paced him carefully, not to rush with my response. Meanwhile, I saw that he had begun to quiet down. I calibrated his facial expressions and breathing. I waited for him to relax a little more.

"I became concerned when I noticed you were ignoring me. I tried to talk with you, but you weren't responsive. I realized you weren't ready just yet. I felt worried. I thought you were angry, but wasn't really sure because I was confused. 'After all,' I said to myself, 'This man is very intelligent.' (This acknowledgement and validation was very important for him to hear.) 'How can he hold me responsible for another person's behavior? She's an adult, and takes responsibility for her own behavior.' I just needed you to validate my concern. When you didn't, I imagined you didn't want to talk about it. I'm glad we're talking now. I also thought it was a bit inappropriate for Linda to express herself like that in a crowd she didn't know. I made a mental note to speak with her in private tomorrow. Perhaps during a walk. It was my intention to do so . . . and I will. I hope you don't hold me responsible for another person's behavior in the future. I'm truly sorry that it spoiled your evening." I shut up.

He looked at me glazed. His mouth was open, but nothing came out. "What did you say? I mean, say that again."

"Say what again?" I had him. This guy was hooked. He was putty in my hand.

"What you just said. I never heard anyone speak like that before. You're right. You're absolutely right. How can I hold you responsible for someone else's behavior?"

We looked at each other. He laughed and apologized.

"You must think I'm an asshole," he said. I did, but I didn't tell him.

This conversation opened the door to our relationship. He sat back, and said, "Tell me more. Just tell me more."

I did, and one year later we were married. The change model has a lot of power, folks—a lot of power.

Marriage and Family

Give one another of your bread but eat not from the same loaf.
Sing and dance together and be joyous, but let each one of you be alone,
Even as the strings of a lute are alone though they quiver with the same music.
Give your hearts, but not into each other's keeping.
For only the hand of Life can contain your hearts.
And stand together yet not too near together:
For the pillars of the temple stand apart,
And the oak tree and the cypress grow not in each other's shadow.

—*Kahlil Gibran,* The Prophet

One of the main reasons why marriages or relationships fail is because of unrealistic expectations. Unknowingly, each person comes into the relationship with an unconscious blueprint of what their union is "supposed" to be. This then becomes projected onto the other, as if the other already knew about it, and is assumed to deliver the expectation. This is the chief cause for disorder of desire. When you set up your partner to become the parent you were most wounded by (which most of us unwittingly do), you're in deep trouble. You get to go to bed with that parent, (and sometimes both). The unconscious expectation is to resolve the conflict with your source relationships that never got resolved. "Be the mommy or daddy I never had. Then, when you become that person (even when you don't bear a single solitary resemblance to them), I'll project all my unresolved feelings onto you, find you exactly like I found my parent, and reject you or make you reject me, so I can reinforce my belief system that I'm really not loveable. Once I make you into my mother or my father, I'll lose complete desire for you."

In the beginning of this book I addressed the issue of making permanent life decisions at an age when you don't even know who you are. So many of us go into committed relationships with positive intentions, for better or for worse, for richer or for poorer, in sickness and in health, till death do us part, without knowing or understanding we are dragging in a collection of unemptied trash that gets dumped in the relationship. Even garbage trucks make dispatches. Human beings don't even know they're carrying around a load to dispatch. All this garbage gets acted out and the relationship usually ends up in the dump.

For some of us it's too late to avoid these mistakes. We found out after the fact. Some never learn. I did this four times. It can easily become a habit.

Sam Keen writes, "Marriage is designed to allow two people to fall out of love and into reality." One wonders, "Why do it?" I wonder, "Why do it four times?" What is that absoluteness (or absolute *mess*) of commitment that urges us to get married? What draws us into this traditional relationship mode, even with evidence that it limits individuation and autonomy, resulting, according to statistics, more often in failure than success? What is it that hurts so good inside that we keep doing it until we think we've got it right?

For me there was never any other option. Not to have done it would have been a nightmare, disappointment and a failure of my womanhood. This was an unwritten injunction of my time and culture. It was what every girl waited for; most got (much too soon), and most gave up at one time or another. And a large percentage of those who hung in there for better or for worse, did so in quiet desperation, either selling themselves a bill of goods such as, "He's only bad when he drinks," or "Maybe the baby will change things," or sublimating their discontent with outside interests that helped meet their needs. Then, there are those lucky ones (very few I might add), who somehow, in spite of all the trials and tribulations of marriage, raising a family and perhaps even having a career, come to terms with the ups and downs of it all, settle in, and are reasonably content. I don't know too many who are truly fulfilled. (I'll probably get letters from this statement.)

In my generation the covenant of marriage was a rite of passage that secured our future. It gave us free passes to get laid, credit cards to make purchases, a false sense of self-actualization for some of us, and a position of acceptance in a society that didn't prepare us for what was to follow—a family.

At least now we've come to understand that marriage and family aren't just society's expectation. They're conscious decisions that involve the ultimate commitment—to choose to become a unit, a team that will become the family unit, and will hopefully provide a healthy environment for our future generations to grow and profit from the mistakes of the generation that preceded them.

Children need at least a mother and a father. My children grew up in a home that served as lodging for their father and three surrogate fathers to follow. The first, their biological father, was barely there. Not his fault. In his words he was "stamping out disease and saving lives to make a better life for his family." So consequently, we rarely saw him, and he rarely got to see what he provided for his family. The second surrogate father withered away into some obscure corner, metaphorically reflecting his displaced position in a Jewish family of five children. This poor Episcopalian Canadian was the fish who fell in love with a bird.

The third surrogate father had his own family down the street, not even a mile away, and was frantically trying to play daddy to my children and his own. Both families were so angry that the sight of him at either home made everybody miserable. The only reason it worked for a while is that he scared the shit out of everyone. This Italian Catholic from South Philly terrorized us with his baby blue Neapolitan eyes, and satisfied us with pasta and gravy.

And finally, last, but not least, came Poppa Hemingway, the 65-year-old Wharton school graduate who was going to right every wrong. Wrong. Each kid moved out, or was thrown out, one by one, until the big bad wolf huffed and he puffed and he blew the house down. And so they all never lived happily ever after. Each, however, has come full circle with him as of this writing.

I have often observed that many marriages suffocate love. In order to be in the moment in your loving, you must be free. When marriage begins to be observed as a sanctified institution as opposed to a free-standing state of beingness, it begins to prohibit the free flow of feelings and intimacy. Institutionalized marriage imposes extensive restrictions and expectations that strangulate freedom and spontaneity. The moment there are expectations, freedom is lost. This is probably why there is a disorder of desire after we say "I do." It's not just that the conquest is over. It's that the freedom has been compromised. In his book, Sam Keen cites Carl Jung who said, "Where there is love, there is not power. Where there is power, there is not love."

How many happily married couples do you know? I mean really happily married. I don't know too many. Marriage, as I have observed in so many of my clients, aborts suspension, interrupts personal growth, fosters control, breeds dishonesty, dependency and enmeshment, and polarizes the partners, causing endless power struggles. Even in its perfect state, with the best of intentions, it fails to fully support the individual in his/her effort to actualize and be autonomous. At best, perhaps with two psychologically and developmentally fully mature, healthy, autonomous (maybe even psychoanalyzed), integrated, whole persons, a state of interdependence might be achieved. So, the success and longevity of marriage is determined by the individuals within the institution, their level of mental health, the compatibility of their goals, values, belief systems, their understanding of true intimacy and the level of their commitment to make it work. It's difficult to imagine that two people can be so synchronized as to pull it off.

So why do we keep doing it? It's like cutting off Cinderella's toes to make her foot fit the glass slipper, so we can say "they lived happily ever after."

We just love happy endings. Human beings have an extraordinary need to conform as well as individuate and separate. We need to belong. At the same time we need to be free. How to balance these two states within the framework of marriage is the quest and the impossible dream. Serial monogamy (and even that has its restraints), may be one answer. Fear of AIDS and other sexually transmitted diseases have certainly limited sleeping around. But sleeping around is not what I mean by freedom. We already know that doesn't work. By freedom, I mean a state of being, loving life, experiencing your aliveness. Feeling your pulse as you are experiencing the moment. Having the permission on a very deep level to be exactly who you are, unstifled, spontaneous and authentic. If marriage can be a state of friendship without constraints or expectations, it then becomes a state of joy.

I'm not sure what the answers are again. I am only reflecting on my personal history, which represents a period of time and tradition in my life. I think about my daughters and what their options are going to be. Perhaps Goldie and Kurt have the right idea. Perhaps once you subject another to a contract, resistance occurs just because of the nature of a contract. Love must come freely. Perhaps all that it really needed is a decision based purely on desire.

I'm beginning to discover that the more autonomous the individuals are within the relationship, the higher the level of intimacy. The more constraints and demands for loyalty placed on the relationship, the less trust exists. Perhaps in relationships that reach the level of autonomy that I am speaking of, which transcends most social and religious dogmas and practices, people will really be free to be who they are. If and when this occurs, we will have reached a new plateau of understanding. Relationships will no longer have the same meaning. Children will be born out of friendship rather than just traditional marriage. The requisite for this kind of relationship would have to include enlightened and evolved individuals. The question is are we ready for it? Perhaps, some of us are and some are not.

Healing Myself and My World

The goal of recovery is to separate, but stay connected. Families are very important. They are the nucleus of our lives. The intention of Inner Child work is not to blame our parents for our miserable childhoods and subsequent unhappy adult lives. Along with our woundedness, in each of us, is a very intelligent, remarkable adult who knows how to parent that child. The focus of this work is not on the past child. It's on the adult of today. We first go back and reclaim that part of ourselves, which due to our misfortunes of unintended dysfunctional family behaviors, got left behind. Once reclaimed, healing can begin. You, as a fully operating, capable adult, can become the champion to that little girl or boy who didn't have the advantages that he or she may have now, due to your own process of growth and development in spite of the shortcomings of your life.

John Bradshaw gave us a paradigm of the "Inner Child" that helped heal our pain, acknowledged our sorrow, shame and suffering, gave permission to feel joy and wonder, and restored us to new possibilities. Much of this work has been misunderstood and highly criticized because of misconceptions. Recovering from the whore and madonna complexes, saying goodbye to our fathers, changing female body images and recovering from source relationships are necessary stages of growth if we are to become self-actualized, autonomous and integrated women. Those of us who continue to stay in those roles are staying loyal to fathers who either oversexualized or abandoned us. The objectification or suppression of sexuality and its reinforcement will put you in either/or roles. We must divorce our fathers before we can be free to have an intimate relationship with another man. We will continue to stay in a squirrel cage unless we finish our business with both our mothers and fathers. This does not mean never having to see or speak to them again. This is saying goodbye to our internal parents who wrote the scripts for our lives. We each have the right to write our own script. Theirs was about them; not about us. Even with the best intentions in parenthood, things go awry.

I met Phil in a restaurant one evening while Tom was in Cancun working on a project with Henri. I was introduced to him by a friend. He looked at me with those baby blue Neapolitan eyes as if I were a lamb chop. That was exactly the kind of attention that I needed. Tom had already forgotten the color of my eyes. "Would you like to dance?" I asked, in my most coquettish manner, wearing a girlish grin that would have been impossible to say no to.

All I remember after that was that we practically had sex on the dance floor. He couldn't keep his hands off my body or his lips off my mouth. My friend went home. Phil came with a friend, so he didn't have a car. I offered to drive him home.

The valet pulled up alongside us in my new baby blue Cadillac Seville with Tchaikovsky on the stereo.

"Get in," I whispered. I took him home with me to five kids sprawled across the family room, all asleep with the television on. Then I introduced him to my 85-year-old Aunt Fannie, who was spending the night.

Tom left one month after I met Phil, who moved in two days later. The first thing he did was change my necklines. Sexy, silk nightgowns were to be worn to bed. (T-shirts were prohibited.) Dresses or polyester suits that looked like the kind worn by Italian housewives from South Philadelphia were mandated for day wear. Arguments about my dress, my makeup, my hairstyle, my "provocative" manner (the kind that turned him on the night we met), were a constant source of irritation. In actuality, his projection, which was never externalized, but rather consistently denied, was that it would probably turn other men on too. Therefore, he justified his need to change me.

He jestfully, however shamingly, told our friends that I had to hire carpenters to help me get ready for an evening out. Phil did all that he could to keep me as the Madonna on the outside and the whore on the inside. I was really more like the reverse. The balancing act became a nightmare.

After five years of him trying to change me into his "ideal woman," things got worse. He just couldn't get me to submit. The harder he tried, the more I'd rebel. It was a constant source of aggravation and disruption between us. He usually won through intimidation. I would change my outfit at least two or three times before he was satisfied enough to go out. It didn't accomplish anything except to turn my love to hate.

One evening we were going out to celebrate my 45th birthday. I had bought an Italian silk hand-painted dress that I found in a trendy boutique. It had once been more than I could afford, but now it had been greatly reduced and I bought it for my birthday. It had a matching full scarf that could be tied around the hip line, so you could blouse the top portion over the scarf. A slit ran up to my thigh. Although it exposed no other body parts, it was sexy and classy, a real show stopper. I had my eye on it for a long time and I was thrilled to get it on sale.

I took a long time dressing, primping and pampering. My daughters were in the dressing room attending me, trying on make-up and fixing my hair. I walked out into the bedroom where Phil was sitting, nursing a drink. "How do I look?" I asked, twirling around once and feeling quite beautiful.

"Like a fifty-dollar hooker."

"That's it? Only fifty dollars?" I joked, but feeling intimidated and uneasy about what might follow.

"Not even that. Take that off. I'm not going anywhere with you looking like that."

"Fine, then don't go," I retorted.

The vodka gave him just enough permission to get mean and nasty, but not enough to cancel the birthday dinner.

We walked into Christine Lee's, a fashionable Chinese-American restaurant that we frequented often. Phil knew the maitre d', John, so it was never a long wait. We went to the bar and he ordered me a drink and one more for himself. Phil was not a drinker, so it was hard to know what two drinks might do to him, but I soon found out.

"Maybe you want to fuck John," he said in a voice loud enough so that everyone turned around to stare.

Shaken, and afraid of what might come out of his mouth next, I tried to calm him down. In a whisper, I begged him to stop.

"I'll say whatever the hell I want. You're just a cheap hooker. I don't give a shit what you want."

"You're embarrassing me, Phil. Please stop this or I'm going to leave."

I was sitting on the last bar stool closest to the wall, and if I could have found a way to go through it, I would have. I felt everyone's eyes on me, and for a few minutes lost all sense of time and thought. I knew I had to get out of there, but I was afraid to move off the bar stool.

"Just who the hell do you think you are? Some hotshot call girl? Some kind of piece of ass? You're nothing but a cheap whore. A real piece of shit," he said with his baby blues spinning in place.

I stepped off the stool and started past him.

"Just where the hell do you think you're going?"

"I'm going to the ladies' room. I need to get away from you too. You're scaring me and your behavior is offensive. I don't know what else to do."

"Just sit down. You don't need to go nowhere."

I withdrew my arm and continued walking past the bar. He never left his stool. I walked through the lobby to the public telephone and called my daughter Emily.

"Emily, come get me. Phil is acting like a lunatic. I'm afraid he's going to get worse. Come right away. I'll be waiting outside."

When she finally arrived and I got in her car, Phil dashed out the front entrance waving his arms frantically in the air for me to stop.

"Hurry Emily. Just hurry. Phil is nuts tonight. This is it. I've got to do something."

We drove home the long way, taking our time so I could think things through. I knew I couldn't take this abuse anymore. I just have trouble ending relationships. They're easy to get into, but so difficult to end.

By the time we reached the house, Phil was already there. When I walked in I was afraid to see what I might find. Linda had some friends visiting, so at least we weren't alone in the house. "Where's Phil?" I asked, not wanting to cause any alarm.

"What's wrong, Mom?" she asked. I knew from her facial expressions that she knew something was wrong.

"Phil was out of control tonight. He didn't like the way I looked, so he made a scene. I've had it," I replied.

"He's in the bedroom," she said.

I cautiously walked into the bedroom. He was alive with fire and pacing like a caged animal.

"Why the hell did you leave? Why would you do a thing like that?" he asked as if I had no reason to leave.

"Would you stick around a public place like that if someone was insulting you?" I asked.

"You deserved it. You know I hate when you look like that. It's degrading. You look like a whore," he said once again.

"You've said that enough times tonight. I think you should get your things and leave."

I started out the bedroom door, and suddenly, without any warning, he flashed a gun in my face.

"I'll tell you who's getting out of here. Not me!" he said with such conviction that I nearly collapsed. He was holding a gun to my face. Me, the mother of five children, and this man was going to shoot me. I could think of only one thing. Take the kids and leave. Fortunately, Emily had already gone, the others were sleeping out, which left only Linda and her three visitors. I walked quickly into the family room.

"Linda," I said in the calmest voice I could muster up. "We all have to leave. Phil is on a rampage, and totally out of control. He's got a gun and I don't know if he's crazy enough to use it. Ask your friends to leave and I'll need you to come with me. Do it now!" I said urgently. She understood. Within a minute we were out of the front door. Linda and I drove together to a coffeehouse in

Hallandale, where I called my brother Mickey and told him what had happened. I asked him to call Phil and make sure he would be gone before we returned home.

I waited a few minutes and called Mickey back. He assured me that I could go home. Phil would be gone and I would be safe. He also told me that Phil said that I overreacted. The gun was never loaded, and it was just a joke. He apologized to my brother for causing any concern. He thought I should realize it was just a joke, a practical joke.

If this had occurred in 1994, his behavior would be considered a felony, punishable by imprisonment. But it never occurred to me to call the police.

This was the same man who drove to Islamorada in the middle of a violent rainstorm to rescue my son Tim. This was the same man that made the gravy and pasta, helped with homework, drove the kids to football practice and Hebrew school, and made sure Emily got on the plane to her father. But until we acknowledge and embrace our shadow side, until we heal our emotional wounds, we are not fully integrated human beings. These repressed parts of our personality will keep interfering with our choices, behavior and relationships. They will eventually destroy us. And, what's worse, our children will inherit the traits of our shadow side.

When I was six I had to walk to school on the very first day by myself. Although my mother would have preferred to escort me she couldn't leave my two-year-old brother, who until that age remained colicky. Crying and screaming was his only means of communication. He didn't speak until he was four. Knowing she may have an impending problem, she made several trial runs from our house to South Beach Elementary. On the days preceding the first day of school, she would walk with me and my brother in his makeshift stroller, to make sure I knew the route just in case I had to make the trip alone. Wouldn't you know it. On the only day that I prayed it wouldn't happen, the very first day of school, entering the first grade, I had to walk it alone. She waved and shouted out from the third-story window, I looked back over my shoulder several times hoping she would say, "Wait. I'm coming. I'll walk with you." But she didn't.

I walked alone down the alley toward First Street, feeling terrified, but aware of a new feeling which seemed to be covering up the one of fear and abandonment. I felt a sense of bravado and what seemed to be a sense of pride; words I didn't even know or understand. I only experienced the feeling. I didn't know there was a language which could describe that feeling. I carried that feeling all the way to the school. I crossed Washington Avenue, one of the busiest streets on Miami Beach. I walked a few more blocks west, towards Alton Road, picking the oleander bushes, looking and feeling for the milky, sticky substance that flowed from their stems when you break the branch. I turned north on Alton Road, growing bigger in my new uniform of pride and courage until I saw the familiar building that was to become my elementary school for the next six years. All the children were gathered with their respective parents, or at least mothers, and in I walked alone. I looked around thinking how big this school was. How would I know where to go? Who would be my teacher? My mother had told me her name was Mrs. Davidoff. What did she look like? How would she know me? Suddenly I felt scared and all alone. The magic cloak of confidence and pride suddenly disappeared and I stood there thinking I might die. Then suddenly a teacher called to me. "Joni? Are you Joni Gilbert?"

"Yes, I'm Joni Gilbert," I replied with great relief.

"I'm Mrs. Davidoff. Come this way. You're in my class."

I knew I wasn't going to die, and I would never give up that cloak again.

The very roles we learn to become as an act of adaptation to help us survive, become double-edged blades for the rest of our lives. The intention of my cloak must never be forgotten or tossed away. It saved my life. I will always honor it. But if I never had taken it off for fear I wouldn't make it without it, I would never have become real. Remember Dumbo? He and I shared the same experience. He needed the feather to learn how to use his ears to fly. I needed the cloak of confidence to get to school and please my mother. But each of us, Dumbo and me, in our own inimitable ways, needed to learn how to integrate the feather and the cloak. We kept them in our hearts whenever we needed them.

In learning how to integrate all our parts, we never really have to give them up. They all serve a positive intention, and we'll always need them. The cloak, Sarah, the Madonna, Delores, the whore, Joni, the curious wonder child and all my other roles have been my friends and neighbors. We are a community of selves living together to build a more integrated self.

Walk into any New Age bookstore and you will see people buying texts about spirituality, ecology, shamanism, mysticism and magic. *The Celestine Prophecy* is always on re-order. The shelves are full of books written by Carlos Casteñeda, Edgar Cayce, Ram Das, Deepak Chopra, Brian Weiss, Clarrissa Pinkola Estes, Tony Robbins, Scott Peck, Marianne Williamson and other literary poets and prophets with new and old revelations on healing the human spirit. If you visit the home of someone who has a book on *A Course in Miracles* you will probably see any or all of the ones written by the above authors. Each day new books flood the market: Books on psychic phenomena; life after death; prophets; soul mates; gods and goddesses; Native American and Eastern Indian folklore, religion and philosophy; feminism; female empowerment (if I see one more of those, I'll vomit); channeling; guides; wizards; saints and even Kabbalah (Jewish mysticism) are selling out. Psychology books, which once could only be found in either libraries or university bookstores, are abundant today. Psychologists and psychotherapists are becoming the new philosophers of our time. They are the professionals who deal with real life—the human psyche. People want to grow. They want to change. They'll buy anything and everything that they think will give them the answers they are looking for. What they don't want to do is go into that experience of change. To feel it in their bodies. They would prefer to read about it.

It was once said that if you put a group of co-dependents into a room with two doors, one having a sign that reads "Heaven" and the other "Lecture on Heaven," all attendees would go in the door that says "Lecture on Heaven."

The buzz words of the 1990s no longer resemble those of the 1980s. Goodbye co-dependency, hello mystification. Goodbye models, hello paradigms. Goodbye coincidence, hello synchronicity. Are we really changing or are we creating a new vocabulary to exchange old labels to make us look and sound more enlightened and evolved? Can we really move into higher consciousness without understanding and acknowledging lower consciousness? I don't think so. Many of my clients have spent years studying with the mystics, shamans, spiritual guides, maharishis and other gurus, some on the mountain, and others not. Yet, when they come to me they don't really know who they are, where they came from and where they are going. They've just evolved into another persona desperately in search of self. They all want the same thing . . . peace of mind. But none of them have the vaguest idea of what that looks like, sounds like or feels like. They only know they want it. They think that if they meditate long enough, pray hard enough and forgive everyone that has ever harmed them, make amends to everyone they have ever harmed, stay in a 12-step program the rest of their lives, rebirth, breathe and shout primal screams, they will reach Nirvana. No way. This is not to say that all the aforementioned modalities and behaviors aren't valid and valuable. They are. But by themselves, they are not enough.

Again, without sounding repetitive, I don't have all the answers. And if anyone says they do, watch out. You're hearing dogma you really don't need. And if they promise you Nirvana, really watch out. You're dealing with a cult.

I do know that before we can heal the world, we must heal ourselves. If each of us takes full responsibility to achieve this personal mission, then we will automatically create a healed world. It's happening all around us. We are truly approaching a new epoch. We are becoming aesthetically nurtured. There will be those who will grow, heal and become the healers of tomorrow, and those who won't. I am not a philosopher. I am a change agent, a psychotherapist, committed to the idea that human beings need to discover themselves and reach their potential in this finite lifetime. Perhaps psychotherapists are in fact the new age philosophers. I believe there is a primordial need for growth. Call it existential. Call it humanistic. Perhaps it's simply being a human being. I believe there is a biological need for becoming what we were intended to be. The essence of "being" is at the root of all humans. Somehow, somewhere it gets lost or disrupted along life's path. In spite of these disruptions and lost dreams, the need to become whole flourishes throughout one's life. If not realized, stagnation and depression result. Some of us are lucky; we have found the lost keys to growth. Others are not so lucky. You know who they are. They carry the rules and regulations, the dogmas and pedagogy of others, never having found their own set of rules. They are the trustees of unfulfilled dreams and ambitions passed down generation after generation. They will unwittingly continue to carry the torch for future generations unless change is affected.

The intention of my book is not to create another "how to." It is not to say that my way is the only way to discover the self. It is not to provide answers where there may never be any. It is a personal journey into myself, into the mystery of my life to redeem my wounded soul. It is the teachings and technology I use in my clinical practice. It has become a way of life. It is me.

When we go deep into the mystery of our lives to redeem our wounded souls, change occurs. We are able to have healthy relationships without losing ourselves. Perhaps the most important result is that we are able to finally look at the world through the wonderous eyes of a child. We are able to enter the kingdom of heaven right here on earth. We each must decide for ourselves. We're all on the spaceship. We are all going to the same place. Do you want to come along?

Epilogue

It is not easy to begin a book. Nor is it easy to end. There is, however, a time for both, and I have now come to that time.

This book has been an epic for me. After all, it was my first. And like all beginnings, we don't know where the path will take us. We can only trust the process. So I had to follow my bliss, to take the path with the heart and let it lead me to whatever my destiny holds.

It's a scary thought to bring this manuscript to a close. After all, it became a part of me for more than two years; like a friend or lover. My companion in the night. It filled empty spots, lonely spots and let me breathe when my breath was shallow. It let me think when I thought I had lost my mind. It let me feel when I felt I had nothing else to feel, or when I was afraid to feel. It's even scarier when I think that people will be reading it. What if they don't like it? What will they think of me now that I am naked? What will this exposure of myself do to me and my family? Will I have any regrets? Only time will tell. I've taken the risk. I worked many long hours into the night. In its pre-edited form it comprised over 400 pages. I've lost text several times due to hitting the wrong buttons too many times. The perils of computer paralysis have made me look at my intentions and goals hundreds of times. Each time I heard my inner voice urging me on. "Just finish it. Damn it! Just finish it!"

I still don't know why I wrote it. I only know that I could not have not written it. I'm not even sure I wrote it. I feel I co-created it with a lot of help from assorted allied forces.

You may have wondered why this book was dedicated to Emily Brontë and my mother. In the beginning, I was reluctant to tell the story of how Emily Brontë became my partner in this book. I was afraid of criticism. At this juncture, it doesn't matter. The truth is the truth.

At the closure of a session with a client (who happened to be a psychic) whom I had been working with for a few months, I was interrupted by the intrusion of a "guide."

"There's a guide in the room," Susan announced. "She's your guide."

"Susan, this is not necessary. You don't have to do this. We need to complete the session," I said firmly, yet curiously.

"I can't help it. She's here and she has a message for you."

"This is not right. Please, Susan, I'm not asking you for a reading. Let's finish the session," I said in my most professional-sounding voice.

"No. I can't," she said. "I'm asked to give you this message."

Not knowing what to do or say with such unexpected information, and trying to stay grounded and sensible, I just sat silently.

"She wants me to tell you she is going to write through you. She is going to help you with your book."

"Book! How did you know I was writing a book?" I asked.

"I didn't. Are you? Are you writing a book?"

"Yes. But I haven't told anyone except my family, a few friends and colleagues," I responded.

By now she had my full attention. I forgot about therapeutic boundaries and allowed my curiosity to get the best of me.

"Who is she?" I demanded. "Who is this guide?"

Susan shifted in the sofa, leaning to one side as if she were trying to communicate with a spirit or entity. Her face grimaced and she looked as if she were trying to understand what was being communicated.

"Emily," she said. "She says her name is Emily."

"Emily who?" I asked.

She leaned again to the same side, screwed her face up, and said, "Brontë. Emily Brontë."

"Emily Brontë. My God, Susan. Do you know Emily Brontë?"

"No. Do you?"

Somewhere in the back of my mind lived the fragments of a memory that suggested an author from long ago. But I couldn't place it. It's not easy to admit, but then again neither was not knowing I was reciting the 23rd Psalm.

"Ask her who she is," I said.

Susan leaned again to the same side and closed her eyes.

"She says she's a writer. An author. She has a sister named Charlotte."

"Ask her what she wrote. Tell her not to be offended that I don't know. It's more about me than her," I said.

Susan listened attentively. She leaned further over. She shook her head.

"I can't make it out. Something like 'wither' or 'withering heads' or 'highs.'"

"*Wuthering Heights?* Was it *Wuthering Heights?*" I nearly screamed.

"Yes. That's it. *Wuthering Heights.*"

"Oh my God. Are you serious? Are you really serious, Susan?"

"Yes, I'm serious. I'm not making it up," she said.

"Susan. Do you know who Emily Brontë is? Have you ever heard of her? Have you ever read *Wuthering Heights?*"

"No. It sounds familiar, but no. I don't remember. Anyway she has a message for you." Susan closed her eyes again, leaned and listened.

"She wants you to light a candle. A white or purple candle. Burn some incense. Cedar. Bless the computer each time you begin to write. She will write with you."

I was flabbergasted. How could this be happening in my office? What do the texts say to do when this happens? I was speechless.

"Are you sure you didn't know about my writing a book? I never mentioned it? Perhaps you overheard it accidentally?"

"No. I had no idea," she said. "But it's no secret now."

Susan left my office. She had been my last client that Wednesday. I had a group to facilitate in one hour. I left my office to meet Mervyn for dinner before I had to return. At dinner I asked Mervyn if he had heard of Emily Brontë.

"Sure," he said. "She wrote *Wuthering Heights.* She had a famous sister, too. Charlotte. She wrote *Jane Eyre.*"

"How did you remember that?" I asked with a bit of amazement. Had I been so illiterate as not to have known something I should have learned in the 10th or 11th grade?

"I had to do a book report on it in high school. Then I saw the movie with Laurence Olivier. He played Heathcliff. She ambled on the moors, calling his name, 'Heathcliff!' Why?"

I told him what had happened, but I sensed he didn't hear me, or perhaps he chose not to. Another mashuganah story. Mervyn has a way of ignoring inexplicable tales. He doesn't respond and goes on to another subject. Then he forgets I ever told him. I can't say that I blame him. It's probably an appropriate response.

So in closing, I especially want to thank Emily Brontë for helping me to "dream my dreams that have stayed with me ever after, and have gone through me like wine through water, and have changed the colors of my mind."

With deep humility I share these events with you. I don't claim to have the answers for why some of these inexplicable experiences occurred. And they may be only my perception. I don't really believe answers are necessary. For me it was only important that they made a difference in my life.

For whatever or however it touches your spirit, brings you back to times forgotten, rings your bell, or resonates somewhere inside your heart, just know that all of it, every word comes from my truth.

N o t e s

Front Matter

The Norton Anthology of English Literature, Sixth Edition by Abrams, et al (New York: Norton, 1994), 133-134.

Chapter One

Augusta J. Evans. *St. Elmo* (New York: Grosset & Dunlap, 1866).

Chapter Two

Keen, Sam. *Fire in the Belly.* (New York: Bantam, 1991), 560.

Shinoda Bolen, Jean, *Goddesses in Every Woman.* (New York: Harper & Row), 36-37

Common Boundary Between Spirituality and Psychotherapy, July/August 1989. Volume 7, Issue 4, 42.

Kester, Nicola Kester et al. "Kundalini: The Serpent Power Comes to the West." *Common Boundary,* July-August 1989, vol. 7, issue 4: 18-31.

Keen, 57.

The Nag Hammadi Library, edited by James Robinson (New York: Harper, 1977).

Jung, Emma. *Animus and Anima* (New York: Spring Publications, Inc., 1957).

Chapter Four

Keen, 830.

Chapter Five

Heschel, Abraham *Between God and Man* p. 114.

Keen, 124.

Keen, Sam. *Hymns to an Unknown God* (New York: Bantam, 1994), 125.

The Journals of Kierkegaard, Storen Kierkegaard, 1934-1854, Alexander Dru, ed. (Huntington, NY. Fontana Pub. 1958). p. 130, #6.

Chapter Six

Life Magazine, June 1993 article as it appeared in Richard Moore, *Miami Herald* "If Women Ran the Country It Would Be a Kinder and Genler Place."

Sharpe, Rochelle "Women Make Strides, But Men Stay Firmly in Top Company Jobs," *Wall Street Journal,* 29 March 1994: A1+.

French, Marilyn. *The War Against Women* (New York: Summit, 1994), 151.

Keen, 161.

Keen, 167.

Morrow, Lance "Men: Are They Really That Bad?" *Time,* 14 February
    1994: 53-54.
Keen, 170.

Brontë, Emily. *Wuthering Heights.* (New York: Bantam Classics,
    1983), 197.

About the Author

Joan E. Childs, J.C., D.C.S.W., is a clinical social worker in private practice in Hallandale, Florida, since 1978. Her center, Joan E. Childs & Associates, is known as the Center for Tao. She was named the first affiliate of the John Bradshaw Center in 1990. She is a lecturer and presenter. This is her first book.

If you are interested in attending A Retreat for Growth, a five-day intensive workshop for co-dependency, in either Florida or North Carolina, or a workshop on *The Myth of the Maiden: On Being a Woman*, please contact her office at 2500 East Hallandale Beach Boulevard, Suite 800, Hallandale, Florida, 33009, (305) 456-0200. If you wish to be on her mailing list, please fill out the bottom of this page and mail to the above address.

Name_____

Address_____

Phone (   )_____

I am interested in obtaining information about:

_____Workshops _____Professional Training _____Retreats

_____Corporate Healing _____5-Day Intensive (Out-Patient)

231

Give the Gift that Keeps on Giving:
CHICKEN SOUP FOR THE SOUL

Inspire the special people in your life with a copy of *Chicken Soup for the Soul* and *A 2nd Helping of Chicken Soup for the Soul.* Sometimes it's hard to find the perfect gift for a loved one, friend or coworker. Readers of all backgrounds have been inspired by these books; why not share the magic with others? Both books are available in paperback for $12.95 each and in hard cover for $24.00 each (plus shipping and handling). You're sure to enrich the lives of everyone around you with this affordable treasure. Stock up now for the holidays. Order your copies today!

Chicken Soup for the Soul (paperback)
Code 262X $12.95
Chicken Soup for the Soul (hard cover)
Code 2913 . . . . $24.00
A 2nd Helping of Chicken Soup for the Soul (paperback)
Code 3316 . . . . $12.95
A 2nd Helping Of Chicken Soup for the Soul (hard cover)
Code 3324 . . . . $24.00

Lift Your Spirits with *Chicken Soup for the Soul Audiotapes*

Here's your chance to enjoy some *Chicken Soup for the Soul* and the ears. Now you can listen to the most heartwarming, soul-inspiring stories you've ever heard in the comfort of your home or automobile, or anywhere else you have a tape player.

Two of America's most beloved inspirational speakers, Jack Canfield and Mark Victor Hansen use their consummate storytelling ability to bring to life their bestselling collection. You'll hear tales on loving yourself and others; on parenting, learning and acquiring wisdom; and on living your dream and overcoming obstacles.

Special Gift-Set Offer: All three volumes
(6 cassettes—7 hours of inspirations) for only $29.95 + S&H
(a 27% discount). *Best Value!*

Volume 1: On Love and Learning to Love Yourself
(2 60-minute cassettes) Code 3070 . . . . $12.95
Volume 2: On Parenting, Learning and Eclectic Wisdom
(2 60-minute cassettes) Code 3081 . . . . $12.95
Volume 3: On Living Your Dream and Overcoming Obstacles
(2 90 minute cassettes)
Code 309X $14.95

Available at your favorite bookstore or call 1-800-441-5569 for Visa or MasterCard orders. Prices do not include shipping and handling. Your response code is HCI.

Your Soul Journey Begins Today

Recovery of the Sacred
Lessons in Soul Awareness
Carlos Warter, M.D., Ph.D.

Here is the book that everyone is talking about by the author who is quickly approaching the status of Marianne Williamson, Deepak Chopra and James Redfield. This may be the most fascinating story you will ever read: and it is all true. *Recovery of the Sacred* is the mesmerizing tale of Dr. Carlos Warter's spiritual journey down paths of which few even dream: Studying with Idries Shaw, Claudio Naranjo, Alain Naude, Frederick Leboyer and Lama Thartang Tulku Rimpoche. Learning rituals of Shamanism, spiritual traditions of Sufism, Christian, Jewish and Islamic mysticism, Buddhist techniques of meditation. Traveling from Chile to Mexico, Machu Picchu, the Rockies, Morocco and the Holy Land. Don't dare miss it!
Code 3138...$9.95

The Quiet Voice of Soul
How to Find Meaning in Ordinary Life
Tian Dayton, Ph.D.

This wonderful book illuminates for you the many ways in which soul can be seen and heard: through family, relationships, feelings, play, the universe and spirituality. Tian Dayton has written a work with the same power as *Care of the Soul.* An uplifting read that will inspire you.
Code 3391...$9.95

The Soul of Adulthood
Opening the Doors . . .
John C. Friel, Ph.D. and Linda Friel, M.A.

The Friels explain to you the connection between true adulthood and the deeper realms of your own soul in this transfixing book. Adulthood is a quality of soul that is chosen and earned through the deepening struggles that life offers as you progress from birth to death. A work that will open the doors to your soul.
Code 3413...$9.95

Available at your favorite bookstore or for Visa or MasterCard orders call: 1-800-441-5569 response code **HCI**. Prices do not include S&H.

Professional Care.
      Professional Concern.
            Professional Counselor . . .
                  just for you!

Brought to you by Health Communications, Inc., the
nation's leading publisher of books and magazines for
counseling and treatment professionals, *Professional
Counselor* is dedicated to serving the addictions and mental
health fields. With Richard Fields, Ph.D., a highly respected authority in the area of dual diagnosis, serving as editor,
and in-depth feature articles and columns written by and
for professionals, you will get the timely information you need to best
serve your clients. *Professional Counselor's* coverage includes:

- Substance abuse and alcoholism trends
- Mental health and addictions research
- Family, group and special populations therapy
- The latest in counseling techniques
- Listing of upcoming workshops and events
- Managed care and employee assistance programs

Professional Counselor: Serving the Addictions and Mental Health Fields is the magazine for
counselors, therapists, addictionologists, psychologists, managed-care specialists, administrators,
employee assistance program and law enforcement personnel.

Order *Professional Counselor* today and take advantage of our special introductory offer: One
year of *Professional Counselor* (6 bimonthly issues) for just $20.00. That's 23% off the regular
subscription price!

CLIP AND MAIL THIS COUPON TO:
Professional Counselor
P.O. Box 607
Mount Morris, IL 61054-7641

YES!

Enter my subscription to *Professional Counselor* for a full year (6 bimonthly
issues) for only $20.00—23% off the regular subscription price.

*If you are not completely satisfied, simply return the subscription invoice marked
CANCEL. The first issue will be yours to keep.*

Name: _____

Address: _____

City: _____ State: _____ Zip: _____

❒ Payment enclosed   Charge my: ❒ Visa   ❒ MasterCard #_____

Exp. Date: _____ Signature: _____

Please allow 4-6 weeks for delivery. FL residents please add $1.20 state sales tax.
